Qualitative Research

for Social Workers

Phases, Steps, & Tasks

Leslie M. Tutty
Michael Rothery
Richard M. Grinnell, Jr.

Faculty of Social Work
The University of Calgary

ALLYN AND BACON

Boston   London   Toronto   Sydney   Tokyo   Singapore

Vice President and Publisher: Susan K. Badger
Executive Editor: Karen Hanson
Managing Editor: Judy Fifer
Editorial Assistant: Jennifer Jacobson
Executive Marketing Manager: Joyce Nilsen
Production Editor: Catherine Hetmansky
Manufacturing Buyer: Aloka Rathnam
Cover Designer: Suzanne Harbison

Printed in the United States of America
10 9 8 7 6 5 4 3   99 98 97

Contents

Preface **iv**
Contributors **ix**

Introduction **2**

PART ONE: THE QUALITATIVE RESEARCH PROCESS **23**

Phase One: *Planning Your Study* **24**

Phase Two: *Collecting Your Data* **50**

Phase Three: *Analyzing Your Data* **88**

Phase Four: *Writing Your Report* **120**

PART TWO: RESEARCH EXAMPLES **151**

Research Study A: *Females Who Sexually Abuse Children* **152**

Research Study B: *Boards of Directors of Social Service Agencies* **174**

Research Study C: *A Child Welfare Tragedy* **208**

Index **227**

Preface

OVER THE LAST SEVERAL YEARS there has been enormous interest in a special kind of social work research method: one that aspires to understand people and their social environments in ways that are as close as possible to normal human experience by studying them in their natural settings. It uses data collection procedures and techniques that try not to distort the experiences it is attempting to illuminate. It seeks to understand the information people share with us without insisting that it be reduced to numbers. And it does not require that information be squeezed dry and juiceless by an indifferent machine with the power to conduct sophisticated statistical manipulations but totally inept when it comes to appreciating the place, in human affairs, of uniqueness and nuance. What we have been describing is the *qualitative research* method.

Its apparent youth is deceptive, however. In social work, and in other disciplines such as anthropology, the qualitative research method has been a mainstay in the development of knowledge for a very long time. Nevertheless, the energy and interest that the rediscovery of "alternatives" to mainstream quantitative research has generated is remarkable. Equally impressive is the number of new books appearing annually exploring and promoting these approaches.

WHAT IS QUALITATIVE RESEARCH?

This burgeoning literature brings with it fresh new ideas and insights, often with a degree of missionary zeal—along with a great deal of terminological confusion. People call the qualitative research method many different things, such as exploratory, naturalistic, phenomenological, ethnography, grounded theory, field, and ethnomethodological, to name just a few.

The above terms are not synonyms, however, since each label suggests a difference in philosophy and approach that is highly important to people with specialized knowledge in the area. At the risk of being too simplistic, we have opted for the term *qualitative research* because we believe it comes closest to capturing what this book is about. The term is much less restrictive than the others, and basically implies:

- research studies that are conducted primarily in the natural settings where the research participants carry out their daily business in a "non-research" atmosphere.

- research studies where variables cannot be controlled and experimentally manipulated (though changes in variables and their effect on other variables can certainly be observed).

- research studies in which the questions to be asked are not always completely conceptualized and operationally defined at the outset (though they can be).

- research studies in which the data collected are heavily influenced by the experiences and priorities of the research participants, rather than being collected by predetermined and/or highly structured and/or standardized measurement instruments.

- research studies in which meanings are drawn from the data (and presented to others) using processes that are more natural and familiar than those used in the quantitative method. The data need not be reduced to numbers and statistically analyzed (though counting and statistics can be employed if they are thought useful).

OUR GOAL AND OBJECTIVES

Given that so much has been written about various types of qualitative research methods in recent years, what justifies yet another book? Our experiences in the classroom and the experiences of our social work students suggest that an important book is missing—an inexpensive, practical, "user-friendly" introduction to doing qualitative research within a social work context, which we intend this book to be. To accomplish our modest goal, we attempt to meet three simple, interrelated objectives.

Our first objective is to include only the core material that a student needs to know to appreciate and understand the role of qualitative research in social work; information overload is avoided. We have also included basic content that must be mastered in order to do a qualitatively orientated master's thesis or research project.

We have struggled to be clear while presenting qualitative research as a natural means of knowledge acquisition using familiar ways of observing and making sense of the world—not as an esoteric domain accessible only to the initiated. We have taken a pledge not to use mystifying terms such as "paradigmatic shifts," "Deridian post-modernist deconstructions of co-authored know-ledges," or "the layering of meaning in textual (narrative) representations of the deep structures of the lived experience." Even the word "heuristic" has been disallowed.

Our second objective is to prepare social work students to become beginning critical consumers of the qualitative research literature.

Our third objective is to provide the student with a solid beginning foundation for more advanced qualitative research courses and texts.

Our Audience

As is probably evident by now, our intended audience is the social work student taking a one-semester (or quarter) beginning social work qualitative research course or doing a qualitatively orientated seminar paper, thesis, dissertation, or project.

With the student in mind, we have designed our book to be flexible. First, it can be used as an inexpensive main text in a qualitative research course where the instructor or student can use other, more advanced, comprehensive texts to support and complement the framework we present. We especially encourage students to seek out the many relevant readings at the library and the available qualitative research texts. (Many of the readings can be found at the end of each chapter.) In short, the instructor can easily tailor the core material of our book (Phases One to Four) to suit a student's individual learning and content needs.

Second, the book can be used as a supplementary text in a social work research methods (or evaluation) course that uses a quantitatively orientated text. Our book is a perfect complement to these texts, as it uses many of the concepts and terminology contained within them.

OUR BOOK'S ORGANIZATION AND PHILOSOPHY

With the above in mind, we begin Part One where every qualitative researcher begins: by finding a meaningful problem area to study within a social work context (Phase One), passing to collecting (Phase Two) and analyzing data (Phase Three), and then to report writing (Phase Four).

We describe each phase of a typical qualitative study and the specific steps and tasks that go with it, in an effort to provide an understandable model that can be taken into the field and modified as circumstances require. The difference between a useful practical model and a rigid prescription is important—the latter is impractical for the real world of social work research, the former is what we want our book to be.

To illustrate how the four phases of the qualitative research method are operationalized in actual social work research studies, we have included three case examples in Part Two.

What Our Book Is Not

First, we attempt neither to present an "original" integration of the various ways of knowing nor to "blend" quantitative and qualitative research approaches to form a "unique research continuum" of some kind or other. There are other books on the market that attempt to do this. More importantly, we believe that the breadth and depth of these tasks extend far beyond what a beginning social work student needs to learn to appreciate the qualitative research literature, to understand it, and to begin to become a critical consumer of it—the goals of our book.

Second, we do not explore the philosophical roots, theories, or rationales that sustain the various qualitative research methods. Many excellent books consider these issues in depth, and we do not wish to add to that literature. We nevertheless do briefly cover some of the basic background issues that impinge on qualitative researchers, mainly to identify these issues and establish the assumptions on which the rest of the book is based. Beyond this, we have attempted to provide a practical student guide rather than a theoretical discourse. In short, we have not attempted to redo what has been expertly accomplished in many of the books that have preceded ours, and potential readers should know what the limits of our ambitions for this volume are, and what needs can best be met elsewhere.

Finally, we have not attempted to be comprehensive. There is a considerable range of published books that discuss qualitative methods, traditions, and perspectives from every conceivable viewpoint known to personkind. For example, we have chosen only one major data collection approach (i.e., interviewing) as it is the means most often used for collecting data within qualitative research studies.

Some student research projects will, however, employ other data collection methods, such as file data, archival data, documentary records, private and public archives, solicited and unsolicited documents, biographies and autobiographies, erosion measures, accretion measures, pictures, and the various types of content analysis. These forms of data collection will obviously follow different phases, steps, and tasks than the interview. Our book will also be useful here, as it can be adapted to these other data collection methods; the qualitative researcher can deviate from the book as circumstances require.

ACKNOWLEDGMENTS

We sincerely thank two of our colleagues who reviewed our book in its entirety as they provided helpful suggestions: Richard Blake of Seton Hall University and Michael Jacobsen of the University of North Dakota. We appreciate the support and expert guidance of four friendly folks at Allyn and Bacon: Karen Hanson, Executive Editor; Judy Fifer, Managing Editor (Social Work); Catherine Hetmansky, Production Editor; and Jennifer Jacobson, Editorial Assistant. Thanks goes to David Este, Heather Coleman, and Yvonne Unrau for assisting with the annotated descriptions at the end of each chapter. We are also appreciative of the *Canadian Social Work Review* for granting permission to use portions of an article written by Leslie M. Tutty titled "After the Shelter: Critical Issues for Women Who Leave Assaultive Relationships" (Volume 10, Number 2, 1993, pages 183-201).

A LOOK TOWARD THE FUTURE

Qualitative research in social work is continuing to grow and develop, and we believe this book will contribute to that growth. A second edition is anticipated and we welcome your suggestions. Please send your comments directly to Leslie M. Tutty, Faculty of Social Work, University of Calgary, Calgary, Alberta, Canada T2N 1N4, or call (403) 220-5040 or fax (403) 289-8969.

JULY, 1995

LESLIE M. TUTTY
MICHAEL ROTHERY
RICHARD M. GRINNELL, JR.

Contributors

CAROL D. AUSTIN, Ph.D., is a professor within the Faculty of Social Work at The University of Calgary, Calgary, Alberta, T2N 1N4. At the time of this writing she was the Assistant Dean (Undergraduate) of the Faculty.

ELAINE BOUEY, BLS, is a Librarian at The University of Calgary, Calgary, Alberta, T2N 1N4.

NICK COADY, Ph.D., is an associate professor within the Faculty of Social Work at Wilfrid Laurier University, Waterloo, Ontario, N2L 3C5. At the time of this writing he was an associate professor within the Faculty of Social Work at The University of Calgary, Calgary, Alberta, T2N 1N4.

HEATHER COLEMAN, Ph.D., is an assistant professor within the Faculty of Social Work at The University of Calgary, Calgary, Alberta, T2N 1N4.

DAVID ESTE, D.S.W., is an assistant professor within the Faculty of Social Work at The University of Calgary, Calgary, Alberta, T2N 1N4.

RICHARD M. GRINNELL, JR., Ph.D., is a professor within the Faculty of Social Work at The University of Calgary, Calgary, Alberta, T2N 1N4. At the time of this writing he was the Acting Dean of the Faculty.

ROBERT MCCLELLAND, Ph.D., is an assistant professor within the Faculty of Social Work at The University of Calgary, Calgary, Alberta, T2N 1N4.

LAURIE ROBINSON, M.S.W., is in private practice in Waterloo, Ontario. At the time of this writing she was a graduate student within the Faculty of Social Work at The University of Calgary, Calgary, Alberta, T2N 1N4.

GAYLA ROGERS, Ph.D., is an associate professor within the Faculty of Social Work at The University of Calgary, Calgary, Alberta, T2N 1N4. At the time of this writing she was the Director of Field Education of the Faculty.

MICHAEL ROTHERY, Ph.D., is a professor within the Faculty of Social Work at The University of Calgary, Calgary, Alberta, T2N 1N4. At the time of this writing he was the Associate Dean of the Faculty.

BARBARA THOMLISON, Ph.D., is an associate professor within the Faculty of Social Work at The University of Calgary, Calgary, Alberta, T2N 1N4.

RAY J. THOMLISON, Ph.D., is a professor within the Faculty of Social Work at The University of Calgary, Calgary, Alberta, T2N 1N4. At the time of this writing he was on sabbatical and is the Dean of the Faculty.

LESLIE M. TUTTY, D.S.W., is an associate professor within the Faculty of Social Work at The University of Calgary, Calgary, Alberta, T2N 1N4. At the time of this writing she was the Assistant Dean (Graduate) of the Faculty.

YVONNE UNRAU, Ph.D., is an assistant professor within the Faculty of Social Work at The University of Calgary, Calgary, Alberta, T2N 1N4.

LESA WOLFE, M.S.W. Candidate, is a graduate student within the Faculty of Social Work at The University of Calgary, Calgary, Alberta, T2N 1N4.

Qualitative Research

for Social Workers

Phases, Steps, & Tasks

Michael Rothery
Leslie M. Tutty
Richard M. Grinnell, Jr.

THE QUALITATIVE RESEARCH APPROACH
  What Do Qualitative Researchers Do?

PHASES IN QUALITATIVE RESEARCH STUDIES

TOWARD ESTABLISHING A KNOWLEDGE BASE
  The Never-Ending Quest for Knowledge

QUANTITATIVE AND QUALITATIVE APPROACHES
  Objectivity / Generalization / Reductionism / The Use of Theory / The Use of
  Numbers and Words / Flexibility

GOOD RESEARCH IS GOOD RESEARCH
  Research and the Profession's Knowledge Base / Research and the Practitioner /
  Research and Gender / Research and Culture

SUMMARY

ANNOTATED BIBLIOGRAPHY / REFERENCES AND FURTHER READINGS

*No profession can afford any
equivocation on the importance of research.*
— DAVID FANCHEL —

Introduction

T HE QUALITATIVE RESEARCH APPROACH is recently enjoying a revitalized interest within the social work profession. It is also being championed as a new option in fields such as nursing, education, and psychology. In social work, however, we are merely getting reacquainted with an old familiar research and practice method that has been around since the beginning of our profession. Consider this report by Mary Richmond (1921), written over 70 years ago:

> I tried the experiment of listing [from case records] each act ... of each social case worker responsible, in the six cases cited, for the treatment described. This gave me six long lists of items, many of which were duplicates. By combining the duplicates and trying to classify the items, I found they fell under the two general headings of "insights" and "acts." Each of these two divided once again—insights to include "an understanding of individuality" and "an understanding of environment"; acts to include "direct action upon the mind" and "indirect action upon the mind."

Mary Richmond's language may not be quite modern, but her use and analysis of natural data (as occurring in case files) is highly congruent with current qualitative research approaches. The first social work textbooks used information derived from the qualitative research approach to develop a working definition of our profession and to delineate our helping skills. Let us now turn our attention to defining exactly what this research approach is.

THE QUALITATIVE RESEARCH APPROACH

There are as many definitions of the qualitative research approach as there are people willing to define it. We have adapted and modified Robert Emerson's (1983) definition of *field research* to offer the following definition of qualitative research:

> Qualitative research is the study of people in their natural environments as they go about their daily lives. It tries to understand how people live, how they talk and behave, and what captivates and distresses them.... More importantly, it strives to understand the *meaning* people's words and behaviors have for them.

What Do Qualitative Researchers Do?

With the above definition in mind, we can now describe what some of your roles and responsibilities would be if you actually carried out a qualitative research study. W. Lawrence Neuman (1994) has provided a helpful summary of what the work may require of you. The qualitative researcher:

- Observes ordinary events and everyday activities as they happen in natural settings, in addition to any unusual occurrences.

- Is directly involved with the people being studied and personally experiences the process of daily social life in the field setting.

- Acquires an insider's point of view while maintaining the analytic perspective or distance of an outsider.

- Uses a variety of techniques and social skills in a flexible manner as the situation demands.

- Produces data in the form of extensive written notes, as well as diagrams, maps, or pictures to provide very detailed descriptions.

- Sees events holistically (e.g., as a whole unit, not in pieces) and individually in their social context.

- Understands and develops empathy for members in a field setting, and does not just record "cold" objective facts.

- Notices both explicit (recognized, conscious, spoken) and tacit (less recognized, implicit, unspoken) aspects of culture.

- Observes ongoing social processes without upsetting, disrupting, or imposing an outside point of view.

- Is capable of coping with high levels of personal stress, uncertainty, ethical dilemmas, and ambiguity.

Many of the above roles and activities are not only carried out in qualitative research studies but are required for good social work practice as well. We will now turn to the general phases of a qualitative research study.

PHASES IN QUALITATIVE RESEARCH STUDIES

Most qualitative research studies share a common set of phases that you must go through. Norman K. Denzin (1989) and Buford H. Junker (1960) have provided us with a composite summary of them:

- Prepare yourself, read the literature, and defocus.

- Select a field site and gain access to it.

- Adopt a social role, learn the ropes, and get along with members.

- Watch, listen, and collect quality data.

- Begin to analyze data, generate and evaluate working hypotheses.

- Focus on specific aspects of the setting and use theoretical sampling.

- Conduct field interviews with member informants.

- Physically leave the field setting, complete the analysis, and write a research report.

We have rearranged the above phases to form four: (1) planning your study, (2) gathering your data, (3) analyzing your data, and (4) writing your report. Each phase will be discussed separately in Part One of our book.

Let us now turn our attention to how qualitative studies can contribute to our knowledge base.

TOWARD ESTABLISHING A KNOWLEDGE BASE

Put simply, like all research approaches, the qualitative approach attempts to strengthen our profession's knowledge base. In addition, it can be useful to you when you want to evaluate your effectiveness with a client. To illustrate how the qualitative research approach to knowledge development operates in social work, we will use one general, common social work problem as an example throughout this book—the plight of women who have been victims of domestic violence and have sought safety in a women's emergency shelter. As you may know, many women, upon leaving a shelter, return to live with the men who victimized them in the first place. Many also do not, and we will make extensive use of a qualitative research study that focuses on their experience as an example throughout this book.

The first group—those who return to their abusive partners—can present perplexing and troubling issues to social workers who work on their behalf. On one hand, there is no disputing the value of a woman's self-determination and her right to freely make a choice to return to her partner (or not to return). On the other hand, when her choice means she could be putting herself at risk of further victimization (and perhaps her children as well), many of us would see this as problematic. This represents an issue about which social workers would like to know more, just as we would be interested in knowing more about the experience of women who decide not to return to live with their abusive former partners.

Hopefully, the more knowledge we have about such situations, the better able we are to provide effective and efficient services to these women when they enter, go through, and leave the shelters. There are two main, complementary ways that this knowledge can be developed—through the use of a quantitative research approach or the qualitative research approach.

This chapter will provide a brief discussion of the qualitative research approach by comparing it with the quantitative research approach, sometimes called the positivistic approach, or the scientific method. There is no doubt that both methods would approach the same research problem differently, and thus generate different research findings and practice implications. Nevertheless, their common long-range goal is identical—to produce useful knowledge for social workers. For now, let us turn to the role of knowledge development within our profession.

The Never-Ending Quest for Knowledge

At one time, many clinical social workers believed that women who reported a history of childhood incest were simply expressing an oedipal wish-fulfilling fantasy, and that "real" cases of incest were extremely rare. Now we know that the objective truth of the situation is different, and that incest and other forms of sexual abuse are a common source of pain for many of our clients. In this case, our framework of beliefs—our "constructed" reality—was not consistent with what was independently true, and many women received incompetent, even damaging professional help as a result. It is often extremely important for us to test our beliefs and to be willing to change our minds when we discover that they have deviated from objective facts.

Let us take a second example to illustrate how research knowledge can challenge established beliefs, positively changing a major social work treatment intervention that was developed several decades ago. The intervention focused on families in which one member suffered from schizophrenia, and tried to change the family system as its primary treatment modality. Authority figures in psychoanalysis and family therapy believed that schizophrenia was caused by faulty parenting. Blame was placed on such factors as parental discord, excessive familial interdependency, and "schizophrenogenic mothers" whose overprotective and domineering behaviors did not allow the child to develop an individual identity.

With the above in mind, some social workers tended to assume that families with a schizophrenic member must be dysfunctional. They focused their interventions on changing the family system, often inadvertently instilling guilt into the parents and increasing tensions rather than helping the parents to cope with their children who had been diagnosed as schizophrenic.

However, more recent research studies have shown that schizophrenia is largely caused by genetic and other biological factors, not by bad parenting, and one of the more effective interventions is to support the family in providing a non-stressful environment. It is not surprising that social workers acted on the beliefs of experts in schizophrenia without personally evaluating the research studies that had led to those beliefs. Had they investigated for themselves, and had they been trained in different research methodologies, they would have found that there was little real evidence to support the bad-parenting theory. They may have been more supportive of parents and thus more effective helpers.

The moral in these examples is simple: social workers, like all professionals, are obligated to constantly test the validity of their beliefs. When we find those beliefs are not objectively true, we must adjust our practices accordingly, staying consistent with our advancing knowledge base. In short, we should always use treatment techniques that have been demonstrated to be effective with certain types of client problems and discard those that are found to be ineffective.

QUANTITATIVE AND QUALITATIVE APPROACHES

As mentioned above, both quantitative and qualitative research approaches contribute to our knowledge base, in different but complementary ways. They are like two good wines, one red, the other white (white wine may go better with fish and red wine with lamb, for example). In short, one may be more appropriate to drink than the other depending on the circumstances—and personal preference.

Let us now turn to a brief discussion comparing the two research approaches in relation to our example. They could easily be directly compared with each other on many criteria, but for the sake of simplicity we will discuss only a small number: (1) the objectivity of their findings, (2) the generalizability of their findings, (3) their reductionistic properties, (4) their differential use of theory, (5) the numbers or words they use, and (6) the flexibility of their research techniques. All of these characteristics are highly interrelated, but again for the sake of simplicity we will briefly discuss each one separately.

Objectivity

Both research approaches strive for objectivity in that they provide ways of helping us assess whether what we believe is actually true. For example, anyone studying why some women return to abusive relationships after they leave the safety of a women's emergency shelter will have a few prior ideas and beliefs regarding that issue. It is possible that some believe such a decision suggests a psychological compulsion for the woman to place herself at risk—a variation on the discredited "female masochism" premise. Both qualitative and quantitative researchers would agree that it is important to assess the objective truth of such an idea, and their findings could influence the treatment social workers provide to large numbers of female clients.

The quantitative research approach accepts that there is a reality independent of what we believe, and its goal is to determine how congruent our beliefs are with the reality as it exists "out there." By contrast, some qualitative theorists have suggested that objectivity is a myth, or is at least unattainable. Some even believe that nothing objectively exists outside of our beliefs about it. We argue, against this, that testing our beliefs for their objectivity is not only possible, but is an ethical requirement for all responsible professionals. Our willingness to do so is the reason that we now know that many men who are violent toward women will victimize women no matter what those women do—the "female masochism" hypothesis has been challenged and found not to be generally objectively true.

Quantitative researchers studying women who return to abusive partners after leaving shelters will attempt to improve objectivity by using research methods that limit their personal involvement with the women, in an effort not to "contaminate" the study in any way. As Mary E. Swigonski (1994) puts it:

Logical positivism builds on the epistemological assumption of the possibility of separation of the observer from the observed, the knower from the known (Lincoln

& Guba, cited in Wood, 1990). This thinking requires that the subject and object of research activities be treated as separate, noninteracting entities. The scientist is viewed as an independent observer who minimizes any relationship between the self and the subject of study. The actions of the researcher are constructed so that they do not infect or alter objective truth.

In contrast to the above, the qualitative research approach expects that a close relationship between the researchers and the women will develop and that they will have a reciprocal influence on each other. Qualitative researchers do not remain indifferent to the lives of the people they talk with, and such personal involvement is welcomed rather than distrusted. The experience of the researchers may also be included as important data for analysis.

Another difference between the two research approaches is that quantitative researchers will often seek objectivity by gravitating to research questions employing variables that can be measured using well-established, standardized measuring instruments. Sometimes, they have to re-word the initial research question to fit their strict quantitative methodological expectations. For example, quantitative researchers exploring why women do or do not return to abusive partners may look to variables such as the extent of their social support network, their economic circumstances, or their levels of self-esteem—variables that can be easily measured.

Qualitative studies, by contrast, favor more open and subjective data collection and analysis approaches, setting out to understand the personal experiences of the women as they wrestle with their options. They may argue that the use of standardized measuring instruments presupposes too much, and prefer to hear about self-esteem issues (if these emerge at all) as they are experienced and expressed by each woman. In our qualitative research study, the quest for objectivity means:

> We want to understand the experience of women who have decided not to return to abusive partners as they really live it, independent of what we or others think is involved in their choice.

Generalization

One of the main objectives of quantitative research studies is to discover facts or principles that are generally true. Though ideals are always compromised when any research study is conducted in the field, quantitative researchers who want to learn more about women who do not return to abusive partners will want what they learn from the women in their study to be generally true for a larger group. Thus, they want the study's findings (derived from relatively few women) to be relevant to other similar women who did not participate in the study. In the pursuit of this ideal, quantitative researchers have developed an extensive knowledge of sampling and statistical procedures for determining how confidently they can believe that what they discovered in a study sample of abused women is true for a larger population of women with similar histories.

On the other hand, qualitative researchers place much less importance on the generalizability of their studies' findings. They correctly assert that the pressure to select a representative sample and then measure the same variable in each member of the sample limits the research inquiry in important ways. More often than not, a quantitative study would collect data that would sacrifice depth and detail, and the unique experiences of the women would be left aside. Qualitative researchers, however, may well talk with a smaller number of women about their decisions concerning their relationship to a violent former partner, aiming to learn about their experience in a more profound and personal way.

The goal of a qualitative study would be to understand each woman's unique experience in depth and with a richness of detail that a quantitative study can seldom achieve. The extent to which what is learned may be relevant to other women is important in many qualitative studies, but it is clear that the priorities between the two research approaches differ in regards to generalizability. This is okay as long as we know the goal of each research approach when it comes to the generalizability of the study's findings. To apply the issue of generalizability to the example that we will be using throughout this book:

> We will be doing a qualitative research study in order to understand each woman's unique experiences related to her decision not to return to her partner after leaving a women's emergency shelter. The women we will be talking with will not be randomly sampled, but selected on the basis of their interest and availability. What we learn from them will probably be relevant to some extent to others in similar situations (other women and the people who work with them will judge), but this is not a primary concern in planning the study.

Reductionism

The matter of reductionism has some parallels to the issue of generalizability described above. Reductionism is the measurement of a complex concept by reducing it to a number of measurable variables. Studying women who do not return to an abusive former partner, quantitative researchers will reduce this complex problem to a set of questions or hypotheses that contain variables that can be easily measured, for example: What is the relationship between available social support and economic resources and the decision to forge an independent life or to resume living with a perpetrator?

No research approach can come close to understanding "the interrelationships between all the elements of reality." However, when qualitative researchers say their approach generates a more holistic understanding of issues, the claim is valid. The qualitative researcher would talk in an open-ended frame of mind with the women who are living the process of deciding to stay separated from violent ex-partners. They would not ask the women to respond to a set of standardized questions, but simply to describe their situation, their experiences, and what it all means to them. This approach will very likely yield information that is richer and more attuned to the complexities of context and individual differences than the quantitative approach could ever produce. To apply the concept of reductionism to the example that we have selected for use throughout this book:

> In a qualitative study, we do not need to restrict ourselves to the measurement of variables that can be measured in the same way for all participants, rendering standardized information. Instead, we will invite each woman to share her unique experience, what that experience means to her, and the context within which these experiences and meanings unfold. This information will be used to try to understand what it is like to be her in her unique situation as a woman forging a new life, independent of the partner who has victimized her.

The Use of Theory

The two research approaches use theory in different ways. For example, based on existing theory, quantitative researchers could, at an early point in their work, easily advance a series of simple hypotheses containing variables that can be measured:

- On leaving a women's shelter, women victims of domestic abuse are more likely to live independently rather than return to their abusive former partner *if they have adequate economic means.*

- On leaving a women's shelter, women victims of domestic abuse are more likely to live independently rather than return to their abusive former partner *if they enjoy adequate social support networks as opposed to being socially isolated.*

- On leaving a women's shelter, women victims of domestic abuse are more likely to live independently rather than return to their abusive former partner *if their self-esteem is high rather than low.*

Each hypothesis above could easily be tested via the quantitative research approach. These hypotheses are not a product of the researcher's unfettered imagination, but are derived from existing knowledge and theory, which the researcher will have delved into as part of planning the study. Quantitative researchers often (not always) work *deductively*; beliefs are identified, stated formally (as illustrated above), and put to the test.

Qualitative researchers, by contrast, do not require rigorously defined questions and hypotheses before they can get to work; in fact, they may argue that the exercise of developing them is counter-productive. It may be enough to pursue the general goal of understanding how women leaving the shelter experience their relationship to the men who victimized them. Clarity about important concepts and variables then emerges in response to what the women have to say, not in response to preordained theory and beliefs. Qualitative researchers thus work primarily (though not exclusively) *inductively*, "from the facts up," rather than deductively, "from theory down." Referring to the use of theory in our example:

> The goal of our qualitative study is to gather information from each woman about her own unique experience, what that experience means to her, and the context within which these experiences and meanings unfold. This goal is not pursued in ignorance of what is already known (we will discuss this more in Phase One), but care is taken to assure that pre-existing knowledge and theory do not interfere with our ability to hear each woman's account afresh, minimizing interference from our biases and preconceptions. What we learn may be informed by theory in various ways, but it is driven by what our participants have to tell us. Theory may tell us that self-esteem influences a woman's ability to separate from an abusive spouse. While that theory may sensitize us to self-esteem issues, we will nevertheless be careful to let each woman we interview tell us how much weight her self-esteem deserves as a consideration. Rather than letting previous research findings dictate how self-esteem must be defined and measured, we will let each woman tell us what that concept means to her in the context of her experience.

The Use of Numbers and Words

On a general level, quantitative studies use numbers to describe their findings, and qualitative studies use words (or other "natural" means of communication, like images). For example, quantitative researchers who are interested in women victims' decision-making will gather data that can be expressed in numbers. Whether or not a woman returns to her abusive partner, the adequacy of her financial resources, how much social support she enjoys, and her level of self-esteem—all these variables can be measured, reduced to numbers, and manipulated statistically in order to discover any meaningful patterns. Is there in fact a relationship between levels of social support and the likelihood that an abused woman will return to live with her abuser? Can such a pattern be detected statistically, and is it strong enough to be considered statistically significant?

Qualitative researchers will often prefer to represent information in non-numerical forms, such as texts (words) or images. These kinds of representation are better suited to capturing and communicating the complexities and subtleties of human experiences. Instead of analyzing such data statistically, qualitative researchers may study a text for meaningful elements, look for similarities and differences between them, and establish how elements can fit into categories and how these categories can form more general themes. This is exactly what Mary Richmond did in the example at the beginning of this chapter.

When women are interviewed regarding their decision-making about the future (if any) of their relationship to their abusive partners, a tremendous range of experiences and meanings will emerge: remembrances of past abuse that led to earlier decisions to leave, concerns about their children, hopes and fears regarding a future as a single person, weighing of the reactions and advice of friends and extended family members, the practical difficulties associated with establishing an independent household, and so on. With reference to our example:

> If our goal were to know clearly how success at leaving an abusive partner relates to self-esteem as measured by a standard instrument, we would certainly consider a quantitative study, where these variables could be expressed in numbers and our findings analyzed statistically. Since our goal is to gain a complex understanding of our participants' experience, and to retain as much of that complexity and subtlety in our eventual presentation of findings, we will leave the information in the form in which the women give it to us—in words. We will still be looking for meaningful patterns and relationships, making sense out of a formidable amount of information, teasing out themes that will have relevance to other women in similar circumstances and to their social workers, but we will not reduce information to numbers and use statistics to assist us in our search.

Flexibility

There is no question that the qualitative research approach is more flexible than the quantitative one. For example, quantitative researchers design studies that utilize strict rules regarding sampling, research design, measurement, and the analysis of data. These rules indicate what researchers need to do to be reasonably sure of the validity, reliability, and generalizability of their studies' findings. When rules must be compromised for one reason or another, the quantitative researcher generally acknowledges this as a limitation of the study and provides an assessment of the degree to which this compromise undermines the overall soundness of the study's findings.

In a way, quantitative researchers place more faith in their research methods than in themselves. Someone conducting a quantitative study needs knowledge of and skills in research methods to employ them properly, but beyond that it does not matter who he or she is. In theory, once the details of the research design are established, anyone with the requisite training could implement the study and the findings should theoretically be the same.

In fact, quantitative researchers hope that others will replicate their work. A single study may find a statistically significant relationship between two variables: the more social support a women has upon leaving the shelter (Variable 1), the better are her chances of terminating an abusive relationship (Variable 2). While this finding alone is certainly useful, if the same research design is implemented with a similar sample of women and generates the same results on subsequent occasions, the believability of those results is vastly improved.

Qualitative researchers also have accomplished much over the years in spelling out guidelines for increasing the rigor of their methods. However, it is still the case that the credibility we assign to qualitative findings depends on our trust in the intelligence and discipline of the researcher as much as our faith in qualitative methods. Further, a qualitative researcher who interviews women who leave the shelter, then studies the transcripts of those interviews and determines the categories of meaning and the themes that they contain, is conducting a unique study. No matter how closely subsequent researchers follow his or her approach, there is no expectation that the results will be exactly the same. A different person with a different mind-set, research experience, knowledge base, and interviewing skills will have a different kind of relationship with the research participants, and thus will inevitably produce a somewhat different set of understandings. Replication is not the major goal in qualitative studies as it is with quantitative ones. With respect to our study:

> While we will approach our study with a conceptual map in mind (see Phase One), this framework will be facilitative rather than constraining. Flexibility is never absolute, but in our interviews (Phase Two), we will be able to take whatever direction is appropriate, within the general goal of the study. In our analysis (Phase Three), we will not be directed by predetermined hypotheses, but will follow concepts and themes as they emerge from our examination of our interview transcripts.

> With this kind of flexibility, eventual outcomes cannot be predicted. Also, while future researchers will, hopefully, learn from and build on our work (Phase Four), there is no expectation that our study will ever be replicated by someone else.

GOOD RESEARCH IS GOOD RESEARCH

Fundamental to knowledge acquisition through quantitative and qualitative research studies is the idea that what we think should be rooted in and tested against good evidence, and that sound articulated methods—systematic, disciplined inquiry—are necessary to bring this about. A good research study respects these essentials, regardless of the tradition within which it is conducted, quantitative or qualitative.

Bad research can also be found in both approaches. Qualitative case studies that pathologized women, and lower income people as well, are abundant in the literature into the 1970s and beyond. Often, quantitative methods are now being used to repair the damage. Quantitative studies that evaluated social work interventions without recognizing their complexity or that dismissed the perceptions of the practitioners and their clients as subjective, and therefore irrelevant, did harm that qualitative researchers are working to correct.

Neither research approach can claim its adherents have never done harm, and neither can deny that the other has made a genuine contribution. Neither deserves blind faith in its inherent virtues, and neither is innately perverse. As we have discussed, however, differences do exist. We now will turn to a brief discussion of the implications of those differences as they relate to: (1) our profession's knowledge base, (2) the practitioner, (3) gender, and (4) culture.

Research and the Profession's Knowledge Base

All approaches to research must generate and test the knowledge we need to be effective with our clients. Quantitative and qualitative approaches alike can contribute significantly in both ways. The main difference between the two is the kinds of knowledge they generate, which overlap but still tend to have different advantages and uses.

The cumulative effect of well-conducted quantitative research methods can be tremendously powerful in establishing client needs and documenting the effectiveness of our interventions. As examples, the steady accumulation in recent decades of evidence about the incidence of child abuse, sexual abuse, and AIDS as well as violence against women has changed the awareness of the public and professionals, and has had a wide-ranging impact on services to those populations. Indifference and skepticism about these issues has retreated as increasingly well-designed research has reinforced the message of earlier studies. Quantitative studies have an enviable ability to say, "This is true whether you want to believe it or not."

On the other hand, we need to know more than just the frequencies of the different forms of victimization, or how often a particular social work program produces particular outcomes for traumatized clients. When we want to understand the impacts of trauma in more depth and detail, when we want rich information about the experience of social workers and survivors working to ameliorate the effects of abuse, when we need to describe healing processes in ways that capture this human experience as something highly individual and sensitive to context—when these are our goals, the qualitative research approach is very useful.

The two approaches can contribute differently at different stages in the knowledge-building enterprise. When not much is known about a problem—in the early days of designing social programs for women who have been physically abused by their partners, for example—qualitative methods are well suited to providing exploratory information about possible needs and interventions. Once a reasonable understanding of such variables has been accumulated, quantitative methods can be efficiently used to provide more precise and generalizable information about the impacts that specific interventions have on needs. Qualitative researchers continue to contribute, however, by persisting in exploring issues, adding depth and texture to quantitative findings.

Considerations such as these lead us to believe that our profession would be foolish to reject the contribution to our knowledge base of either research approach. Irwin Epstein (1988) had a few strong words to say about the complementarity of the two research approaches over a decade ago:

- Thus far we have maintained that quantitative and qualitative methods each has its special uses—it is only the uneducated person who states that one method is unequivocally better than the other. As a result, rather than asking which is best, it makes more sense for us to ask under what conditions each method is better than the other as a research strategy.

- To imply that we, as professional social workers, must make a choice between one or the other research method is senseless, idiotic, and simple-minded, to say the least. Both methods make meaningful contributions to our understanding of the social world and, when used together, can obviously augment it.

Research and the Practitioner

In recent years, some educators have suggested that front-line social workers should integrate quantitative research techniques into their practices. This was to be accomplished by educating students to become "scientific practitioners" who regularly employ quantitative research methods to evaluate the effectiveness and efficiency of their practices.

Arguably, there is little evidence that the researcher/practitioner model has succeeded in winning significant numbers of adherents. One of the many reasons for this is that the quantitative research methods that were offered to practitioners for their consideration were too foreign to practice to be easily integrated with day-to-day activities. The tasks of administering standardized measuring instruments and collating, coding, and statistically analyzing client data are unnatural and intrusive when they are introduced into a practice setting. Additionally, and probably more importantly, they were too time consuming to use on a regular basis.

It has been hinted within the literature that qualitative research methods may be more promising than quantitative methods when it comes to evaluating the effectiveness of our treatment interventions. Unfortunately, it does not seem to us that this is likely, for reasons of feasibility: qualitative research remains a highly demanding exercise, and the time involved in preparing transcripts and subjecting them to a systematic qualitative analysis (see our discussion in Phase Three) is no less formidable than the demands of quantitative research. A somewhat different issue is that of research utilization: will practitioners find the information generated by either approach more accessible and relevant to their work? Only time will tell.

Research and Gender

There have been rumblings throughout the literature that there are gender issues associated with the quantitative and qualitative research approaches. The suggestion, in brief, is that since the quantitative approach strives for objectivity (read "distance") at all costs, dispassionate logic, and well-engineered and thought-out research designs, it is rooted in male values.

A more extreme extension of this argument is that quantitative researchers, subjecting the people in their studies to procedures imposed with no consultation or agreement and reducing peoples' experience to numbers, are acting in patriarchal ways. Therefore, some believe that the quantitative research approach is inherently oppressive and morally inferior to the qualitative options. We know of women researchers with clear feminist commitments who have had difficulty getting their work published because its quantitative approach was ideologically unpalatable.

The qualitative research approach, on the other hand, has been said to employ research methods that value relationships, egalitarianism, and empowerment of all research participants, sometimes called co-researchers. With their respect for individual experience, subjectivity, and subtlety, qualitative methods have been said to be more compatible with women's ways of knowing and experiencing the world. Whatever the general validity of this position, it can easily be seriously overstated. While there appears to be current evidence that women and men are cognitively different, or have "different ways of knowing," the evidence also suggests that these differences are not particularly strong.

Differences within the sexes are much greater than differences between them—men and women may experience life somewhat differently, but they do not inhabit separate cognitive worlds. For this reason, it is easy to identify well-known male qualitative researchers as well as female quantitative researchers who do very good research studies—regardless of the research approach used.

As well, quantitative research studies and qualitative ones alike have been oppressively used. For example, practitioners who dismissed women's reports of sexual abuse as wish-fulfilling fantasy had solid support for their position in an extensive body of qualitative research findings beginning with the case studies of Sigmund Freud. To a large extent, quantitative studies have exposed this falsehood—an example of how this research approach had a liberating and empowering effect of considerable importance.

Research and Culture

Considerable concern has been expressed in recent years about research studies that involve people from diverse cultures. The concerns have indicated difficulties with both quantitative and qualitative approaches. Quantitative researchers have used standardized instruments developed in studies of one culture when studying others, without recognizing the problems this can create. A measure of social support employed with women who have been abused by their partners in a Haitian community in Florida, for example, might be quite inappropriate if it was developed with white college students in New York.

Language, assumptions, and values implicit in an instrument's questions and the way they are interpreted could be foreign to research participants, making the process confusing or difficult and rendering the study's findings invalid. It is also possible that the lack of any meaningful relationship between the researcher and the research participant can be experienced as strange or even intimidating by someone from another culture. Many research studies conducted with diverse cultures have been qualitative in nature (the studies of cultural anthropologists, for example), and these have also been subject to an over-whelming amount of criticism.

To the extent that qualitative researchers carry their own cultural assumptions into the field, they risk imposing a foreign frame of reference in interpreting the experience and meanings of the people they study. The problem is severe enough in the eyes of some critics that they have suggested the only people who should study a culture should be members of that culture.

There are no easy answers to these complex problems. Quantitative researchers are working to develop methods and measures that are sensitive to cultural diversity. At the same time, some qualitative researchers are hopeful that their efforts to develop research approaches that are sensitive to social contexts and different ways of interpreting human experience will help them answer the concerns that have been raised. In part, the issue will be less of a problem to the extent that members of different cultural groups develop ways of using both research approaches in the service of their own communities' agendas.

As we have noted more than once, research in either tradition can be used oppressively. There is truth, however, in the cliché that knowledge is power, and there are certainly examples of culturally disadvantaged groups who are doing good research studies to further their legitimate aims.

SUMMARY

The purpose of this brief chapter was to briefly explore the differences between quantitative and qualitative research approaches in a conciliatory spirit. We have argued in favor of pluralism, where differences in approach and emphasis are valued and the contributions of each approach are welcomed and seen as complementary to those of the other.

Hopefully, our respect for both qualitative and quantitative methods is clear, and our arguments for methodological pluralism in social work research are convincing. Ideological disputes may be diverting for academics, but the realities of practice are that the need for a research-informed, broad, diverse knowledge base has never been stronger. What is true of social life generally is also true for social work researchers: respect for diversity and valuing difference is the best recipe for a rich and well-differentiated profession, flexible and effective in its response to the complex needs that our clients present.

We will now turn our attention to the first phase of a qualitative research study, the topic of the following chapter.

ANNOTATED BIBLIOGRAPHY

SHERMAN, E., & REID, W.J. (Eds.). (1994). *Qualitative research in social work*. New York: Columbia University Press. This book is a "must" on the shelves of social workers with an interest in qualitative methods, as a compendium of the latest thinking and insights of social work scholars examining the full range of issues and options that qualitative researchers in our profession confront.

Sherman and Reid examine the emergence of qualitative methods as a response to social work's need for knowledge building. Many other chapters, too numerous to review separately, provide discussions of almost any "qualitative issue" that you may wish to explore. This book, however, does not tell you how to do a qualitative research study.

STRAUSS, A., & CORBIN, J. (1990). *Basics of qualitative research: Grounded theory, procedures, and techniques*. Newbury Park, CA: Sage. This book thoroughly details the concepts and skills of the grounded theory approach to qualitative research. Part I of their book is particularly relevant to Phase One of this book. The authors set the stage for doing a qualitative research study by presenting the philosophical view underpinning a grounded theory approach, defining the basic components of a grounded theory research study, addressing the personal role of the researcher, and discussing the various roles of the literature review process in qualitative research studies.

REFERENCES AND FURTHER READINGS

Anderson, M. (1993). Studying across difference: Race, class, and gender in qualitative research. In J. Stanfield & R. Dennis (Eds.), *Race and ethnicity in research methods* (pp. 39-52). Newbury Park, CA: Sage.

Berg, B.L. (1989). *Qualitative research methods for the social sciences*. Needham Heights, MA: Allyn & Bacon.

Berg, B.L. (1995). *Qualitative research methods for the social sciences* (2nd ed.). Needham Heights, MA: Allyn & Bacon.

Creswell, J. (1994). *Research design: Qualitative and quantitative approaches*. Newbury Park, CA: Sage.

Denzin, N.K. (1989). *The research act: A theoretical introduction to sociological methods* (3rd ed.). Englewood Cliffs, NJ: Prentice-Hall.

Denzin, N.K., & Lincoln, Y. (1994). Introduction: Entering the field of qualitative research. In N. Denzin & Y. Lincoln (Eds.), *Handbook of qualitative research* (pp. 1-17). Newbury Park, CA: Sage.

Ely, M. (1991). *Doing qualitative research: Circles within circles*. New York: Falmer Press.

Emerson, R.M. (1981). Observational fieldwork. *Annual Review of Sociology, 7*, 351-378.

Emerson, R.M. (1983). Introduction. In R.M. Emerson (Ed.), *Contemporary field research* (pp. 1-16). Boston: Little, Brown.

Epstein, I. (1988). Quantitative and qualitative methods. In R.M. Grinnell, Jr. (Ed.), *Social work research and evaluation* (3rd ed., pp. 185-198). Itasca, IL: F.E. Peacock.

Erlandson, D., Harris, E., Skipper, B., & Allen, S. (1993). *Doing naturalistic inquiry: A guide to methods*. Newbury Park, CA: Sage.

Gabor, P.A., & Grinnell, R.M., Jr. (1994). Should program decisions be based on empirical evidence? Yes! In W.W. Hudson & P. Nurius (Eds.), *Controversial issues in social work research* (pp. 142-146). Needham Heights, MA: Allyn & Bacon.

Gabor, P.A., & Grinnell, R.M., Jr. (1994). Rejoinder to Dr. Taber. In W.W. Hudson & P. Nurius (Eds.), *Controversial issues in social work research* (pp. 153-154). Needham Heights, MA: Allyn & Bacon.

Glasser, B., & Strauss, A. (1967). *The discovery of grounded theory: Strategies for qualitative research.* Chicago: Aldine.

Glesene, C., & Peshkin, A. (1992). *Becoming qualitative researchers: An introduction.* White Plains, NY: Longman.

Grinnell, R.M., Jr., Austin, C., Blythe, B.J., Briar, S., et. al. (1994). Social work researchers' quest for respectability. *Social Work, 39,* 469-470.

Guba, E., & Lincoln, Y. (1994). Competing paradigms in qualitative research. In N. Denzin & Y. Lincoln (Eds.), *Handbook of qualitative research* (pp. 105-117). Newbury Park, CA: Sage.

Harding, S. (1991). *Whose science? Whose knowledge? Thinking from women's lives.* Ithaca, NY: Cornell University Press.

Junker, B.H. (1960). *Field work.* Chicago: University of Chicago Press.

Lincoln, Y.S., & Guba, E.G. (1985). *Naturalistic inquiry.* Newbury Park, CA: Sage.

Lofland, J., & Lofland, L. (1984). *Analyzing social settings: A guide to qualitative observation and analysis* (2nd ed.). Belmont, CA: Wadsworth.

Marshall, C., & Rossman, G. (1989). *Designing qualitative research.* Newbury Park, CA: Sage.

Miles, M.B., & Huberman, A.M. (1994). *Qualitative data analysis: An expanded source book* (2nd ed.). Newbury Park, CA: Sage.

Neuman, W.L. (1994). *Social research methods: Qualitative and quantitative approaches* (2nd ed.). Needham Heights, MA: Allyn & Bacon.

Olesen, V. (1994). Feminisms and models of qualitative research. In N.K. Denzin & Y. Lincoln (Eds.), *Handbook of qualitative research* (pp. 158-174). Newbury Park, CA: Sage.

Patton, M. (1990). *Qualitative evaluation and research methods.* Newbury Park, CA: Sage.

Richmond, M.E. (1921). *Social diagnosis.* New York: Russell Sage Foundation.

Schatzman, L., & Strauss, A. (1973). *Field research: Strategies for a natural sociology.* Englewood Cliffs, NJ: Prentice-Hall.

Sherman, E., & Reid, W.J. (Eds.). (1994). *Qualitative research in social work.* New York: Columbia University Press.

Stanfield, J. (1994). Ethnic modeling in qualitative research. In N.K. Denzin & Y. Lincoln, (Eds.), *Handbook of qualitative research* (pp. 175-188). Newbury Park, CA: Sage.

Swigonski, M.E. (1994). The logic of feminist standpoint theory for social work research. *Social Work, 39,* 387-393.

Tyson, K. (1994). Author's reply: Response to "social work researchers' quest for respectability." *Social Work, 39,* 737-741.

Tyson, K. (Ed.). (1994). *New foundations for scientific social and behavioral research: The heuristic paradigm.* Needham Heights, MA: Allyn & Bacon.

Williams, M., Tutty, L.M., & Grinnell, R.M., Jr. (1995). *Research in social work: An introduction* (2nd ed.). Itasca, IL: F.E. Peacock.

Wood, K.M. (1990). Epistemological issues in the development of social work practice knowledge. In L. Videka-Sherman & W.J. Reid (Eds.), *Advances in clinical social work research* (pp. 373-390). Silver Spring, MD: National Association of Social Workers.

Part One

The Research Process

Phase One: Planning Your Study   **24**
   Michael Rothery, Leslie M. Tutty, & Richard M. Grinnell, Jr.

Phase Two: Collecting Your Data   **50**
   Gayla Rogers & Elaine Bouey

Phase Three: Analyzing Your Data   **88**
   Heather Coleman & Yvonne Unrau

Phase Four: Writing Your Report   **120**
   Robert McClelland & Carol D. Austin

Michael Rothery
Leslie M. Tutty
Richard M. Grinnell, Jr.

Phase One

PLANNING YOUR RESEARCH STUDY

    Step 1: Defining Your General Problem Area
    Step 2: Identifying Why the Problems Are Problematic
    Step 3: Determining the Preliminary Groundwork Needed
    Step 4: Developing a Conceptual Map

CONSIDERING PROCEDURES AND ETHICS

    Step 5: Recruiting a Supervisor
    Step 6: Determining Needed Resources
    Step 7: Choosing a Site for Your Study
    Step 8: Identifying and Dealing with Ethical Considerations
    Step 9: Writing a Proposal
    Step 10: Obtaining Permission and Ethical Clearances

SUMMARY

ANNOTATED BIBLIOGRAPHY

REFERENCES AND FURTHER READINGS

Planning Your Study

H AVING BRIEFLY VISITED a few key theoretical issues in the previous chapter, we can now turn to the heart of our book—a practical, straightforward model that discusses the phases, steps, and tasks that you can follow as you conduct your qualitative research study. Our model is open to modification as circumstances require, and we would be astonished if you followed it exactly as outlined in the pages to follow.

Dividing the qualitative research process into discrete phases, steps, and tasks is partly arbitrary. We have exercised our judgement regarding how this process can be usefully broken down, but other writers may present it differently. The reality of doing a qualitative research study is never as tidy as it appears in our book; instead of moving through our model in an orderly linear fashion, you will inevitably find yourself moving back and forth between and among the steps and tasks within each phase. You will also find yourself going between and among the phases themselves. All this is as it should be, and we hope you will not be perplexed to discover that our guidelines, while hopefully useful, cannot be used as an invariable formula. Even our best hints and suggestions will not spare you the occasional struggle, periods of confusion, or the need to flounder at times until the way becomes clear.

Those who are relatively new to the literature on qualitative research can also be confused by inconsistent use of common terms. Different authors use the same technical terms to refer to somewhat different things. We have tried to be clear what we mean by the words we employ in this book, but you should be aware that another author may attach a different sense to the very same words.

PLANNING YOUR RESEARCH STUDY

When you decide to undertake a qualitative research project you are making a major commitment. You will be investing huge amounts of time (your own and other people's) and, to a lesser degree, resources. Careful planning is necessary to be sure your study proceeds as efficiently as possible and produces results that make you feel the hours of difficult work you have put in were worthwhile.

As you know from the previous chapter, at the beginning of a research study, qualitative researchers do not necessarily have to spell out their hypotheses or research questions as precisely as do quantitative researchers. The stipulation of variables to be measured and their operational definitions are not required at the outset of a qualitative study. Nevertheless, a well-thought out focus for your study is vitally important and heavily influences the study's success.

Step 1: Defining Your General Problem Area

As we indicated in the last chapter, the problem area that we will be using throughout this book has to do with the experiences of women who have been physically abused by their partners. More specifically, our study will include women who have sought safety in a women's emergency shelter and who have decided not to return to their ex-partners after they leave the shelter. In a nutshell, we want to know what happens to them as they attempt to establish separate lives away from their ex-partners.

This specific problem area did not come to us in a dream, or in the mail, or as a serendipitous insight. It emerged out of our professional work and our experiences as social work researchers and practitioners with an interest in family violence. From our own observations and from what colleagues in the field have told us, these women are at a critical juncture in their lives. Few, if any, research studies have identified their experiences and needs at this point in their lives. Thus, there is little reliable information to help us understand how we, as professional social workers, can best help them as they decide to live new lives away from their abusive ex-partners. It would be helpful if we could provide the appropriate social services and support systems for these women, as these could make a big difference for them as well as their children.

Task 1a: Reflecting on Your General Problem Area

Obviously, your own personal interests will take you in your own direction. The first step is for you to determine, *in general terms*, what that direction will be. This direction will be guided by writing things down. Writing is a tremendous help with thinking, and we strongly suggest that you proceed with pen and paper at hand, or sitting at your personal computer. Take notes as you reflect.

Your starting point for defining your general problem area can vary. You may have a situation (past or present) in your practice experience that troubles you, or you may have read about a problem that engages your interest for some reason. You, or a family member or close friend, may have gone through an experience that remains as a piece of unfinished business for you, which you would like to understand in more depth.

A classmate, colleague, or supervisor may tell you about a group of people, or *population*, that needs to be studied and that you think may be an interesting focus. Whatever the route by which ideas come to you, and however vague they may be when they first present themselves, *write them down*.

Keep in mind (as you note possible populations to study) that a research problem should be interesting to *you*. While this may seem a statement of the obvious, it is not unusual for novice researchers to find themselves studying certain types of populations that were suggested by others and are not strong personal interests to them. It is doubly hard to complete a sometimes arduous process if your personal interest in your population is not strong.

A final issue to think about is the precise operational definition of your population. More often than not, your initial ideas about your population will be general: for example, "I am interested in studying family violence"—those families experiencing family violence would in this case be the population for your study.

This is okay at first, but soon you will need to be much more specific. With your initial population so abstractly stated, there are too many possible directions you could go: child abuse, sexual abuse, elder abuse, domestic assaults within cultural groupings, the role of alcohol abuse in domestic assaults, and so on.

Your final objective is to state your population with enough specificity that you have a reasonably clear sense of exactly whom you want to study and where you will go to find these people.

Once you find them, what will you ask them? And, much more importantly, *why* will you ask the questions that you do?

Task 1b: Narrowing Down Your Population

Defining the general focus for your study is often a matter of narrowing down the population you are interested in. In our example, our population is women who have been physically abused by their partners. However, your interests could draw you toward any other population of people that social workers serve: the elderly, children, male perpetrators, people with AIDS, the homeless, or families with schizophrenic members, for example. As you reflect and write ideas down, you may find yourself narrowing the definition of your potential population in exceptionally important ways.

In our example, the population we finally chose to study was *not* "women who have been physically abused by their partners," but consisted of four interrelated components, or concepts if you will:

- Women

- who have been physically abused by their partners

- and have sought safety within a women's emergency shelter

- and have decided not to return to their ex-partners upon leaving the shelter.

The above is a reasonably specific population to study, to say the least, and we can easily enough determine where to go to find them.

Task 1c: Exploring Potential Problems Within Your Population

Having identified a specific population that you are interested in, you will need to think through what it is about these people you want to study—what is your problem focus? A problem exists when there is something you do not know about, and this "not knowing" matters to you. The point here is that if you have more information about the problem, you will be able to act more competently and provide better social work services to these women. Unless you have some clear idea about what you are uninformed about within the population you want to study, and *why* that matters not only to the population but also to you, you have not identified a topic for a research study and you should stop your study and go back to Task 1*a*.

Read books and journal articles; talk to yourself, fellow classmates, and colleagues; and take notes as you pursue the answer to the question: What is *it* I want to know about this population? The "it" is the problem(s) you want to study. It is possible, however unlikely, to proceed to interview these women having simply defined the population—we could set out knowing that we want to talk with them in an effort simply to better understand their experiences. Our initial focus would be: "What is it like to be you in this situation?" However, as we reflect further on what we do not know about these women, we may well identify more specifically what it is we want to know about them.

In our example, we could have explored many problems relevant to these women. After long talks with each other, fellow colleagues, and social workers who work directly with these women, we decided to focus our study on seven problems areas we believed each woman would be facing:

- Her relationship with her ex-partner

- Her court experiences, for those women who were pressing charges or dealing with divorce or custody issues

- Her self-esteem

- Her coping capacities with her children and the children's feelings toward the separation

- Her financial situation and vocational training possibilities (along with finding a job)

- Her housing situation

- Her safety

Obviously, we could have explored many other problems with this population that would be well worth pursuing—no two researchers (or research teams) will ever conduct an identical qualitative research study. It should also be noted that some qualitative researchers would scold us for defining the problem areas to the extent that we have. This issue will be discussed in more detail shortly.

Step 2: Identifying Why the Problems Are Problematic

As you are brainstorming about the possible problems (Task 1c) of your population (Task 1b), the "So what?" question should be regularly raised. We all have an infinite number of unanswered questions in our lives; fortunately, most of these are not highly relevant. With respect to our example, the importance of knowing what happens to women who have been physically abused by their partners and have decided not to return home may seem obvious—of course this would be relevant information for social workers who work with these women. Still, it is very useful to ask ourselves, "So what?" What difference will it make when we better understand how these seven problems affect the women in our study?

The "So what?" question is useful because it opens the door to a host of other practical considerations. The seven types of information we want to gather (i.e., problem areas), of course, have wide-ranging possible impacts. The women themselves may well benefit by reflecting upon and clarifying important further problems, such as their safety.

For clinical social workers involved with this population, an increased awareness of the problem of safety for women in this situation can help them be more deeply empathic, and can alert them to a potentially important focus for intervention. For program developers and policy makers, a more accurate and in-depth appreciation of how safety issues affect such women and their children can assist in the creation of better services and policies.

For some qualitative researchers, the question of possible impacts may be secondary. Achieving a deeper understanding of a problem area and bringing that understanding to greater public awareness may be a sufficient goal. As a social worker, and given your responsibility to our profession, it is more important for you to think through how your study's findings are to be used. Certainly, an impact at all conceivable levels of social work practice, from clinical work through to international social policy, can be entertained as your study's goal if you are highly ambitious, extraordinarily talented, inexhaustible and, most importantly, naive.

If on reflection you decide that your lofty goal should be more modest—that your most important contribution will be information for the front-line worker, for example—this realization will be very useful in subsequent steps of the research process. We urge you to have a small and well-defined realistic goal for your study. We would rather see you do a small study well than a large study poorly.

The seven problem areas that we focused on are hardly the only ones we could pursue with these women. There are, in fact, hundreds of perfectly legitimate alternatives. The reason we selected these is that we have conducted prior work in this area and have come to appreciate how little is known about women at that decision-point in their lives. Our own observations, supported by colleagues in the field, confirm that it is a critical juncture, and one about which social workers would like to know more.

Our general problem area and the more specific seven problems we are going to tap into are rooted in our own values, interests, professional priorities, and curiosity. They are also considered relevant by the professional community we work in and by similar women who have been physically abused by their partners. Finally, it is feasible for us to study these women since we have developed formal and informal networks that will facilitate our access to them.

These women in turn will provide us with the information we will need to address each of the seven problems we have identified.

Step 3: Determining the Preliminary Groundwork Needed

This step could be placed earlier, since it raises considerations that require attention early in your research endeavor. The issues to be resolved are partly practical and partly ideological—and they are therefore worthy of careful attention.

The amount of "front-end" planning you should do before you actually begin collecting data is a matter of debate among qualitative researchers. Some people believe you should plan as little as possible, arguing that the more prior reading, thinking, and discussing you do, the more you will approach your research participants with preconceptions. (Preconceptions operate as mental filters, or worse yet, blinders that may make it more difficult for you to be completely open to what your research participants have to say.) Others argue for more flexibility, and suggest you exercise a degree of professional judgement. If you are working in an area where good work has previously been done and solid information or theory exists, you may well decide to build on that rather than starting from the beginning as if nobody had studied your population before you. Since we do research studies to add to our profession's knowledge base, we must also recognize the practical need for studies that build upon what is already known. Time, money, and ethics (bothering the people whom we want to study) do not afford us the luxury of rediscovering well-explored territory, whatever the academic and philosophical rationale for doing so.

Task 3a: Negotiating a Clear Contract

As you decide how much groundwork is desirable for your qualitative research study, you must remember that you are dealing with a matter (the *qualitative* research approach) about which everyone has an opinion and ideological positions are often fervently held. It is therefore important to have a clear contract with your supervisor(s), co-researcher(s), and/or funder(s) as to your intentions regarding groundwork. Our own position (with which you may or may not concur) is that knowledge of prior research and theory development in the area you choose to study is worth acquiring: it makes you less likely to repeat other people's mistakes or to waste time rediscovering what is already well known.

Also, while we can understand the suggestion that you should approach your study without preconceptions as an ideal, we think it is impossible to achieve. Inevitably, you will have prior beliefs about problem areas that interest you.

Indeed, some definition of the problem is necessary if your study is to proceed: unless you know what you want to study and why, you are unlikely to go to the trouble of doing the research study in the first place. Further, any definition of a problem area involves a degree of cognitive mapping. How much is useful and how much is too much is a judgement call. Like us, you will make your own decision based on the particular area you are working in, and in negotiation with the people who will be important to the success of your work.

A point on which most, if not all, qualitative researchers agree is that you are required to think through your preconceptions, writing them down and assessing how they might affect your ability to be open to new information from your research study. People tend to see what they expect to see, and the best safeguard against this is to clearly note your biases and stay alert to how they influence you, rather than to pretend they are not there.

Step 4: Developing a Conceptual Map

As we have suggested, all of us create cognitive maps of the situations we have to deal with. The creation of mental "schemas" is an activity that appears very early in life, and is something that we all do in order to deal with the world in a reasonably organized way. The map you will develop with respect to your study will be largely conceptual, the goal being to identify the main concepts that will guide your work and to determine what they mean to you.

The map you create at the beginning of your study will be incomplete in many important respects. The goal of qualitative studies is often to explore the meanings that study participants attach to their experience, and those meanings cannot be known to you in advance; if they were, it would be pointless to conduct your study.

Before various regions of the world had been fully explored, cartographers labeled some areas *terra incognita*—unknown territory. Their maps therefore described what was known and what was unknown, and this was very useful. Explorers knew where their services were required, and they also had good information as to how to get there. Similarly, in planning your own explorations you will greatly benefit from a conceptual map that is as clear as possible about where the *terra incognita* is that you intend to visit, and will help you get to it efficiently.

Task 4a: Listing Essential Concepts

In our study, our conceptual map addresses a number of concepts and can be broken down into the population we wish to study and the problems we wish to address within the study:

Population (from Task 1b)

- Women

- who have been physically abused by their partners

- and have sought safety within a women's emergency shelter

- and have decided not to return to their ex-partners on leaving the shelter.

Problems (from Task 1c)

- Women's perceived relationships with their ex-partners

- Women's perceptions of their court experiences, for those women who were pressing charges or dealing with divorce or custody matters

- Women's self-esteem

- Women's coping capacities with their children and the children's responses to the separation

- Women's financial situations and vocational training possibilities (along with finding a job)

- Women's housing situations

- Women's safety issues

If we thought it useful, some of these concepts could be broken down further. "Housing situation," for example, subsumes ideas such as cost, comfort, location, adequacy, and desirability.

Task 4b: Refining Concepts and Specifying Their Meaning

Of the several concepts listed above, some need to be defined (population ones) and others should be left as *terra incognita* (problem ones). Luckily for us, the population ones are easy to define—we can simply accept that our main concept applies to anyone who has been given refuge in a women's shelter, defines herself as victimized, and plans to leave her ex-partner. In other studies, this concept could require considerable thought. Should domestic assault be taken to mean physical violence only, or should it include emotional abuse?

Does it matter if the perpetrator is unequivocally responsible for his behavior, as opposed to instances where neurological impairment or mental illness is implicated? Many such issues may or may not be important, but they need to be thought through.

Similarly, we can simply rely on shelter staff and the women themselves to identify women who are leaving the shelter. Thinking the issue through, however, is still important, and will raise such issues as whether to include only women who have *actually left* the shelter versus those who are *preparing to leave*. Whether a woman has decided to live independently can be defined through self-report, or may be taken to include only women who have stayed separate from their ex-partners for a specified period of time, or who have taken concrete steps to establish independent households. The decision of how detailed your map needs to be is a matter for your own best judgement, using practicality as your guiding principle. Taking time and care in developing a proper map is excellent insurance against getting lost or pursuing false leads once your study is underway.

Task 4c: Reviewing the Literature

The timing of a literature review is a point of disagreement among qualitative researchers. Some suggest it should be delayed until after your interviews are completed and your analysis is done (or is underway). Our view is based on arguments that have already been stated in the discussion of the pros and cons of planning and conceptualizing a study—we think that you should review the literature relevant to your problem area as soon as possible (though you should also plan to revisit it later). If you were also interested in studying the experiences of women victims of domestic assaults, your search of the literature could help with developing your conceptual map in many ways:

- How have other researchers conceptualized this type of violence? If they included psychological and emotional abuse in their definition, how did they conceptualize that?

- What methods have previous researchers used in their efforts to understand women's experiences. More importantly, how well did different options work?

- What ethical dilemmas have previous researchers encountered?

Questions such as these (and many others) may be addressed in the literature, and the chance to learn from explorers who have gone before you is invaluable. It will give you a better focus and sense of direction for your study.

The amount of information you need to address most problem areas is increasing daily, and extremely rapidly. Fortunately, the technologies that help us cope with the information explosion are also improving quickly. Using these technologies to master the literature in a given area is a complex set of tasks, and in order to do justice to these without losing the flow of our discussion of phases, steps, and tasks, we suggest that you read Elaine Bouey and Gayla Rogers (1993) and Gayla Rogers and Elaine Bouey (1993) before you start reviewing the literature.

CONSIDERING PROCEDURES AND ETHICS

With the preliminary conceptual development of your study complete, you can turn to another part of your planning: the procedural aspects of your study. These involve arranging the resources your study will require, thinking through the logistics of carrying it out, and addressing ethical concerns.

Your life as a qualitative researcher is partly scientific and partly political. Students conducting research studies to meet academic program requirements will have to give some thought to the personalities, priorities, and research expertise of members of their social work department or school who may be a resource to them. Much of social work research takes place in agency settings, and this means negotiations with agency personnel are necessary to obtain support for your study.

Step 5: Recruiting a Supervisor

Students completing a research study as part of their academic programs are the major audience for this book, and this step has been written with their special needs in mind. If you are not a student but are planning a qualitative study, the material in this section may still be useful in thinking about soliciting support for your study and, perhaps, recruiting members to a research team.

By the time you begin to plan your study, you should have a list of potential academic supervisors that you would like to work with. At the point where you know what your problem area is (Task 1b) and have developed initial ideas on how you would like to go about studying it (Task 1c), you can also begin finding someone to be your supervisor. While Step 5 is described here for organizational purposes, it overlaps with the previous four steps.

A potential supervisor will probably want to contribute to the conceptualization of your study, and the amount of front-end planning that is desirable is a matter about which both of you will have an opinion. For this reason, it is wise to begin discussion with as many potential supervisors as possible early in your planning process.

Task 5a: Writing a Brief Synopsis of Your Proposed Study

You have decided to study a particular problem area—you have a reasonably clear idea regarding the population that interests you and what the unknowns are that you wish to explore. You know why the problem area is important and have decided you wish to explore it using a qualitative research approach. Summarize this information in a brief document that will inform potential supervisors about your intentions and excite their interest in your work.

Task 5b: Stipulating What You Want in a Supervisor

Different supervisors have different strengths, and what students want from a supervisor also varies. Obviously, you will be interested in someone with whom you think you can enjoy a productive relationship, whose knowledge you respect, and who will challenge you to work to a high standard, producing work you can confidently defend. Beyond this, there are any number of issues you can think about:

- How essential is it for your supervisor to have a great amount of expertise regarding the population you have elected to study?

- Do you want a supervisor who can help you gain access to your population?

- How much help do you need in identifying the relevant literature, or with the conceptualization of your study?

- Do you want a supervisor who is a committed and experienced qualitative researcher, or one who is flexible and open-minded regarding the qualitative research approach?

- Do you need a supervisor who can advise you regarding research methods and procedures, or can you get this information elsewhere?

- Do you work relatively independently, or do you want a supervisor who is able and willing to be available on a frequent basis and who will help you structure your work by suggesting deadlines for particular tasks?

- What degree of compatibility do you require between you and your supervisor on some of the debatable methodological points we have discussed, such as the need to conceptually map a study in advance or the function and timing of the literature review?

As you write down the answers to the above questions (others may well occur to you and/or your supervisor), you will establish the criteria that are important to you. You can also prioritize them and think about which you want to be rigid about and where you can be more flexible. As your ideal supervisor profile becomes clearer, you will also likely begin thinking about particular professors, and adjusting what you would ideally like to the realities of who is actually available, ready, and willing. Your supervisor does not have to offer everything you need in relation to your study; usually, it is necessary to consult with others about your substantive area or method as your study proceeds.

Task 5c: Talking with Potential Supervisors

Once you have identified one or more potential supervisors, provide them with a copy of your synopsis and make an appointment to discuss your ideas further. Keep your criteria (Task 5*b*) in mind during these discussions, so you can weigh how well each person will meet your educational and research needs.

Task 5d: Contracting with a Supervisor

Once you and a supervisor have agreed to work together, the terms under which you will proceed should be clearly stated. Some may wish to limit their commitment to collaborating until you develop a full-blown research proposal, with a review and recontracting to occur at that point. The amount of conceptual work that is to be done before data gathering commences, the handling of the literature review, and the type of proposal that needs to be developed are other points about which you should seek explicit agreement. Also important is agreement about how you would like the supervisory relationship to work: how often do you anticipate meeting, how much direction and support do you want, and what substantial or methodological issues might require supplementary help from someone else?

Step 6: Determining Needed Resources

Intellectual stimulation, support, and technical assistance are all important resources that you will have thought about while recruiting a supervisor. Your study will need other resources to succeed, and it is a good idea to itemize these as thoroughly as possible. Resource requirements vary widely from study to study, though we can suggest common issues to consider. These are: your time, your access to your population, your equipment and supplies that are available to you, your space, and your friends.

- *Time* — Qualitative research studies are extremely labor intensive, and the demands they make on your time are worth thinking about (though precise estimates are difficult). You will need time to prepare your research proposal. For data collection, budget time for meeting with agency representatives who may help you access participants, for contacting participants to arrange appointments, and travel (in addition to the actual interviews). If you intend to transcribe tapes of your interviews (discuss this with your supervisor—some will consider it important for you to do this yourself), you will find the task time consuming even if you are a skilled typist. Finally, the analysis of qualitative data is a slow and painstaking task, as you will learn if you talk to others who have completed qualitative studies. These same people will probably tell you that you have underestimated the amount of time your study will take.

- *Access* — You have defined the population of people you wish to invite to participate in your study, and you know what it is about their experience that interests you. Sometimes access to a population is easy, but this is not always the case. You need to question your own resources in this regard. Do you have contacts within agencies that serve this population? Can you reach people by publicizing your study and asking them to contact you? What is involved in getting permission to carry out your study in the agency you hope to utilize?

- *Equipment and Supplies* — If your study will require transportation, this can be a relevant expense. If you intend to tape your interviews, you will need a good tape recorder (it must be reliable, with a high-quality microphone) and tapes. You may also need equipment to make transcription of the tapes less onerous, and access to a computer for word processing. If other people than yourself have access to that computer, it is absolutely necessary that you know you can work on transcripts in privacy and can secure your files so that there is no possibility of anyone else reading them. If you intend to analyze your interviews using a computer program, you will need a copy of the software (again, talk to your supervisor, since some believe that computers detract from the relationship you have with your data). The production of your final report requires access to printers, binders, and other such equipment or services. Finally, think about small things that can add up: paper, postage, telephone bills, and so on.

- *Space* — You will need a comfortable work space (you will be spending many hours in it) and a secure place to store tapes and transcripts where no unauthorized person can get at them.

- *Friends* — It is not your supervisor's role to listen to you ventilate or ramble on about giving it all up for a small cabin on a distant island, or to validate your feelings of being uniquely victimized. Friends, intimates, family—even pets who *appear* attentive—are better suited to the important task of providing emotional bolstering. Some qualitative researchers find a support group of interested colleagues is very important for providing emotional support as well as concrete advice. Evaluate your own networks with respect to the availability of the social supports you will need, and consider if you need to supplement them in any way. You are not a client in your supervisor's eyes—you are a student who is learning how to do a qualitative research study.

Step 7: Choosing a Site for Your Study

Choosing a site for your research study is a matter of identifying places where you can meet people from the population you wish to study and encourage them to participate. It is very important to talk to people in likely sites early in your planning process (the synopsis you prepared to recruit supervisors may be useful in introducing your study to potential agency hosts).

Representatives of the agency and future participants, if they find your ideas interesting, may well respond with useful feedback. Participation of this sort leads to increased interest, so it has the secondary benefit of cultivating a potential future resource. If interest is weak, you are at least learning this early and can consider options.

When you and your host agency clearly share an interest in working together, find out what formal steps are needed to ensure your access to the site. A letter of permission to proceed with your study from someone in authority is often advisable, and a host agency may well have their own ethical review process that you will have to go through. The more you can learn early on about such requirements, the exact steps involved in meeting them, and even the people who will play a part in formally approving your study, the better able you will be to assess the feasibility of carrying out your study in that site.

Part of your job in relation to your host agency(s) may be educative. The people with whom you will be dealing may have conceptions of research based on the quantitative model that prevailed when they were in school, and an opportunity to discuss the procedures and goals associated with a qualitative study may be of value. If a larger agency has its own researchers on staff, it will be important to know if they are sympathetic to qualitative studies, and to think through the implications if they are not.

Choosing a site for your study is probably one of the hardest parts of doing any research study (quantitative or qualitative) as the site finally chosen must be willing for you to "intrude on its territory."

Step 8: Identifying and Dealing with Ethical Considerations

Finally, you must address the ethical issues associated with your study. For all research studies, primary concerns are informed consent, confidentiality, and management of information. Management of information includes issues such as where tapes, notes, and transcripts will be stored, what will happen to them when the study is concluded, and what will become of your findings.

Some qualitative researchers also emphasize the research relationship as an ethical issue. The suggestion is that some quantitative researchers tend to relate to the people they are studying from a position of superior expertise and status, and do not always fully inform them of the research goals, process, and outcomes. It is seen as desirable for qualitative researchers to strike a more egalitarian relationship, referring to those who take part in the study as participants or co-researchers. Equality may also be promoted by emphasizing all participants' involvement in establishing goals for your research study, participating in planning your study, confirming the validity of your findings, and sharing in decision making about writing up your final report.

You will need to establish your own value position regarding the degree of involvement and decision making all participants will share. It is our observation that the ideal suggested in the previous paragraph is seldom if ever completely achieved. A bottom-line value, however— one that all researchers are ethically bound to honor—is the need for informed consent. Nobody should be included in your study who has not explicitly agreed to take part in it, having been fully informed as to the purposes of your study, the uses to which your findings will be put, and what their participation will involve.

Writing with a quantitative research audience in mind, Margaret Williams, Leslie M. Tutty, and Richard M. Grinnell, Jr. (1995) provide these observations on the importance of obtaining informed consent:

> The word "informed" means that each person fully understands what is going to happen in the course of the study, why it is going to happen, and what its effect will be on him or her. If the interviewee is psychiatrically challenged, mentally delayed, or in any other way incapable of full understanding, the study must be explained to someone else—perhaps a parent, guardian, social worker, or spouse, or someone to whom the interviewee's welfare is important.
>
> It is clear that no person may be bribed, threatened, deceived, or in any way coerced into participating. Questions must always be encouraged, both initially and throughout the course of the study. People who believe they understand may have misinterpreted your explanation or understood it only in part. They may say they understand, when they do not, in an effort to avoid appearing foolish. They may even sign documents they do not understand to confirm their supposed understanding, and it is your responsibility to ensure that their understanding is real and complete.
>
> It is particularly important for interviewees to know that they are not signing

away their rights when they sign a consent form. They can decide at any time to withdraw from the study without penalty, without so much as a reproachful glance. The results of the study will be made available to them as soon as the study has been completed. You must never promise anything that you cannot fulfil.

A promise that is of particular concern to many interviewees is that of anonymity. A drug offender, for example, may be very afraid of being identified; a person on welfare may be concerned whether anyone else might learn that he or she was on welfare. Also, there is often some confusion between the terms "anonymity" and "confidentiality."

... [Usually, we know] how a particular participant responded and have agreed not to divulge the information to anyone else. In such cases, the information is confidential [but it is not anonymous]. Part of our explanation to a potential interviewee must include a clear statement of what information will be shared with whom. All this seems reasonable in theory, but ethical obligations are often difficult to fulfil in practice.

For example, there are times when it is very difficult to remove coercive influences because these influences are inherent in the situation. A woman awaiting an abortion may agree to provide private information about herself and her partner because she believes that, if she does not, she will be denied the abortion. It is of no use to tell her that this is not true as she may feel she is not in a position to take any chances. There are captive populations of people in prisons, schools, or institutions who may agree out of sheer boredom to take part in a research study. Or, they may participate in return for certain privileges, or because they fear some penalty or reprisal. There may be people who agree because they are pressured into it by family members, or they want to please the social worker, or they need some service or payment that they believe depends on their cooperation. Often, situations like this cannot be changed, but at least we can be aware of them and try to deal with them in an ethical manner.

A written consent form should be only part of the process of informing interviewees of their roles in the study and their rights as volunteers. It should give them a basic description of the purpose of your study, the study's procedures, and their rights as voluntary participants. All information should be provided in plain and simple language, without jargon. A written consent form should contain the following items, recognizing that the relevancy of this information and the amount required will vary with each study:

- A brief description of the purpose of the research study, as well as the value of the study to the general/scientific social work community (probability and nature of direct and indirect benefits) and to the participants and/or others.

- An explanation as to how and/or why they were selected and a statement that their participation is completely voluntary.

- A description of conditions and/or procedures. Some points that should be covered are:

  - The frequency with which the participants will be contacted.

- The time commitment required by the participants.

- The physical effort required and/or protection from overexertion.

- Emotionally sensitive issues that might be exposed and/or follow-up resources that are available if required.

- Location of participation (e.g., need for travel/commuting).

- Information that will be recorded and how it will be recorded (e.g., on paper, by photographs, videotape, audiotape).

- Description of the likelihood of any discomforts and inconveniences associated with participation, and of known or suspected short- and long-term risks.

- Explanation of who will have access to information collected and to the identity of the participants (i.e., level of anonymity or confidentiality of each person's participation and information) and how long the data will be stored.

- Description of how the data will be made public (e.g., scholarly presentation, printed publication). An additional consent is required for publication of photographs, audiotapes, and/or videotapes.

- Description of other research projects or other people who may use the data.

- Explanation of the interviewees' rights:

  - That they may terminate or withdraw from the study at any point.

  - That they may ask for clarification or more information throughout the study.

  - That they may contact the appropriate administrative body if they have any questions about the conduct of the people doing the interview or the study's procedures.

We would add a caveat regarding confidentiality that is of special interest to social workers conducting qualitative research studies. When your research participants are invited to share their experience in a relatively unstructured fashion, they should know in advance that there is some information that you cannot legally keep confidential. In our study, one area identified for exploration is the task facing these women in redefining their relationship to their former partners after deciding to permanently separate.

As you may know, this often involves working out such issues as custody and visitation rights. Suppose, in exploring these issues, one woman discloses to us that she has knowledge that her child was sexually abused by her partner during unsupervised visits. In most jurisdictions, you would be legally obligated to report this information to the appropriate authorities; this obligation would override any prior promises of confidentiality. Whenever there is a chance of such a situation arising, your research participants, when they give their informed consent, need to know what the limits to confidentiality are.

Though the question of personal risk is a general ethical issue in research, it deserves emphasis as something especially pertinent in qualitative research studies, where the data collection approach often encourages exploration of personal, possibly emotionally difficult material. In our study, for example, we had to consider that some participants might get in touch with aspects of their experience that would be highly upsetting—something that is reasonable to anticipate in an exploration of safety issues involving oneself or one's children.

The ethical response to this problem included the following measures:

- We provided a prior warning (while obtaining written informed consent) that potentially difficult issues would be discussed.

- We made it clear with each woman that if she was finding the interview too difficult at any point she could say so, and we would agree to change the course of the interview or stop altogether.

- We utilized interviewers who were fully professionally trained and experienced in talking with people about emotional concerns.

- We made sure that back-up supports (e.g., shelter staff, counselors) were available to whom a woman could be referred if necessary.

Step 9: Writing a Proposal

As with many other aspects of conducting a qualitative research study, conventions regarding preparation of proposals are not as well established as they are in the quantitative research approach. You will need to discuss with your supervisor, or potential supervisor, and others who will be approving your study the form your proposal should take and the content it should address. Our proposal was written for potential funders and followed an outline that mirrors our discussion of the steps and tasks in this chapter, and is presented in Figure 1.1 as a possible model that you can modify for your own purposes.

Your proposal will guide you through the entire research process and will serve as a valuable road map as you do your study. Your proposal will be helpful when you write up the results of your study as it can be used as the outline for your final report (Phase Four).

INTRODUCTION

    Identify Your General Problem Area
    State Your Population to Be Studied
    State the Problems within Your Population
    State Your Research Goal
    State a Rationale for Your Study: Why Is it Important?

CONCEPTUALIZATION AND LITERATURE REVIEW

    Review the Literature on Your General Population Area
    Review the Literature on Your Population
    Review the Literature on the Problems within Your Population
    Delineate Your Key Concepts (i.e., population and problems)
    Outline Your Preconceptions and Biases

THE RESEARCH APPROACH

    State Your Rationale for Using a Qualitative Research Approach
    State Anticipated Benefits: Type of Knowledge Sought
    Relate Strengths of Research Approach to Your Research Goal
    Describe Proposed Procedures
        Identify Options and Rationale for Alternative Chosen
        Describe Your Desired Populations Size and Characteristics
        Describe Your Proposed Data Collection Procedures
    Describe Your Proposed Data Analysis
    List Ethical Considerations
        List Steps for Obtaining Informed Consent
        List Risks and Protections Against Them

OUTLINE RESOURCE REQUIREMENTS

    Review Specific Tasks to Be Accomplished
        Estimate Time Required for Each Task
        Assign Tasks to Research Team Members (if applicable)
        Provide Time Lines for Accomplishment of Each Task
    Estimate Equipment and Supplies Required
    Estimate Demands Your Study Will Place on Participants and Agency

BUDGET (if applicable)

APPENDICES

    Provide Sample Letter(s) of Introduction
    Provide Sample Informed Consent Forms

FIGURE 1.1   OUTLINE FOR A QUALITATIVE RESEARCH PROPOSAL

Step 10: Obtaining Permission and Ethical Clearances

Though the research world is changing, it is still the case that in undertaking a qualitative study you are doing something unusual, and in some eyes your work will be suspect. It is also true that you are using a method where the rules and standards are less clear than those of quantitative studies. At the end of your study, you do not want to be challenged for having disregarded or violated some expectation that you were unaware of and never agreed to in the first place. Your best protection against this is a clear, formal contract with relevant people at the outset.

Hopefully, you have written a proposal that covers as many bases as possible, explaining what your goal is, the steps you will take to achieve it, and how ethical issues will be addressed. This proposal should be distributed to your supervisor, committee members (if any), and relevant people in the host agency or setting. Our advice is that you subsequently meet with them, verbally review the contents of your proposal, and ask for discussion of any concerns. From key people such as your supervisor and agency directors, it is a good idea to obtain a letter acknowledging your proposal and agreeing that the study outlined in it is acceptable.

SUMMARY

We have briefly touched upon the basic aspects of getting your qualitative research study off the ground. It has been our experience that the more attention you pay to the planning aspects of your study, the better off you will be in the long run. The contents of this chapter should help you write a research proposal, which is one of the final steps in Phase One.

ANNOTATED BIBLIOGRAPHY

BERG, B.L. (1989). *Qualitative research methods for the social sciences* (Chapter 6). Needham Heights, MA: Allyn & Bacon. Berg's chapter on ethical issues presents a brief history of the rise of concern about safeguarding research participants, from classic examples such as the Milgram experiment to the Tearoom study of homosexuals. A brief, but well-written review of how to address ethical issues is presented in this chapter.

ERLANDSON, D., HARRIS, E., SKIPPER, B., & ALLEN, S. (1993). *Doing naturalistic inquiry: A guide to methods* (Chapters 3 and 4). Newbury Park, CA: Sage. Erlandson and his colleagues devote two chapters to designing a qualitative study. Chapter Three centers on the typical steps associated with the initial stages of the design process: (1) identifying a problem, (2) completion of a literature review, (3) stating the research problem and questions, (4) site selection, and (5) gaining access to a site to carry out the research. The authors, in an effort to highlight the salient points made in each of the above-mentioned topics, provide examples from completed pieces of research. The authors maintain that it is critical that researchers pay attention to these steps as they impact on the success of the study.

In Chapter Four, the authors highlight key points originated by Lincoln and Guba (1985, below), an especially useful aspect being a listing of activities a researcher can plan in advance to develop an "emerging" design. These include such things as planning for the data collection and analysis, purposive sampling, developing a logistical plan, negotiating conditions of entry, and determining how the study will be disseminated.

GLESNE, C., & PESHKIN, A. (1992). *Becoming qualitative researchers: An introduction* (Chapter 2). White Plains, NY: Longman. Glesne and Peshkin present a detailed overview of the various stages of designing qualitative research, emphasizing that designs are blueprints which will often change as fieldwork proceeds. The material provided by the authors is especially suited for those who are new to qualitative research. However, experienced qualitative researchers will find the clearly written material to be an excellent refresher.

Particularly useful are discussions dealing with the stages of the design process: (1) review of the literature, (2) the cover story, and (3) gaining access. Glesne and Peshkin acknowledge the debate within the literature regarding the place of the literature review in qualitative research. Although they are cognizant of the dangers of doing the literature review prior to beginning data collection, they contend that the benefits of reviewing the literature early outweigh the risks. The benefits they identify include: verifying the relevance of the topic, sharpening the focus of the research, and developing the best possible design and potential interview questions.

The "cover story" is a statement written to introduce the researcher and the proposed study to potential participants, and the authors provide a list of major points that should be part of this document. Gaining access to a site is presented as a process of contracting, with a useful summary of the issues that need to be negotiated.

JANESICK, V. (1994). The dance of qualitative research design: Metaphor, methodology, and meaning. In N.K. Denzin & Y. Lincoln (Eds.), *Handbook of qualitative research* (pp. 209-219). Newbury Park, CA: Sage. Janesick provides a succinct overview of the design process in qualitative research, identifying three stages. Stage One, the "Warm-up," deals with the array of decisions made at the beginning of the study: (1) determining what one wishes to research, (2) formulating questions, (3) selecting a site and participants, (4) gaining access, (5) establishing timelines, (6) selecting appropriate research strategies, and (7) determining the relationship of the study to theory.

Stage Two, the "Total Workout," deals with decisions that are made as work progresses. Janesick stresses the importance of piloting the study prior to formal commencement. The researcher can incorporate the feedback received from the pilot test to strengthen the study. During this second stage, she also stresses the need for the researcher to be adaptable and flexible.

Stage Three, "Cooling Down," deals with the issues of leaving the field and completing the final data analysis.

Of particular importance is the author's discussion of the value of five types of triangulations: (1) comparison of different types of data, (2) comparison across investigators, (3) comparisons with prior theory, (4) comparison with findings generated with different methods, and (5) comparisons between disciplines.

LINCOLN, Y., & GUBA, E. (1985). *Naturalistic inquiry* (Chapter 9). Newbury Park, CA: Sage. Lincoln and Guba have written extensively on qualitative research, and this book is a classic in the field. The chapter dealing with designing qualitative research is detailed and requires a number of careful readings.

Prior to launching into the discussion dealing specifically with stages associated with the design process, the authors compare and contrast the nature of qualitative and quantitative designs. Like other writers, Lincoln and Guba strongly emphasize the emergent, unfolding nature of the qualitative design.

Two distinctive features of the work presented by the authors are their discussions dealing with the issues of determining instrumentation to be used in a study and planning for ensuring the trustworthiness of the data being collected. With respect to trustworthiness, they provide a discussion of key design issues—credibility, transferability, dependability, and confirmability.

MARSHALL, C., & ROSSMAN, G. (1989). *Designing qualitative research* (Chapter 2). Newbury Park, CA: Sage. An easy-to-read discussion of research questions and their relationship to theory. As such, this chapter also presents a strong rationale for conducting a preliminary literature review. A short section outlining a qualitative research proposal completes the content in this section.

PATTON, M. (1990). *Qualitative evaluation and research methods* (Chapter 5). Newbury Park, CA: Sage. In his extensive discussion of qualitative research designs, Patton stresses clarity of purpose as a foundation for decision making regarding other design issues. These other issues include:

- The place of the literature review in qualitative studies (the advantages and disadvantages of doing the review before, during, or after the study).

- The question of breadth versus depth—deciding whether to work with a small sample (capturing detailed information) or a large sample (forgoing the opportunity to gather in-depth data).

Patton's detailed treatment of twelve sampling strategies that may be employed in qualitative research is a strong contribution; also useful is his discussion of different types of triangulations. In particular, he focuses on methodological triangulation.

An equally useful aspect of Patton's presentation is a table at the end of the chapter which summarizes the design issues previously discussed and the options available to the researcher for each of the issues. Overall, Patton's work on designing qualitative research is recommended as required reading. The clarity of his writing, along with the provision of examples, provides a valuable contribution to the literature.

ROTHERY, M. (1993). Problems, questions, and hypotheses, In R.M. Grinnell, Jr. (Ed.), *Social work research and evaluation* (4th ed., pp. 17-37). Itasca, IL: F.E. Peacock. This chapter is about choosing a research problem and identifying whether it is relevant, feasible, researchable, and what ethical considerations need to be addressed.

The chapter suggests analyzing whether a problem might best be researched using qualitative or quantitative methods rather than assuming one approach or the other. As such, it is a good general guide to thinking about the decision-making process in research.

REFERENCES AND FURTHER READINGS

Berg, B.L. (1989). *Qualitative research methods for the social sciences* (Chapter 3). Needham Heights, MA: Allyn & Bacon.

Bouey, E., & Rogers, G. (1993). Retrieving information. In R.M. Grinnell, Jr. (Ed.), *Social work research and evaluation* (4th ed., pp. 402-426). Itasca, IL: F.E. Peacock.

Burgess, R. G. (1984). *In the field: An introduction to field research.* Boston: Allen & Unwin.

Creswell, J. (1994). Research design: Qualitative and quantitative approaches (Chapters 1-9). Newbury Park, CA: Sage.

Ely, M., Anzul, M., Friedman, T., Garner, D., & McCormack-Steinmetz, A. (1991). *Doing qualitative research: Circles within circles* (Chapters 1 and 2). New York: Falmer Press.

Erlandson, D., Harris, E., Skipper, B., & Allen, S. (1993). *Doing naturalistic inquiry: A guide to methods* (Chapters 3 and 6). Newbury Park, CA: Sage.

Glesene, C., & Peshkin, A. (1992). *Becoming qualitative researchers: An introduction* (Chapter 2). White Plains, NY: Longman.

Kuzel, A. (1992). Sampling in qualitative inquiry. In B. Crabtree & W. Miller (Eds.), *Doing qualitative research* (pp. 31-44). Newbury Park, CA: Sage.

Locke, L., Spirduso, W., & Silverman, S. (1987). *Proposals that work: A guide for planning dissertations and grant proposals.* Newbury Park, CA: Sage.

Marshall, L., & Rossman, G. (1989). *Designing qualitative research.* Newbury Park, CA: Sage.

Miles, M.B., & Huberman, A.M. (1994). *Qualitative data analysis: An expanded source book.* Newbury Park, CA: Sage.

Morse, J. (1994). Designing funded qualitative research. In N.K. Denzin, & Y. Lincoln (Eds.), *Handbook of qualitative research* (pp. 220-235). Newbury Park, CA: Sage.

Patton, M. (1984). Data collection: Options, strategies and caution. In L. Rutman (Ed.), *Evaluation research methods: A basic guide* (pp. 39-63). Newbury Park, CA: Sage.

Punch, M. (1994). Politics and ethics in qualitative research. In N.K. Denzin & Y. Lincoln (Eds.), *Handbook of qualitative research* (pp. 83-97). Newbury Park, CA: Sage.

Rogers, G., & Bouey, E. (1993). Reviewing the literature. In R.M. Grinnell, Jr. (Ed.), *Social work research and evaluation* (4th ed., pp. 388-401). Itasca, IL: F.E. Peacock.

Schatzman, L., & Strauss, A. (1973). *Field research: Strategies for a natural sociology.* Englewood Cliffs, NJ: Prentice-Hall.

Seidman, I. (1991). *Interviewing as qualitative research: A guide for researchers in education and the social sciences* (Chapter 3). New York, NY: Teachers College Press.

Weller, S.C., & Romney, K.A. (1988). *Systematic data collection.* Newbury Park, CA: Sage.

Williams, M., Tutty, L.M., & Grinnell, R.M., Jr. (1995). *Research in social work: An introduction* (2nd ed., Chapters 1-5). Itasca, IL: F.E. Peacock.

Gayla Rogers
Elaine Bouey

Phase Two

THE QUALITATIVE RESEARCH INTERVIEW

TYPES OF INTERVIEWS

Structured Interviews / Unstructured Interviews / Semi-Structured Interviews

ISSUES IN QUALITATIVE INTERVIEWING

Equality of the Interviewer/Interviewee Relationship / Dealing With Strong Emotions During the Interview / Research Interviews vs. Therapeutic Interviewees

STEPS IN INTERVIEWING

Step 1: Preparing for the Interview / Step 2: Choosing a Recording Method / Step 3: Conducting the Interview / Step 4: Reflecting About the Interview / Step 5: Completing the Process

SUMMARY

ANNOTATED BIBLIOGRAPHY / REFERENCES AND FURTHER READINGS

Collecting Your Data

I N PHASE ONE of the qualitative research process, you did the basic groundwork for your study in relation to refining your study's problem area and addressing any methodological issues. Now that Phase One is complete you can start Phase Two. In this phase, you are going to think about what kind of data you will need to answer your research question. Also, you are going to have to determine how your data will be collected. Luckily, there are many different kinds of data that can be collected. For example, you might use client file data, agency file data, archival data, documentary record data, private and public archive data, solicited and unsolicited document data, biography and autobiography data, erosion measure data, accretion measure data, picture data, the various types of content analysis data, and interview data. All of these different types of data, and the methods used to collect them, have advantages and disadvantages. Nevertheless, the most important thing to remember is that the purpose of your study will determine which type(s) of data to gather.

Without a doubt, the most utilized data collection method in qualitative research studies is the interview. Thus, this chapter will briefly discuss the interview as the principal means to gather data for your research study and the key steps and tasks involved in the interview process. It is also important to note that while we will be discussing the separate steps and tasks one after the other, it is with the understanding that in many research studies they usually occur simultaneously, may overlap each other, and may be repeated in a back-and-forth manner. Let us now turn our attention to the main topic of this chapter, the qualitative research interview.

THE QUALITATIVE RESEARCH INTERVIEW

Simply put, interviewing is a conversation with direction. Its purpose is to gain an understanding of the perspective of the person being interviewed. A successful qualitative research interview can be an especially effective method of data gathering in the field of social work. Interviews provide you with an opportunity to learn about that which you are unable to directly observe in a person's natural environment. This is particularly true when you are interested in learning about a person's experiences, behaviors, thoughts, and feelings. In addition, interviews can assess a person's perceptions of how significant they are to him or her.

Qualitative research interviewing, like all forms of interviewing, involves a complex set of dynamics between the interviewer and the interviewee—or in this case, the researcher (which is you), and the research participant. The quality, quantity, and type of data gathered are substantially influenced by the nature of the interaction between the interviewer and interviewee. However, the quality of information gathered in an interview is largely dependent on your knowledge base, interviewing skills, and sensitivities.

More recently, it has been acknowledged that the qualitative interview process itself may be a stimulus for individual and social change on the part of the interviewee. There is also a new awareness of the dynamics that may be involved in working with different characteristics of interviewees such as gender, race, ethnicity, and social status. This has led to developments in the way in which qualitative research interviewing is both conceptualized (the thinking part) and operationalized (the doing part). For example, it is now believed that there should be an equality between the interviewer and the interviewee in the research partnership.

TYPES OF INTERVIEWS

As we will see shortly, there are three complementary types of interviews which you can choose from. The type(s) of interview you select for your study will have an impact on the quality and quantity of data that you collect. As with most things in life, there are strengths and weaknesses to each type of interview. In addition, the amount and kind of preparation that you will need varies from one type to another. Sometimes all three types of interviews are used in a single qualitative study. The decision regarding the type of interview to use is usually made in the planning phase (Phase One). However, this may change as your study progresses since the information you gather as your study goes along may automatically lead you to a different interviewing plan.

The type of interview you choose can also depend upon the number of interviewers and interviewees you have at your disposal and whether the interviews are to be conducted individually or in groups, sometimes called focus groups. You can also interview one individual several times, or several individuals one time. It is important to note that in qualitative interviewing, even a small number of interviewees can easily provide a large amount of quality data.

An interviewer can work alone, or in a team where each interviewer conducts a certain number of interviews and later on pools the information each one has gathered into one large pot. They can also work in pairs where each shares the interview experience with a co-researcher. Interviewing in pairs is especially useful for reasons of safety and security, for ethical protection, or to have another pair of ears and eyes to observe and record the interviews.

Whether working alone, on a team, or in pairs, you will be doing at least one of the three major types of interviews: (1) structured or standardized interviews, (2) unstructured or open-ended interviews, and (3) semi-structured or guided interviews.

Structured Interviews

The structured interview, sometimes called a standardized interview, uses a common interview schedule that contains specific questions, or items. Its rationale is to offer all interviewees approximately the same set of questions so that each person's responses can be compared with one another. It is assumed that the questions within a structured interview are sufficiently comprehensive to gather all (or nearly all) the information relevant to your study's topic. It is further assumed that the questions have been worded in a manner that allows the interviewees to understand clearly what they are being asked. Finally, it is assumed that the meaning of each question is identical for every person being interviewed.

Since we know virtually nothing about women who leave their ex-partners after having resided in a shelter, a structured interview format would not likely be our first choice. However, questions for a structured interview could be compiled based on what little we know about a sub-group of our sample, women who leave but then reunite with their abusive ex-partners. We know through other research studies that many of these women are on social assistance (and are therefore poor), that having children makes it difficult to stay separated, and that many return to their ex-partner because they fear for their own safety once they no longer live in the security of the women's emergency shelter.

We would use these findings to form the questions that comprise a structured interview. Examples of a few questions that we would have asked if we used a structured interview during our study are the following:

- What was your experience after you and your children left the emergency shelter?

- How are you supporting yourself and your children? Are you employed? If so, what do you do?

- Do you have enough money to live comfortably? Is your housing adequate? If so, in what ways?

- How have your children reacted to living apart from your ex-partner? How are you finding being a single parent?

- What kind of contact (if any) do you now have with your ex-partner? How do you feel about this contact?

- After you left the women's emergency shelter, did you experience fear for your own safety or the safety of your children? If so, in what ways?

- Have you ever obtained a restraining order for your ex-partner to protect you and the children? If so, was this effective?

Notice that in a structured interview more sensitive or potentially controversial topics such as the type and amount of contact a woman currently has with her ex-partner are situated later on in the interview. This process allows time for the researcher and the interviewee to develop a more relaxed and congenial relationship so that the woman will, hopefully, decide that she can trust us with answers to such personal questions.

When it is important to your study that the data you gather are to be compared, and when there are several interviews being conducted by more than one interviewer, then you should choose a structured type of interview. The structured interview is also useful in cases where you may have little interviewing experience. In that situation, more structure would help you to develop and refine your interviewing skills so that later in the research process you might develop the confidence to conduct less structured, more interactive interviews.

Another advantage of using a structured interview is that you will be asking individuals about matters that they might not necessarily think of without such a prompt. Perhaps, for example, a woman would not consider that the interviewer would be interested in whether or not she feared for her own safety or that of her children, and so would not mention it. With the structured interview format we would ask each respondent about her level of fear to ensure that this critical topic is addressed by everyone.

On the other hand, a disadvantage of such structure is that you may find that particular questions are irrelevant to some women and that you have wasted valuable interviewing time ruling out these topics. It is important to note that, while there may be good reasons to use a structured interview, there is a tendency for the interviewer to elicit rational responses with little emotional content, an aspect which can be more easily expressed in the other two types of interviews, unstructured and semi-structured.

Unstructured Interviews

Unstructured interviews, sometimes called open-ended interviews, are generally considered to be the best way to gain an understanding of people's perceptions. In contrast to the rigidity of the structured interview mentioned above, the unstructured interview does not use an interview schedule that contains a common set of standardized questions. Interviewers using an unstructured approach operate from a different set of assumptions than interviewers that use a structured approach. First, they begin with the assumption that they may not know in advance what all the necessary questions might be, thus the interview is essentially exploratory in nature. They also assume that not all interviewees will find equal meaning in like-worded standardized questions.

In an unstructured interview, you must develop, adapt, and generate questions appropriate to a given situation and the central purpose of your study. In our study on women leaving the shelter we could start the interview with a single question such as, "What have you experienced since you left the emergency shelter?" From that point on, we would simply respond to whatever dimension of her experience our interviewee chose to discuss, encouraging her to "tell us more...," or asking questions as they occurred to us as we listened to her story. In essence, the questions emerge from the interactive process between the interviewer and interviewee. Furthermore, the responses from one interviewee may become questions that we will want to include in subsequent interviews.

While researchers new to qualitative methods commonly worry about how they could possibly conduct an interview with so little pre-planning, most are pleased to discover that, armed with a sense of curiosity and respect for another's unique experiences, the interview will proceed smoothly. In many ways, unstructured interviews are not unlike social work interviews with clients, where workers start by asking "What problem would you like to work on?" The worker's reactions to a client's story can help the client to elaborate with rich details and new insights that may lead the client to see his or her situation in a different light. The same is true in research interviews. In summary, you should select an unstructured interview when you want to obtain an in-depth, thick description and understanding of an interviewee's world.

Semi-Structured Interviews

Between the two extremes of structured and unstructured types of interviewing is the semi-structured interview, sometimes called a guided interview. In this case there are usually some predetermined questions or key words used as a guide. For our study of women who leave the shelter the general areas that we speculated would be important include the relationship with her ex-partner, the children's reaction to the separation and the abuse, the economic circumstances of the woman, and her safety.

Unlike the structured interview, we do not formulate specific questions about each issue, but ask about each in an open-ended manner and at a time when it seems to fit with each woman's narrative. In other words, we asked questions or touched on points in an order that suited the flow of the interview, adjusting the wording of the questions, and digressing and probing in a way that went beyond what could have been accomplished with a set of prepared questions.

Thus, the semi-structured interview has some of the advantages of both the structured and unstructured formats. While it allows questioning with respect to specific topics, it poses these questions in a more open-ended manner than is typical in structured interviews. For example, we would reword a question from our previous example of a structured interview, "Have you ever obtained a restraining order to protect you and the children?" to "Have you taken any precautions to protect yourself from your ex-partner?" to use in a semi-structured interview.

Obtaining a restraining order is only one example of how a woman could protect herself: contacting the police, and ordering call display on her telephone are two other options. The second, less restrictive question allows each woman to answer in a way that reflects her experience, while opening up the number and type of potential responses.

In summary, semi-structured interviews are particularly appropriate when you want to compare information between and among people while at the same time you wish to more fully understand each person's experience.

ISSUES IN QUALITATIVE INTERVIEWING

There are three particular issues that you must consider before you do a qualitative research interview. These have to do with: (1) the nature, or equality, of the research relationship, (2) dealing with strong emotions during the interview, and (3) the distinction between qualitative research interviewing and therapeutic interviewing. Let us now turn to the equality of the research relationship.

Equality of the Interviewer/Interviewee Relationship

A long-held view about the role of interviewers in a research interview stressed their "neutrality and distance" from the people they interviewed. This was believed to be necessary in order for them to maximize the opportunity to "objectively" learn about the interviewees' perspectives. Recently, however, there has been a shift in this kind of thinking. Interviewers are increasingly joining with interviewees on a more equal, shared basis during the interview. The interviewee is seen as the "expert" in terms of her unique perspective, while the interviewer becomes simply an interested audience whose goal it is to learn as much as possible about the interviewee's experience.

Over the years, we have become much more mindful of the dynamics in working with people who have different ways of knowing, beliefs, values, and experiences. Instead of continuing to mold the experiences of people of different cultures, sexual preferences, and faiths into a western-Anglo perspective, we are beginning to value such diversity for its own sake. In our interviews with abused women who had left their ex-partners, for example, it quickly became apparent that women of many cultures seek refuge in emergency shelters.

Talking to women of various ethnic groups highlighted the differences that cultural and family beliefs make in whether the abuse was seen as reprehensible or simply a normal part of married life. In cultures where abuse was seen as a necessary way that a man controlled his wife when she did not "properly" fulfil her role, her family was much less likely to support her decision to leave him. Thus, in the analysis, culture emerged as an important theme in the social support that women received from friends and family.

Finally, as an interviewer, you can now share more of your own perceptions with the interviewees than you could in the past. This provides you with an opportunity to enter into more of a dialogue and partnership with each interviewee while still working within professional ethical parameters. For example, in our interviews with the women who have been physically abused by their ex-partners we did not sit silently while a woman described the abuse that she had endured at the hand of her ex-partner. Rather, we felt free to briefly express our own reactions to her plight. Comments that arise from an honest response to the interviewee's story give the relationship a sense of "give and take" that feels more balanced to interviewees.

In sum, we are starting to conduct research interviews in more of a non-oppressive, empowering way. One implication of this stance is the need to be alert to indications by the interviewee of any feelings of defensiveness, anger, discomfort, or disinterest. If you do get a sense of any of these feelings or reactions, then you will need to restore an effective partnership before you can proceed with your interviewing agenda.

Dealing With Strong Emotions During the Interview

While qualitative research interviews are not likely to produce or cause pain or problems in the interviewees' lives, they may elicit or release strong feelings. Obviously, when we asked women to talk about their recent separation from an abusive ex-partner, they recalled many painful moments. One woman was in tears as she described her bewilderment that her boyfriend was suing her for custody of her very young daughters who were not even his biological children. Her fear about losing them and her anger at the control that her ex-boyfriend still exerted over her life, even half a year after she had left him, left her shaking with self-doubt and rage. Another woman spoke angrily as she recalled her neighbor phoning her at midnight two days earlier to alert her that her ex-husband was hiding in the bushes outside her ground-level apartment. This incident was only one of many where he had stalked or harassed her.

Clearly then, when you ask people to share the critical events in their lives, more likely than not they will have powerful recollections about these. When an interviewee does become overwhelmed with emotion, it is best for you to sit quietly and wait for him or her to regain some composure. You might ask, "Is it all right to go on?" before continuing or indicate your understanding, stating something like, "It's been very hard on you." It is important not to step out of the role as researcher and inappropriately take on the role of "social work practitioner" or "friend."

As will be clarified in the next section, it is a mistake to try to "do therapy" with the interviewee as it is unethical for you to attempt to modify, change, or justify the interviewee's feelings. At the same time you must maintain respect for the people who you are interviewing and be sensitive and tactful toward the pain that they may be suffering. In addition, you must be prepared to call a halt to an interview if it appears that your interviewee is becoming too upset to continue. The interviewer's relationship to the interviewee should not change because of the display of strong emotions. Regardless of the type or strength of feelings expressed, your relationship with the interviewee can continue to be a partnership based on mutual respect and trust, while focusing on gathering useful data for your research study.

Research Interviews vs. Therapeutic Interviews

There are some similarities between a qualitative research interview and a therapeutic interview. The qualitative research interviewer resembles a social work practitioner by encouraging the interviewee to express private thoughts and observations, recalling and reflecting on memories, by eliciting underlying emotions, and by listening closely to what is being said—and sometimes more importantly—what is not said.

With the above similarities in mind, Robert Weiss (1994) has noted three ways in which qualitative research interviewing is different from therapeutic interviewing. First, their goals and practices are different. In therapeutic interviewing the functioning of the client is the object of concern and the goal is to help the client in some way. This is often accomplished by getting the client to talk and offering interpretation, advice, alternatives, empathy, through the use of a therapeutic relationship. On the other hand, in qualitative research interviewing, your questions should be motivated according to the purpose of your research study with the goal of eliciting useful data. The interviewee is a partner in developing the data. You do not have permission to produce change in the interviewee's functioning and have no right to provide interpretations, make connections, or furnish advice.

Second, the actual content that is drawn out of the two different interviews is different. The research interviewer is much more likely to want to hear about scenes, situations, and events that the interviewee has witnessed or been involved in and only focuses on the amount and degree of information as required for the study. On the other hand, the social work practitioner is likely to allow the client to explore the scenes, situations, and events along with the client's internal states, past history, and childhood as fully and for as long as the client wishes and is necessary for the therapeutic process.

Third, the interviewer/interviewee relationship is different between the qualitative researcher doing an interview and the social work practitioner doing an interview. Practitioners are responsible to clients for helping them improve or enhance their functioning. Because clients look to social workers for help, they can easily become influential and powerful people (even while being empowering) in the lives of their clients and usually remain important people for some time to come. In contrast, the research interviewer is a partner, with the interviewee, in information development.

It is important to remember that in qualitative research interviewing, the interviewer/interviewee (researcher/research participant) relationship is usually short-term when directly compared to the social worker/client relationship. Remembering that your role is not to be therapeutic is important because you may well be faced with invitations to provide such help. For example, in the middle of one interview that we conducted with a 19-year old woman, her boyfriend phoned from the jail where he was serving time for assaulting her.

After the phone call, the woman was clearly distraught. She was torn between her loneliness and her wish to reunite with her ex-partner, who remained one of the few people supporting her, and her fear that he would hurt her again. Given her dilemma, it was tempting to shift the interview into a counseling one and to work with her to solve her problem. Instead, we reflected that this was a difficult and upsetting situation for her, and one that her Outreach Counselor could help her with.

STEPS IN INTERVIEWING

Now that you know the three basic types of interviews and several of the issues that influence them, you are in a position to actually start doing qualitative research interviews. Most interviews follow five steps where each step has one or more associated tasks. The five steps in a qualitative research interview are: (1) preparing for the interview, (2) choosing a recording method, (3) conducting the interview, (4) reflecting about the interview, and (5) completing the interviewing data gathering process. As usual, they all interact with one another but for the sake of simplicity we will discuss each step and its corresponding tasks separately.

Step 1: Preparing for the Interview

Preparing to do research interviews has to do with getting yourself ready to do them—gaining access and entry into the study site and preparing interviewees to contribute in a meaningful way. You need to accomplish three tasks in this step: (1) preparing yourself, (2) preparing the way, and (3) preparing the interviewees.

Task 1a: Preparing Yourself

During Phase One you have planned your study and have consulted with others. By now, you have an initial sense of what you want to know, who you should interview, and who will be doing the interviewing, and the type of interviewing you plan to conduct. We know, for example that we want to learn more about the positive and negative experiences of women who decided to separate from abusive ex-partners after they had resided in a shelter. The interviewing would be done by two individuals using semi-structured interviews. This type of interview was selected because we had previously identified meaningful areas that we suspected would be critical to surviving separately from an abusive ex-partner. In addition, we did not want to impose structured questions that might not fit the circumstances of some of these women. As we know, the semi-structured interview format provides us with some structure as well as considerable flexibility.

All preparatory interviewing training of yourself and other interviewers should be done by now. When preparing for the actual encounter with an interviewee (or a group of interviewees) it is important for you to be aware that you are not just extracting data from people but joining together with them in a research partnership.

Get ready for an intense process. You are now starting to set sail on a path that will have an impact not only on you but also on those whom you interview. As William B. Shaffir, Robert A. Stebbins, and Allan Turowetz (1980) point out:

> Fieldwork must certainly rank with the more disagreeable activities that humanity has fashioned for itself. It is usually inconvenient, to say the least, sometimes physically uncomfortable, frequently embarrassing, and, to a degree, always tense.

Robert Bogdan and Steven J. Taylor (1975) also have a few words to say about qualitative research studies:

> The price of doing fieldwork is very high, not in dollars (fieldwork is less expensive than most other kinds of research) but in physical and mental effort. It is very hard work. It is very exhausting to live two lives simultaneously.

Read the above two quotes carefully. The more prepared you are for possible setbacks, the better you will be able to handle them when they come up during your study.

During Step 1, plan to keep a personal journal where you can record and track your thoughts, feelings, and reactions. This will prove very useful when you are sorting through the raw data and attempting to make sense of someone else's experience as it is filtered through your own frame of reference. The more you can identify how and when your world view (your experiences, biases, assumptions, values, and feelings) colors your interpretation of your interviewee's world, the better you will be able to understand and accurately articulate your interviewee's perspective.

The process of ridding yourself of your own biases and assumptions is known as "epoch." Before you talk to research participants, your goal is to have achieved as much epoch as possible so that you do not impose your own beliefs on your interviewees. Your journal can assist you with this sorting process.

Arrange for regular conferences with experienced qualitative researchers who can provide you with advice and guidance regarding the qualitative interviewing processes. Reviewing books and other information relating to the process and techniques of research interviewing will be very helpful, particularly if you are new to doing interviews within a research context. You should also gain further experience in interviewing through role playing.

Another way to prepare yourself is to pilot test the interviews. In preparation for interviewing the women in our study we were able to pilot test the interview with one of the shelter staff who had previously been abused herself. A pilot test helps you to decide if the type of interview you are using and the kinds of questions you are asking provide you with the quality and quantity of information you need to answer your research question. It will also give you some insight into your own reactions to the information you obtain from the potential interviewees in addition to giving you a brief chance to evaluate the efficiency and effectiveness of your recording method.

In preparation for pilot testing the interviews it is useful to construct an interview schedule. This will be more or less structured and used in a more or less standardized manner based on the type of interview you will be conducting. A written interview schedule is a useful tool even in the most unstructured of interviews. It can serve as a prompt or as a checklist. At a minimum it should list key words that can be seen at a glance indicating topic areas to be pursued. In its most structured form, the interview schedule will list the exact questions you must ask and the probes that follow each question.

Even with this preparation, your future interviews will likely be modified as you learn more about your study's problem area through successive interviews. Rarely will you begin your interviews knowing what is truly important or critical to your study. This will emerge as the study unfolds and so your interviews will shift in focus as you discover and learn what is more-and-more salient.

Task 1b: Preparing the Way

Depending on the purpose of your study, there are two distinct categories of potential interviewees: (1) those who are uniquely able to be informative, known as a panel of knowledgeable informants, and (2) those who, taken together, represent what happens within a population affected by a situation or event, known as a sample of representatives.

If you want to study the experiences of people who share something in common, then you need to interview a sample of people who represent the phenomena in question. On the other hand, if you want to learn about an event or topic, then you need to interview experts in the area or those who witnessed the event. You could draw on a panel of informants to provide as many perspectives as possible. In many cases, both key informants and representatives may be interviewed to more fully learn about a phenomenon you wish to study.

In our study, the abused women were clearly the key respondents. However, we also interviewed a panel of informants including shelter staff and several social workers in private practice who led a support group for women after their shelter experience. While much of the information from the two different groups of research participants overlapped and provided validation for the other, there were advantages to speaking to the panel of informants. For example, the support group leaders talked about being aware of the grief for the lost relationship expressed by women in sessions. In their interviews the women were more likely to emphasize anger and fear with respect to their ex-partners. The perspectives of the two sets of interviewees are both valid but have different implications in regard to providing social support.

Preparing the way, in terms of gaining access to key informants and representatives requires sensitivity and persistence on your part. You may find potential interviewees on the basis of knowing someone who can refer you to others. You may need to contact gatekeepers who may be in a position to give you permission to access certain people. In our study we relied on staff from the emergency shelter to provide us with the names of former residents who had left to establish independent lives. Without their help, it would have been extremely difficult to connect with women who would have been willing to be interviewed. Dealing with gatekeepers is a recurrent issue as you enter new levels or areas. In addition, a gatekeeper can shape the direction of your study as Martyn Hammersley and Paul Atkinson (1983) point out:

> Even the most friendly and co-operative gatekeepers or sponsors will shape the conduct and development of research. To one degree or another, the ethnographer will be channeled in line with existing networks of friendship and enmity, territory and equivalent boundaries.

As W. Lawrence Neuman (1994) notes:

> In some sites, gatekeeper approval creates a stigma that inhibits the cooperation of members. For example, prisoners may not be more cooperative if they know that the prison warden gave approval to the researcher. As Gordon W. West (1980, *p.* 35) remarked regarding juvenile delinquents, "I am convinced that such access routes almost always retard—or in some cases prevent—the establishment of rapport with delinquents."

You may plan to interview someone who will make you appear more legitimate as you approach others who are perhaps harder to access. In order to gain entry to any of these key individuals or situations, you will need to develop strategies to deal with resistance to or disinterest in research. In addition, you will need approvals from committees for the protection of human subjects, and you will have to deal with problems associated with being an outsider.

You will need to be sensitive and respectful in approaching potential interviewees as well as persistent and committed to fully working through any of the necessary preliminary activities in order to assure that your research study proceeds successfully within ethical and professional parameters. This is often an area where an experienced research advisor can provide you with valuable assistance.

Task 1c: Preparing the Interviewees

Assuming you have dealt with initial ethical and other access issues in Phase One, obtaining the cooperation of the interviewees will likely begin with a phone call or a letter to request an interview. If you start with a phone call, it is often a good idea to follow it up with a descriptive letter. If you start with a letter, it is useful to follow it with a phone call. Figure 2.1 presents the letter that we used in our research study.

[Agency Letterhead]

Dear Former Shelter User:

Your name was given to us by one of the workers from Transition House, the local emergency shelter. We are requesting your participation in a research project to study the experience of former shelter residents (like yourself), who are establishing new lives separate from abusive partners.

Our study was developed because of our past work in counseling women who have been abused by their partners. The study is being funded by a grant from the Thomlison Foundation. The information gathered from our study will be used to identify unmet needs of people like yourself in order to develop relevant social services that could be of some assistance in meeting these needs.

We are asking you to participate in a one-hour interview to discuss your experience since you left the shelter. With your permission, the interview will be audio-taped. We will also be utilizing selected information from the client intake form which you completed when you entered the shelter.

Your responses to the interview will be kept strictly confidential, and individual responses will not be shared with shelter personnel. The audio-tape will be coded so that your name does not appear and the tape will be stored in a locked office at the University of Calgary campus.

The audio-tapes will be destroyed at the completion of the research study. Identifying information will be deleted or disguised in any subsequent publication of the research findings.

Obviously, you have the right to withdraw from the research project at any time. Your decision to participate, or not to participate, will not affect your relationship with Transition House in any way or manner.

If you are willing to participate in our study, please read and sign the attached consent form [Figure 2.2]. Thank you for your assistance.

Your help in our research project will be greatly appreciated and could make an important difference to other women who hope to leave abusive situations.

FIGURE 2.1   SAMPLE LETTER ASKING FORMER CLIENTS TO PARTICIPATE IN THE RESEARCH STUDY

Regardless of your initial approach, be prepared to clearly explain to potential interviewees the purpose of your study and under what auspices it is being conducted. Tell them who you are, how you got their name, and why they are being asked to participate. You need to explain what will be asked of them, where the interviews will take place, how long they will take (e.g., length and number of interviews), use and purpose of any mechanical recording devices, and what else might be expected of them (e.g., reviewing transcripts or notes, discussing the interpretation).

Finally, you must address the ethical issues of confidentiality, management of the information (e.g., where tapes, notes, and/or transcripts will be stored and what will happen to them when the study is concluded), and what will become of the findings. Handling volatile or illegal information is another ethical concern inherent in qualitative studies. With the promise of confidentiality, participants may disclose or confess illicit material. For example, when we were talking to assaulted women, one divulged that she was using a belt to discipline her six-year-old son. How should we have handled this information? In this case, we had the same obligation to report the incident to child welfare authorities as we would had we been counseling the mother.

To avoid similar incidents, Patton (1990) recommends that an ethical framework for dealing with such issues be developed before the study begins. This framework should be consistent with the social work professional *Code of Ethics*. As such, you must inform your research participants of any personal risk connected to their participation in your study. Although the purpose of your research study is to further knowledge, social scientists do not have privilege of client confidentiality as do clergy and lawyers, and you may be summoned to court and asked to testify about information divulged to you in interviews.

It is good practice to prepare two copies of a written informed consent form containing the above information for each interviewee to sign. One copy will be for your records and one copy is for the interviewee to keep. Figure 2.2 is the consent form we used in our research study.

In thinking about how many interviews to conduct with interviewees, consider that it may be desirable to interview people more than once, unless you are very clear and quite specific about the information you wish to gather. Usually the first interview is partly about establishing the research partnership, building trust, and establishing rapport. The second interview tends to increase the interviewee's willingness to disclose information, allows you to probe much more deeply and/or broadly, and gives you an opportunity to check out your initial perceptions, observations, and interpretations.

The main reason you might conduct several interviews over time with the same interviewee is when the purpose of your study relates to the ongoing and unfolding story of the interviewee's life. For example, we interviewed several of the women twice, over a six month period, to see how their lives were progressing, and what was improving or becoming increasingly difficult. Normally, up

---

Dear Researcher:

    I agree to voluntarily participate in your research study about former shelter residents who are establishing new lives away from abusive partners. I understand that all responses will be kept *completely confidential* and that I may withdraw from the study at any time, without affecting my relationship with Transition House in any way.

    Your Signature: _____

    Today's Date: _____

FIGURE 2.2   EXAMPLE OF A VOLUNTARY CONSENT FORM

to three interviews with the same person should be sufficient for the purposes of most studies.

    Two other issues involved in preparing people prior to conducting interviews with them are related to the length and location of the interview. The optimum length of an interview is approximately an hour and a half. It is possible to gather useful information in as little as half an hour or to retain someone's interest and cooperation for as long as two hours. Therefore the length of a meaningful interview can vary from one situation to the next. Do remember, however, that an interview can be exhausting for you as well as to your interviewee. Make sure you plan to have enough time between interviews so that you are not rushed and can be fully ready for the next one. This time interval will also allow you to make notes and reflections.

    In some instances it may be appropriate to conduct the interview in the interviewee's home or workplace, and in other cases it may be more expedient or convenient to conduct the interview in your office, home, or even over the telephone. The issue to be considered in making the decision about location is the extent to which the environment has an impact upon the quality and quantity of the information you wish to obtain.

    If there is a lot of background noise or frequent interruptions, the flow of the interview can easily become disrupted. If the place is unfamiliar to your interviewees, they may become uncomfortable. If they are at work, they may be preoccupied with what is on their desk or yet to be accomplished that day. If they are at home, they may be limited in what they can say if others might hear them or they may be distracted by happenings going on around them. All of these factors also affect you and your ability to tune into the interviewee and attend to the interview.

We chose to interview the women in our study in their homes. Although, in several instances, the activities and noise of young children did, in fact, interrupt the interview, because children were considered to be an integral part of the life experience of women who separate from abusive ex-partners, we decided that to visit them in their homes would give us the best sense of their lives. In several cases the reality of coping with children's behavior highlighted the desperation and loneliness experienced by these women.

One woman's four-year-old daughter had recently been diagnosed with developmental problems. She had difficulty understanding language, slept little, and, during the interview, constantly attempted to open the fridge to eat food that she was medically restricted from eating. Her mother was coping admirably with her daughter's disability, in addition to her other worries about her ex-husband suing her for custody.

Although the flow of the conversation was interrupted often, holding the interview with mother and daughter together conveyed the demanding aspects of their lives in a way that would not have been apparent if she had been interviewed alone. Thus, the nature of the inquiry should guide your decision about the best location to hold your interviews.

Step 2: Choosing a Recording Method

Recording deals with the mechanics of collecting the information obtained through the interview so that it can lend itself to analysis. Regardless of the type of interview you conduct, the purpose of it will be lost if you fail to capture the actual words and the essence of the interview. There are three typical approaches to recording the information gathered in qualitative research interviews: (1) tape recording the interview (either audio or video), (2) taking notes during the interview, and (3) taking notes immediately following the interview.

Task 2a: Tape Recording

There are both pros and cons to tape recording interviews. For the interviewee, the presence of a recorder may be intrusive and a barrier to full disclosure. Nevertheless, it may be the only way to capture the richness and subtleties of the speech of the person being interviewed. In the case of video recording, it may be the only way to capture the nonverbal language of the interviewees, or to accurately identify each speaker in a group interview. Recording devices may also provide a means of self-monitoring and improvement for the interviewer, particularly if you are new at interviewing. The tape recorder may give you the confidence to focus all of your attention on the interviewee and the interview itself, knowing you do not have to worry about remembering details or writing notes. At the same time, knowing the tape will record everything that is said, you might be tempted to let your mind wander.

Ultimately, the decision about whether to tape depends on what you want to do with the data you gather. If you want to include many direct quotes from the interviewees in your study, then it is useful to have the verbatim account which can be transcribed at a later date. If capturing the exact phrasing of all interview responses is not critical to your study, then note-taking may suffice. Nevertheless, the power of a direct quote from an interviewee can far exceed that of a summary statement from the researcher. Compare the statement "It is important to offer further counseling services to shelter residents even after they have moved out" to the following quote from one of the interviewees in our study:

> If you're not going to offer follow-up help you shouldn't have a shelter. All you're doing is giving that woman temporary assistance for her to go back to what she just came from. And you're going to kill that woman...

The above direct quote from a woman who has used a shelter makes a tremendous impact because it comes directly from the one who has lived the experience.

Once you have the interview on tape you can use it in several ways. If time and money are not an issue, it is clearly best to fully transcribe all your interviews from the tape. If your time and budget are limited, you might listen to the tape and use your notes to help you decide what parts to transcribe and what parts to paraphrase.

Task 2b: Taking Notes During the Interview

Many qualitative researchers advocate taking notes during the interview in addition to tape recording. The notes can serve as a back-up or safeguard against mechanical difficulties. Such difficulties are likely to occur at some point despite precautions to the contrary. In one instance, after we had decided that it was safer to plug in the tape recorder than to use batteries, a thunderstorm interrupted the electricity. Batteries are a useful back-up, but seem to have an annoying habit of running out of energy in the middle of an interview, rather than at the end.

Notes also serve as a guide to the tape in helping you decide what to transcribe and what to leave out. In some cases, where tape recording is not possible, brief notes may be the only way of recording the data. We've certainly been in situations where a woman was willing to be interviewed, but preferred that we not use the tape recorder. In this case you would try to write down some exact quotations and brief comments, supplemented by notes after the interviews.

Be aware, though, that some people may react negatively to your taking notes during the interview; they may feel that you are evaluating or judging them in some way. If you sense that taking notes is having an effect on the interview, it would be preferable to wait to write a summary until afterwards.

If you interview in pairs, then you may take notes, leaving your co-researcher to be the primary interviewer. This is particularly useful in group interviews where you can observe and note (no pun intended) who speaks, who listens, who follows, and what is said (or *not* said) and your co-researcher can guide the discussion.

Task 2c: Taking Notes After the Interview

The third approach to recording is to make a written record of the interview soon after it occurs. This can be done in a variety of ways, but it is important to allow sufficient time for this activity. One hour of interviewing can require as much as three to four hours of time to develop the notes afterward, particularly if this is the only record of the interview. One way is to write a process recording of the interview as soon as is possible afterwards.

A common format used in writing a process of qualitative research interviews is to use two columns. In the first column you write as close to a verbatim account of the interview as you can recall. This would include your questions, probes, and statements as well as the interviewee's responses. Use the adjacent column to make reflective comments and observations: what you were thinking or feeling at the time, other things that were occurring that may have caused interference (e.g., room was too warm or too noisy, or other distractions), and any insights or themes that occur to you.

It is also recommended that you make summary notes and write in your personal journal after each interview. This will enable you to note your impressions, reactions, hunches, and general comments about what you have learned. In this way you can capture any particular intra personal or interpersonal experiences that might affect the way you make sense of the data.

If you write about your personal reflections in conjunction with a record of what transpired, then you will have a set of notes containing the content of the interview alongside your notes reflecting the interview process. The process has an effect upon the quality of the content you gather, your interpretation of the content and of what steps you decide to take next. Identifying these effects as they are revealed to you will also facilitate your interpretation and reporting of them later on in your study (Phase Four).

W. Lawrence Neuman (1994) has provided some recommendations when it comes to taking notes in Step 2:

- Record your notes as soon as possible after each interview, and do not talk with others until your observations are recorded.

- Begin the record of each interview with a new page, with the date and time noted.

- Use jotted notes only as a temporary memory aid, with key words or terms, or the first and last things said.

- Use wide margins to make it easy to add to notes at any time. Go back and add to the notes if you remember something later.

- Record events in the order in which they occurred, and note how long they last (e.g., a 15-minute wait, a one-hour ride).

- Make notes as concrete, complete, and comprehensible as possible.

- Use frequent paragraphs and quotation marks. Exact recall of phrases is best, with double quotes; use single quotes for paraphrasing.

- Record small talk or routines that do not appear to be significant at the time; they may become important later.

- "Let your fingers flow" and write quickly without worrying about spelling or "wild ideas."

- Never substitute tape recordings completely for note taking.

- Include diagrams or maps of the setting, and outline your own movements and those of others during the interview.

- Include your own words and behaviors in the notes. Also record emotional feelings and private thoughts in a separate section.

- Avoid evaluative summarizing words. Instead of "The sink looked disgusting," say, "The sink was rust-stained and looked as if it had not been cleaned in a long time. Pieces of food and dirty dishes which looked several days old were piled into it."

- Reread notes periodically and record ideas generated by the rereading.

- Always make one or more backup copies, keep them in a locked location, and store the copies in different places in case of fire.

Step 3: Conducting the Interview

Conducting the interview is concerned with the specific activities involved in the interview itself. It is important to approach this step with the mind set that you are trying to obtain the perspective of the people who you are interviewing. Your interviewing skills, past experiences, and interviewing techniques will assist you in learning about others' perspectives, combined above all with your honest respect for people. Remember, research interviews are the primary purpose of gathering data, as distinct from therapy. They have the potential to open new areas of personal awareness for both you and your interviewees and can be change-inducing.

There are four key tasks to be accomplished in conducting a qualitative research interview: (1) engaging, (2) contracting, (3) implementing, and (4) terminating.

Task 3a: Engaging

Two issues must be considered during this task: (1) developing a relationship or a research partnership, and (2) establishing trust and building rapport. These issues must be attended to throughout the interview but are of primary focus at the beginning. According to Robert Weiss (1994), the interviewer/interviewee partnership involves several aspects:

- The interviewer and interviewee work together to produce information relevant to the study.

- The interviewer defines the areas (in more or less structured ways) to be discussed; the interviewee provides information in the directed areas.

- The interviewer's questions are always asked for purposes directly related to the study; the interviewee regards the interviewer as a privileged inquirer and may give information that is not generally available.

- The interviewer respects the interviewee's integrity and in so doing does not question the interviewee's personal worth, motives, or choices.

- The interviewer makes every effort to ensure the interviewee is not harmed by participating in the interview.

Establishing trust occurs at the beginning of the interview with some disclosure of who you are and the reasons for wanting the interview. In our case, we talked about our experiences counseling women who have been battered and our interest in learning about what they needed to do to get on with their lives.

Building rapport is related to an ability to make interviewees comfortable and to put them at ease. This is most commonly accomplished by giving them information about what will transpire, what is expected of them, and inviting them to join with you in the process.

We found that one way to further connect with interviewees at the outset of our study was to state our interest in hearing what they had learned from their experience, clarifying that others may well benefit from their knowledge. Such an invitation opens the way to the task of contracting.

Task 3b: Contracting

This task involves obtaining the interviewee's agreement to involve him- or herself in the interview in a meaningful way. It is more than simply agreeing to the interview itself. It represents the interviewee's understanding of the purpose of the interview and willingness to work within the conditions under which it is being conducted. To foster this, you can give an outline or agenda to potential interviewees, either verbally or in writing. They can also be given a copy of the interview schedule informing them about the questions they will be asked.

As mentioned in Task 1c, contracting includes obtaining written informed consent, which represents a mutual recognition and acknowledgment of the ethical considerations and implications of your study. Typically, engaging and contracting occur simultaneously at the outset of the interview and precede the actual conducting of the interview itself.

Task 3c: Conducting

During the interview, it is your job to guide the interviewee to the topics that relate to your study. In most cases you will want the interviewee to describe an actual instance or a specific experience in considerable detail, giving you his or her particular story from his or her own perspective. You will need to be aware that many interviewees initially seem to prefer to provide (or think they ought to give you) generalized accounts rather than concrete instances. Therefore you need to be reasonably specific in asking them to tell you about their internal and external experiences. For example,

Could you tell me about the last time _____ happened to you, right from the beginning?
— or —
Is there a specific incident you can recall when you felt (acted or thought) that way?

If you are concerned that this is or is not a typical instance or representative of the phenomena in question, then you might ask,

Is this occurrence or incident different from other times? If so, in what ways?

There are two particular considerations associated with the task of conducting an interview: (1) interview dynamics, and (2) types of questions.

INTERVIEW DYNAMICS. As should be evident by now, an interview involves an interaction between the interviewer (the researcher) and the interviewee (the research participant). In any interview there are certain tips that can optimize the interview dynamics and thus, the quality of the research partnership.

- *Tip 1* — When you start off conducting an interview it is helpful to encourage the interviewee to begin by describing present experiences or activities of a noncontroversial nature to help create rapport and a reference point for other questions. Present experiences generally are easier for interviewees to deal with. They lead the way into past and future explorations which require a different mental set.

- *Tip 2* — It is best to keep background and demographic questions to a minimum. Most people find these kinds of questions boring and de-energizing. It is a good idea to collect this type of information near the end of the interview rather than at the beginning. Asking for demographic information at the beginning sets the wrong tone and gives the wrong message about what the purpose of the interview is and the kind of contribution and involvement you want from the interviewee. You might ask interviewees to fill in a form with these data in advance of the interview or alternatively ask these types of questions when you have finished conducting the interview.

- Tip 3 — It is a good idea to get into the habit of asking open-ended, neutral/nonjudgmental questions worded in language that the interviewee understands, and can easily relate to. Try to use some words from their context so you have a shared sense of meaning in the interview partnership.

- *Tip 4* — Ask one question at a time with a single idea in each question, otherwise it is confusing for interviewees. They will either respond to the last question they heard or the one which is easiest for them to answer.

- *Tip 5* — It is important that you find ways to demonstrate that you are listening carefully. Using brief verbal cues mirrors that you are interested and following what they are saying. Asking clarifying questions from time to time and using neutral but encouraging phrases provides feedback about the progress of the interview.

- *Tip 6* — You need to allow interviewees sufficient time to organize their thoughts and respond to your questions. Find ways to gently and respectfully guide them to other areas of focus in your study to make the most of the time available. This includes being careful in asking "Why" questions as they tend to assume cause and effect, and they can have the effect of putting interviewees on the spot and making them feel defensive. If you do want to understand reasons why, then try asking this as a "What" question.

- *Tip 7* — In group interviews, be aware it is not a problem-solving session or group discussion *per se* but a purposeful, data-gathering interview. It is not necessary for the group to come to a consensus, as the essential tasks involve getting different points of view on a specific situation or phenomenon. Be resourceful in finding ways to involve all the people in the group, including tactfully dealing with those who may be dominating the group interview.

- Tip 8 — Be mindful of your own cultural norms and considerate of other peoples' cultural norms, values, beliefs, and learning styles when conducting an interview. Stay attuned to the interview progress and dynamics so that you can adjust and adapt accordingly.

- *Tip 9* — Read interviewing books that will help you develop your knowledge and skills.

- *Tip 10* — Role-play with fellow students.

If you check in briefly with interviewees on how they perceive things are going and you keep the above tips in mind while conducting the interview, then you will probably find that you have gathered useful and meaningful data for your study.

TYPES OF QUESTIONS. Many beginning qualitative research interviewers actually believe if they can just ask "The Right" question, then magically the interviewee will divulge "The Perfect" answer. While experience in interviewing will be helpful in generating good questions, what is most important is to develop good rapport with the interviewee and to fully attend to the dynamics of the interview process. Many people who are interviewed follow a less than direct path toward revealing information and it is not just the question itself that brings them to do so. The interview is often a part of a learning process not only for the interviewer but for the interviewee as well. In fact it may be the first time they have organized and verbalized their thoughts on a particular subject. It could be a profoundly emotional experience for them to recall certain events.

There are many different ways to ask good questions. In fact, any question is a good question if it respectfully guides the interviewee to reveal information and the kind of detail needed for the study. Michael Q. Patton (1990) suggests some of the different dimensions of experience you might access through questions include the following, any of which may be asked with respect to the past, present, or future.

- Experience/Behavior — a person's actions, behaviors, activities, experiences. (e.g., What did you do after your husband threatened to kidnap the children? What was it like for you, hearing that threat?)

- Opinions/Values — how a person interprets a situation, what he or she thinks of it. (e.g., Knowing what you know now, how do you explain the abuse to yourself? What would you tell women at the shelter about the difficulties in leaving an assaultive ex-partner?)

- Feelings/Emotion — feelings, emotions in response to very personal experiences and thoughts. (e.g., How did you feel when your boyfriend sent you roses and begged you to reunite? Do you believe that your relationship is worth saving?)

- Knowledge/Facts — what the person considers to be factual and what factual information is known by a person. (e.g., What did you learn about the cycle of abuse when you attended the support group at the shelter?)

- Sensory — captures a person's experience of the senses of what is seen, touched, tasted, smelled, or heard. (e.g., What do you experience living in this new apartment?)

- Background/Demographic — routine information about personal characteristics: age, education, current occupation, etc. (e.g., When were you born? Do you work outside the home?)

Asking the "tough" questions involves entering into areas that are sensitive or painful and requires a certain degree of skill. This is where your earlier attention to establishing rapport and building a solid relationship pays off. To begin with, you must believe in your study's purpose giving you the need to know and the permission to ask certain questions. As mentioned previously in our study, it was evident that many of the issues that might be important could be upsetting to remember or to admit to, including the pain of leaving a long-term relationship, fear, low self-esteem, and despair.

Nevertheless, in order to understand the needs of women in this situation, we needed to have a clear sense of the extent to which they experienced such difficulties. It is a good idea to identify potentially tough questions ahead of time and to practice the best way to introduce them with a sense of purpose. If you do not believe in your study, then you will communicate to your interviewee your own sense of hesitation, uncertainty, and discomfort in asking tough questions.

Next, you must clearly communicate to your interviewees why you are going to be venturing into a potentially difficult territory so that they will believe in your need to know. Their confidence that these questions, albeit difficult, are worthwhile answering is a direct reflection of your ability to prepare them for your questions and your comfort level in asking them. One useful idea is to preface difficult questions with a phrase such as "This may be a painful issue...," or "At the risk of seeming too personal, would you be willing to tell me about...," or "It would be helpful for me to hear about how you ended up in the shelter."

Of course, as with any part of the interview, and in keeping with ethical standards, the interviewee always has the option of refusing to answer a particular question. Often, however, interviewees are willing to answer most questions given the appropriate rapport, timing, and phrasing of questions.

To give you a sense of how an interview would proceed, we have included an excerpt below from our study. In this example, the interviewee was very open about her relationship with her abusive boyfriend. We took every precaution not to prompt or to question her often in order to encourage the continuation of her story.

Interviewer: So now that we've got the (ethics) forms out of the way, I'd like to tell you how much I appreciate you taking this time to talk about your experience after leaving Transition House.

Joy: I have only good things to say about that place. It was so peaceful being there, you know, you don't have to worry, you don't have to be concerned. You know your children are safe and everything (pause) and you're safe. The counselors were really helpful, too. No, I really liked that place. That was my second time there. Silly me, I've got involved in the same relationship twice. I decided to give it another chance because of the baby. Yeah, no...I liked that place a lot, it was just excellent.

Interviewer: Well, that's good to hear.

Joy: Nice people. And then the residents that live there also—they back each other up on a lot of things. If someone's depressed, or busy with another kid, or whatever—they all help each other out. It's good that way.

Interviewer: When was the previous time you were there then?

Joy: That was last year, I was there in April. I was about seven months pregnant then. And I was there for the full 21 days, the full time you're allowed to stay.

Interviewer: So it sounds like you've got a good impression about Transition House.

Joy: Oh, yeah. The first thing I thought of when I started having ... like my boyfriend hadn't kept his promise to stop alcohol, go to A.A., us to go to family counseling and so when we had a big blow-out in front of everyone down at the fairgrounds, and he was grabbing the baby trying to pull her out of my arms and he was too drunk. You know, I don't know whether he hurt the baby but the fact was there that he could have. And then, he slammed the stroller into my son, so that was just enough right there. He couldn't control himself on booze, and the first place I thought of was Transition House. I called the police, too, to protect me from him, and they escorted him off the grounds and made sure that I got on the bus safely. Yeah, the first place that I thought of to go to was the Transition House.

Interviewer: So you took the bus there?

Joy: Yeah, I had to transfer once. The police were on duty, they couldn't escort me the whole way. They made sure I got off the fairgrounds safely.

Interviewer: Did they lay charges?

Joy: No, it wasn't a chargeable situation. Because he wasn't actually beating on us, but he grabbed the baby, threatened me—he had his hand in a fist and he was threatening me. He didn't go through with it, but he did threaten me. He did slam the stroller into my son, but I think it might have been because he was drunk and mad at the same time, so in a way it was intentional, and in a way it was probably an accident too. I just can't stand the booze. I don't drink myself, so I can't get along with it.

Interviewer: Yeah, that makes it even more difficult...

Joy: The booze was just too much. He destroyed our house and two apartments—things broken everywhere, holes in the wall, doors torn off hinges, all kinds of stuff. Yeah, after the last time at Transition House my initial thought was to leave him and not go back, pregnant or not. And then we got talking. I didn't phone him for a long time but he kept phoning me at work, trying to see me at work, you know, saying "I want to work this through." That was great, I believed him, I trusted him, and then when I finally said, "Okay, I'll come back," he kept to it for a little while. And then he just started breaking his promises again. And then he started sneaking drinks. It kept on increasing ... problems, fights kept on intensifying and that was all I could take. The final blow down at the fairgrounds because he wanted a gun, a little carved gun that shoots elastics...

Interviewer: You're kidding!

Joy: What a silly thing to blow up about! First off I said, "Okay, but I won't get it for you today, I'll get it when I come back on Friday." That wasn't good enough for him. So then when I finally agreed to get the gun for him, that wasn't good enough for him. He was complaining that I changed my mind. So, I couldn't win, I couldn't win any way. During this time abusive language, yelling and screaming right in front of all this crowd of people. So embarrassing. I couldn't control him.

I couldn't talk to him, couldn't even calm him down, so I just went and he slammed the stroller into my son, that was the final straw ... It was all I could take. I wasn't willing to deal with it anymore. I'm doing better on my own ... it's best that I don't get involved with him anymore. He can see his baby girl when he wants, you know, the three of us can just live our lives and he can live his own. Just visit his daughter when he wants to. As long as he phones first. And I told him he has to be sober when he comes by. I'm not going to have him come by—if he's drunk, he just doesn't get in.

Interviewer: How's that working out so far this time?

Joy: He's not drinking, but when he comes over we still fight a lot. I guess it wouldn't be so bad if we hadn't had my daughter. I haven't gone for legal custody yet. But, I don't know ... some days I feel like I should and somedays I feel like I shouldn't, it's hard to say.

Interviewer: So, that's not one of those things that you have to do right now...

Joy: No, he hasn't threatened to take Annie for six months, so ... that's nice (Annie spills a drink, Joy cleans it up, changes his diaper).

Interviewer: So how are you getting on financially?

Joy: I'm on Social Assistance ... when you only have $800 a month it's kind of hard, but we're making out okay. I planted a garden this year. I work part-time on Thursdays and Fridays. My hours aren't very long ... like Fridays could be longer, it depends on how business is...

Task 3d: Terminating

The central consideration in the terminating task is to complete the interview at an appropriate point. The way in which an interview is completed needs to be thought out just as carefully as all the preceding steps and tasks of the interviewing process. It involves disengaging gracefully and respectfully from an interview session which may have been very intense for everyone involved—including you. As the time scheduled for the interview draws to a close, it is helpful to signal about ten minutes beforehand that the interview is coming to an end. Then you can ask if there is anything more the interviewee wishes to convey.

Bringing closure to the interview can be done by summarizing briefly the areas you have covered in the interview. Reiterate how this information fits into your research study, and review ethical considerations such as confidentiality that we have previously mentioned.

If feasible and appropriate, provide interviewees with an opportunity to give you additional data in a written format later on. Depending on the type of interview, offer them an opportunity to review your transcribed notes. This is one way to ensure you heard them correctly and have accurately recorded their thoughts, feelings, and meanings. In some cases it would be appropriate to give them a copy for their personal information.

When terminating an interview, you could make arrangements for any follow-up interviews. It is also appropriate to ask them for feedback on how the interview went for them, and if there are any suggestions they would make to help you prepare for your next interview with another person. At all costs, consider their feedback seriously. As appropriate, share your thoughts as well. The women in our study often noted that they enjoyed the chance to talk about what they had accomplished since they had left the shelter.

Make sure that you thank them for their time and willingness to take part in your study and for the information they have shared with you. Reiterate how they will be involved next (if any) in your study, and tell them how they can contact you if they have any questions whatsoever.

It is your responsibility to be aware of any other concerns or needs that they may have (e.g., medical, psychological, social services) that have been revealed in the interviews that could require immediate attention. Encourage them to attend to these or see if you can assist them through referrals to appropriate resources. For example, we encouraged a women who was so upset about the phone call from her boyfriend to call her Outreach Counselor that day. At the same time, be aware of maintaining an appropriate and ethical boundary. It is a thoughtful gesture to follow up the interview with a thank you note.

Because interviewing is such an intensive process, you may be tempted to wait to reflect and make notes on the interviews and your personal reactions. However, it is crucial to take the time immediately following the interview to carry out these tasks.

Step 4: Reflecting About the Interview

Reflecting is an activity that must take place in all qualitative research studies, and especially throughout the data gathering phase. It involves reviewing and analyzing the interview process itself as it unfolds. Reflection informs your decisions that you must make at each step. It is what gives qualitative research its strength and its uniqueness, as well as assuring its methodological rigor. It is also one of the reasons why those who have done qualitative research often find it to be a highly intensive process.

With respect to interviewing, engaging in reflective activity involves your consciously reviewing, analyzing, and making decisions at every step and task, and carefully and fully recording these events in a personal journal to accompany the interview transcripts and notes. Data collection and analysis are thus simultaneous. This requires strong commitment, good planning, and flexibility to foster the emergent nature of your study.

The kind of information recorded in your journal includes your insights, reactions, questions, self-analyses, biases, impressions about emerging patterns, ideas about connections to other knowledge, decisions about next steps, and why. You should always be scrupulous in distinguishing reflections from interview data, this often being accomplished by using special symbols, dividing interview note pages into two or three sections, and keeping a separate journal for personal process documentation.

Without reflection and analysis during data collection, your study may be unfocused, repetitive, and the amount of data collected overwhelming. Coupled with interview data, your reflections will provide the essential foundation for more in-depth analyses later on.

There are two key tasks associated with the reflecting step in qualitative research interviews: (1) reflecting *in* action, and (2) reflecting *on* action. There is often a great deal of interaction and overlap between them.

Task 4a: Reflecting in Action

Reflecting in action as applied to qualitative interviewing involves your being able to develop an evaluative observer part of yourself that is active at the same time as you may be planning the interview, conducting the interview, or recording the interview.

In order to successfully reflect while in action, you need to be as fully present as possible and open to the process as it unfolds. You are thus able to monitor what may be happening with yourself as well as with others, question any strategies, plans or assumptions, and decide if actions are required and when and how to implement them.

During the interview, it is paramount that you continually reflect on the quality of information you are receiving. Two guiding questions to help you monitor this situation are:

- Is this information really needed for my study?

- Is the information of a high enough quality that I can use it in my study?

These two questions will inform your decision-making processes as you guide the flow of the interview. You will encounter situations where interviewees are giving you information that does not directly answer your questions, or may be off-topic. For example, one woman in our study insisted on describing details about the extramarital affair her husband had several years before she left the marriage. Since it was difficult to see how this information added to our knowledge about the struggles that she currently faced, we asked her if the affair continued to have an effect on her relationship with her ex-husband. She quickly shifted the focus to the present issue in our study of how uncomfortable she feels when her husband comes to pick up the children, a topic that was a better fit with the purpose of our research study.

As you are reflecting in action, you may find it useful to make brief notes to yourself if conditions permit. For example, while conducting an unstructured interview you might note an important but possibly risky question that has emerged during the interview that you want to ask later if it seems appropriate. You might note your personal reaction to how you phrased a question or to how an interviewee's comments impacted on you, or questions he or she may have asked you.

Task 4b: Reflecting on Action

Reflecting on action is the process by which you review the actions you have taken, as well as the underlying assumptions. Planning to reflect on actions at various time intervals in the interview process will add a depth and perspective that will greatly enhance your study.

Some examples of the kinds of questions you might ask when you are reflecting on action are:

- Am I getting the kinds of data that are relevant for my study?

- Was this interview too structured?

- What should I do to get more in-depth information on a pattern that seems to be emerging?

- Is the interviewee withholding something—and what should I do about it?

- What impact could my race, social status, gender, ethnicity, or political beliefs have on my study, or the interviewee?

- Did what the interviewee say ring true—did he or she want to please me, look good, idealize a situation, or push a particular agenda?

- Why am I feeling so stressed after this particular interview?

- What assumption did I make when I asked a particular question of the interviewee?

Reflection on action may occur immediately subsequent to an action, overlapping and interacting with the reflection in action process. An example of this would be when you do ask the tough or risky question identified through reflection in action in an interview, then you double back and review what happened for you and your interviewee as a result of taking the action of asking. Reflection on action is also necessary and important to your study when you have the time to more fully explore your thoughts.

An important time for reflection on action is immediately after any interactions with an interviewee or those people (gatekeepers) who are giving you access to them. Other times include during regular personal journal keeping, after discussions with research advisors, or with other colleagues. You should keep a piece of paper or electronic notebook with you at all times so you can jot down any ideas or thoughts that come to you, often at the most unexpected times and places!

Step 5: Completing the Process

Deciding when you have collected enough interviews to support your research study will be informed by your ongoing reflections and analyses as well as some practical parameters such as the amount of time you have available to interview other people. As this phase of your study draws to a close, you will find yourself concerned more with verification and understanding (Phase Three) of what you have collected and less concerned with adding new data. In our study, we noted that after about nine interviews no new themes were emerging. Since we had already set up several other interviews we continued, but these reaffirmed our thinking that the major issues had been identified. At this point, we elected to stop the interviewing process. Yvonna Lincoln and Egon Guba (1985) suggest some guidelines in making the decision to stop data gathering:

- All of your resources have been exhausted (e.g., time, budget, limitations on access).

- All categories in which you hoped to collect data have been covered.

- Emergence of regularities, overlaps, possible patterns, and duplication of data collected are now occurring with more and more frequency.

- Information divergent from your study's central focus is beginning to be collected.

Prior to making the decision to stop interviewing, you must go over any information you have already gathered to see if it is complete, makes sense, and is legible, audible, or visible. Try to fill in any gaps. This will assure that your data lends itself to a more proper intense analysis (Phase Three).

SUMMARY

Interviewing is one of the primary ways in which information may be gathered from the perspective of others. We have attempted to provide practical information on how to proceed through the process of gathering information from interviews. It requires that you do so in a respectful, ethical, and mindful manner. We have described the different types of interviewing and the key steps and associated tasks involved within them. We have emphasized how these activities may occur simultaneously, recursively, as well as sequentially, consistent with the emergent and organic nature of the qualitative research process. After you have collected all the necessary interview data, they need to be systematically analyzed, the topic of Phase Three that follows.

ANNOTATED BIBLIOGRAPHY

BERG, B.L. (1989). *Qualitative research methods for the social sciences* (Chapter 2). Needham Heights, MA: Allyn & Bacon. This chapter describes practical concepts such as types of interviews, types of questions, and common problem questions. In the last half of the chapter, Berg draws a parallel between the interviewer as an actor, a director, and a choreographer and describes how to "get the show on the road." Within the drama metaphor, he includes a host of practical suggestions about overcoming common problems when conducting research interviews.

ELY, M., ANZUL, M., FRIEDMAN, T., GARNER, D., & McCORMACK-STEINMETZ, A. (1991). *Doing qualitative research: Circles within circles* (Chapter 3). New York: Falmer Press. The authors provide a short, informative presentation on interviewing in a chapter that is sprinkled with examples, which strengthen the many useful points they have to make. After describing informal and formal interviews, the authors pose a series of questions designed to assist researchers in planning interviews.

The questions the researcher should attend to include: "What do I know about the interviewee?" "How will I gain access?" "How will I begin my questions?" and "How will I conclude the interview?" This chapter also deals with pragmatic issues, like strategies designed to keep the researcher in tune with the interviewee and avoiding inappropriate probing or intrusiveness.

Another focus is on the questioning aspect of interviewing. Ely maintains that researchers must pay attention to the rhythm, form, and impact of questions. Commentary is also presented on the types of questions used by qualitative researchers and the importance of probes that are designed to enhance the quality of data obtained.

ERLANDSON, D., HARRIS, E., SKIPPER, B., & ALLEN, S. (1993). *Doing naturalistic inquiry: A guide to methods* (Chapter 5). Newbury Park, CA: Sage. After describing the purposes of interviewing, Erlandson and his associates proceed to discuss keys to completing a successful interview, including question construction, active listening, and proper recording. Although brief, the discussion on the ethical issues pertaining to interviewing is helpful. Interviewing is viewed as a partnership; the importance of respect for participants is stressed. The pragmatics involved in preparing and conducting the interview are addressed, highlighting strategies to ensure the interview achieves its goals.

FONTANA, A., & FREY, J. (1994). Interviewing: The art of science. In N.K. Denzin, & Y. Lincoln (Eds.), *Handbook of qualitative research* (pp. 361-376). Newbury Park, CA: Sage. Of particular interest to researchers are the detailed descriptions in this chapter of three types of interviews: structured, unstructured and group. In their discussion of these basic approaches, the authors present advantages and disadvantages, and identify skill requirements. The inclusion of a table describing different types of group interviews is extremely helpful.

Fontana and Frey then identify and summarize issues that the interviewer may confront during interviewing. These include: (1) gaining access to the setting, (2) understanding the language and culture of the respondents, (3) determining how one should present him- or herself, (4) locating key informants, (5) gaining trust, (6) establishing rapport, and (7) collecting empirical materials.

The focus of the chapter then shifts to three types of unstructured interviews—oral history, creative and postmodern interviewing. Of particular importance is the author's discussion on gender, and the need for researchers to remember that the sex of the interviewer and the respondent does make a difference.

The final section of the chapter deals with issues such as the type of interview to be used, specific interview techniques, methods of recording and interpretation, and ethical concerns (such as informed consent, the right to privacy, and protection from harm).

Some ethical concerns are discussed in detail, including the controversy pertaining to the use of covert fieldwork and the degree of involvement of the researcher with the group under study.

GLESNE, C., & PESHKIN, A. (1992). *Becoming qualitative researchers: An introduction* (Chapter 4). White Plains, NY: Longman. Glesne and Peshkin focus on both structured and open (unstructured) interviews. The first section of their work deals with creating "useful questions," and offers suggestions in this regard. Following this, attention is paid to decisions regarding where interviews will be held, how long they will be, and how data will be recorded.

An unusual aspect of Glesne and Peshkin's work is their presentation of interviewer attributes that contribute to the completion of successful interviews: (1) being prepared for the interview, (2) rapport with the person being interviewed, (3) openness to learning from the interviewing process, (4) being analytic and considering meanings and explanations in the data you gather, and (5) patience in the effort to enrich the data that are collected.

The final section of the chapter deals with some typical problems encountered in interviewing: dealing with resistant individuals, dealing with the nonstop talker, and ensuring that equipment is working properly.

PATTON, M.Q. (1990). *Qualitative evaluation and research methods* (Chapter 7). Newbury Park, CA: Sage. Of particular importance in the chapter by Patton is material describing three types of interviewing: (1) the informational conversational interview, (2) the general interview guide approach, and (3) the standardized open-ended interview. Patton highlights the strength and limitation of each interview approach in a comparative manner, while he also stresses that the common characteristics of all three approaches is "that the persons being interviewed respond in their own words to express their own person perspectives."

The chapter then addresses common issues about interviewing: (1) What types of questions should be posed? (2) How should questions be sequenced? and (3) How should questions be worded? Useful examples enhance the discussion of these concerns.

A strength of Patton's work is his discussion on the use of probes and follow-up questions. He provides the reader with definitions of various types of probes, and a clear demonstration of how their use enhances interviewing. Also, a section dealing with recording data is pragmatic and very useful, especially comments on taping and transcribing interviews.

REFERENCES AND FURTHER READINGS

Berg, B.L. (1995). *Qualitative research methods for the social sciences* (2nd ed). Needham Heights, MA: Allyn & Bacon.

Bogdan, R.C., & Biklen, S.K. (1982). *Qualitative research for education: An introduction to theory and methods.* Needham Heights, MA: Allyn & Bacon.

Bogdan, R.C., & Taylor, S.J. (1975). *Introduction to qualitative research methods: A phenomenological approach to the social sciences.* New York: John Wiley.

Brady, J. (1976). *The craft of interviewing.* New York: Vintage Books.

Cormier, W.H., & Cormier, L.S. (1987). *Interviewing strategies for helpers.* Boston, MA: Jones and Bartlett Publications.

Crabtree, B., Yanoshik, M., Miller, W., & O'Connor, P. (1993). Selecting individual or group interviews. In D. Morgan (Ed.), *Successful focus groups: Advancing the state of the art* (pp. 137-149). Newbury Park, CA: Sage.

Denzin, N.K., & Lincoln, Y.S. (Eds.). (1994). *Handbook of qualitative research.* Newbury Park, CA: Sage.

Easterby-Smith, M., Thorpe, R., & Lowe, A. (1991). *Management research: An introduction* (Chapter 5). Newbury Park, CA: Sage.

Fontana, A., & Frey, James H. (1994). Interviewing: The art of science. In N.K. Denzin & Y.S. Lincoln (Eds.), *Handbook of qualitative research* (pp. 361-376). Newbury Park, CA: Sage.

Frey, J., & Fontana, A. (1993). The group interview in social research. In D. Morgan (Ed.), *Successful focus groups: Advancing the state of the art* (pp. 20-34). Newbury Park, CA: Sage.

Gilchrist, V. (1992). Key informant interviews. In B. Crabtree & W. Miller (Eds.), *Doing qualitative research* (pp. 70-92). Newbury Park, CA: Sage.

Gorden, R. (1992). *Basic interviewing skills.* Itasca, IL: F.E. Peacock.

Guba, E.G., & Lincoln, Y.S. (1989). *Fourth generation evaluation.* Newbury Park, CA: Sage.

Hammersley, M., & Atkinson, R. (1983). *Ethnography: Principles in practice.* London: Tavistock.

Kruger, R. (1994). *Focus groups: A practical guide for applied research.* Newbury Park, CA: Sage.

Lincoln, Y.S., & Guba, E.G. (1985). *Naturalist inquiry.* Newbury Park, CA: Sage.

McCracken, C. (1988). *The long interview.* Newbury Park, CA: Sage.

Merriam, S.B. (1988). *Case study research in education: A qualitative approach.* San Francisco, CA: Jossey-Bass.

Miller, W., & Crabtree, B. (1992). Depth interviewing: The long interview approach. In M. Stewart, F. Tudiver, M. Bass, E. Dunn, & P. Norton (Eds.), *Tools for primary care research* (pp. 103-119). Newbury Park, CA: Sage.

Mishler, E. G. (1990). *Research interviewing.* Cambridge, MA: Harvard University Press.

Morgan, D. (Ed.). (1993). *Successful focus groups: Advancing the state of the art.* Newbury Park, CA: Sage.

Neuman, W.L. (1994). *Social research methods: Qualitative and quantitative approaches* (2nd ed.). Needham Heights, MA: Allyn & Bacon.

Patton, M.Q. (1990). *Qualitative evaluation and research methods.* Newbury Park, CA: Sage.

Schatzman, L., & Strauss, A. (1973). *Field research: Strategies for a natural sociology.* Englewood Cliffs, NJ: Prentice-Hall.

Schon, D. (1983). *The reflective practitioner: How professionals think in action.* New York: Basic Books.

Seidman, I. (1991). *Interviewing as qualitative research: A guide for researchers in education and the social sciences.* New York: Teachers College Press.

Shaffir, W.B., Stebbins, R.A., & Turowetz, A. (1980). Introduction. In W.B. Shaffir, R.A. Stebbins, & A. Turowetz (Eds.), *Fieldwork experience* (pp. 3-22). New York: St. Martin's Press.

Spradley, J.P. (1979). *The ethnographic interview.* New York: Holt, Rinehart, & Winston.

Stainback, S., & Stainback, W. (1988). *Understanding and conducting qualitative research.* Dubuque, IA: Kendall/Hunt.

Weiss, R. (1994) *Learning from strangers.* New York: Free Press.

Werner, O., & Schoepfle, G. (1987). *Systematic fieldwork: Foundations of ethnography and interviewing* (Vol. 1). Newbury Park, CA: Sage.

Heather Coleman
Yvonne Unrau

Phase Three

THE PURPOSE OF DATA ANALYSIS

ESTABLISHING AN INITIAL FRAMEWORK

    Step 1: Preparing Your Data in Transcript Form
    Step 2: Establishing a Plan for Data Analysis
    Step 3: First-Level Coding
    Step 4: Second-Level Coding

LOOKING FOR MEANING AND RELATIONSHIPS

    Step 5: Interpreting Data and Theory Building
    Step 6: Assessing the Trustworthiness of Your Results

SUMMARY

ANNOTATED BIBLIOGRAPHY

REFERENCES AND FURTHER READINGS

Analyzing Your Data

S O FAR, WE HAVE DISCUSSED the initial steps in designing and organizing a qualitative research study. The last phase covered the tasks in gathering qualitative data using the interview method: the next important phase is to analyze the data you have collected.

By now it should be apparent that qualitative data are typically in the form of words. According to Matthew B. Miles and Michael A. Huberman (1994), words contain both rich descriptions of situations and an understanding of their underlying meaning. Words are "fatter" than numbers and have multiple meanings, making the analysis of qualitative data quite a challenge.

We will detail the steps of qualitative data analysis. As with the previous two phases (and the next), data analysis is presented here as a straightforward, step-by-step process. However, you will not find it so in the real world of qualitative research. In contrast to quantitative studies, where you collect your data and then analyze them using an appropriate statistical procedure, in qualitative studies it is not uncommon to conduct further and/or new interviews after you have analyzed the data collected from your previous research participants. Furthermore, the analysis is not a one-step process, but involves considering the fit of each piece of data in relationship to all the other pieces.

Thus, you must continually move back and forth between initial and later interviews, identifying units of meaning, coding, and interpreting the data as you go along. Such a blending of data collection and data analysis permits you to continue interviewing people for as long as is necessary until you truly grasp the meaning of your study's findings.

There are several ways to approach the task of analyzing interview data. One way to analyze interview data is to look for the major themes and patterns in the data, and then to break these down into subthemes and categories as such distinctions become important. In essence, you start out with a broad look at the data and then break them into smaller issues.

This chapter, in contrast, suggests that you start your analysis by looking at the smaller units. Later, you will identify similarities and differences between these, to formulate how they fit together as themes and patterns. With this approach, then, you begin with the smaller issues but ultimately identify the broad themes.

Both forms of analysis are appropriate, and the two can converge to yield a similar interpretation of the data. We decided to present a systematic analysis of small units in this chapter for one reason only: we believe that this approach is more likely to allow the results to emerge from the data. The process of systematically comparing and contrasting the small segments of interviews will keep you thinking about what each individual is saying. There is a greater risk when you start with the broad perspective that once having identified important themes, you will apply these to segments with less attention to what is actually being said.

Nevertheless, you have the capacity to consider both broad themes and small meaning units almost simultaneously. The main point is, experiment with the best method for you, and do not be disconcerted by the existence of different approaches.

THE PURPOSE OF DATA ANALYSIS

The central purpose of analysis in qualitative studies is to sift, sort, and organize the masses of information acquired during data collection in such a way that the themes and interpretations that emerge from the process address the original research problem(s) that you identified in Phase One. The strength of the conclusions drawn from your study ultimately rests with the plan for *data analysis*. If you develop a research project without a systematic plan to guide the data analysis you are likely to produce biased results. Nevertheless, as with the use of an unstructured interview where the questions unfold throughout the process instead of being fixed at the outset, the data analysis will develop differently from study to study, depending on what your research participants reveal. Rather than present a set of concrete rules and procedures about how to analyze qualitative data, we will describe the general process of such an analysis. The interaction between data collection (Phase Two) and analysis (Phase Three) will allow you greater flexibility in interpreting your data and will permit greater adaptability when you draw your conclusions.

There are assumptions underlying the qualitative research approach that we discussed earlier and that are directly relevant to the analysis phase. A very brief reminder of those assumptions is therefore in order:

- The goal of your research study (and thus of the analysis) is to understand the personal realities of research participants in-depth, including aspects of their experience that may be unique to them.

- You should strive to understand human experience in as much complexity as possible. This means aiming for a deep understanding of the experience and the meanings attached to it, but also of the context within which the experience is reported. The context includes the research study itself—for example, your relationship with the research participants is part of what needs to be understood when your findings are analyzed.

- Given the complexity of social behavior, there are many topics in social work that are difficult to measure in the way that you would in a quantitative study. For example, in our study one woman was beaten to the point of needing medical treatment and another's life was threatened regularly with a gun. It would be a questionable goal to attempt to establish which woman experienced more fear. With such research topics, quantification reduces the data to trivial levels. In contrast, in a qualitative study we could describe the experience of each woman in a meaningful way. In the data analysis phase you should organize the information in such a manner that the words, thoughts, and experiences of the research participants can be clearly communicated.

- The extent to which previous research studies and theory should influence your study has been identified in Phase One as a contentious issue, and one about which you will have to exercise your own best judgement. The arguments for and against familiarity with the literature do not need repetition here, but we do need to note that the issues remain relevant. For example, you may find a literature search is relevant in the middle of data analysis. As you are analyzing your transcripts, the concepts and relationships between the concepts that you identify may suggest more reading to discover what others have thought of similar ideas.

In our study, the extent to which the women expressed difficulties about going to court over custody, access to children, and divorce issues prompted us to search for literature identifying this as a problem. Similarly, when you approach the end of your analysis, a literature search comparing your conclusions with the findings of other studies is often advisable.

ESTABLISHING AN INITIAL FRAMEWORK

There are two major steps involved in establishing an initial framework for data analysis. First, you must prepare your data in transcript form, and second, you should develop a preliminary plan for proceeding with your data analysis.

Step 1: Preparing Your Data in Transcript Form

A transcript is the written record of your interviews and any other written material that you may have gathered. As the core of your analysis, it will consist of more than merely the words spoken by each person during the interview. In addition, you will include comments that reflect non-verbal interactions such as pauses, laughing, and crying.

Preparing transcripts involves five basic tasks: (1) choosing a method of analysis, (2) determining who should transcribe the data, (3) considering ethical implications in the data analysis, (4) transcribing raw data, and (5) formatting the transcript for analysis.

Task 1a: Choosing a Method of Analysis

As mentioned previously, the qualitative research process usually results in masses of data. A tape-recorded interview lasting an hour may result in a typed transcript of 20 to 50 pages. Interview data can be collected using a variety of aids, such as tape recordings, videotapes, and your field notes. You may gather additional data from preexisting documents, such as newspaper clippings, abstracts, diaries, and letters. Throughout data collection, you will actively examine any relevant written materials and take copious notes on your reactions and ideas.

Word-processing programs have made the task of transcribing large amounts of data much simpler. Besides presenting the data in a uniform way, such programs allow you to make changes to the interviews quickly and easily, producing a clean copy of the data to analyze. Nevertheless, it is important to remember that after being transcribed, the original sources of data must be safely stored away in case you wish to use these sources again.

Part of the reason that qualitative analysis is considered to be a massive responsibility is that you ultimately end up comparing and sorting multiple segments from the large amount of information that you collected previously. Several methods of analysis are possible, and this choice will affect the manner in which you transcribe your data. The first option is to analyze your data using the traditional "cut-and-paste" method, whereby you use scissors to cut the typed transcript into the categories you have decided on, and to sort these into relevant groupings. Some qualitative researchers still prefer this method, remaining skeptical about the use of computers.

A second option is to use a regular word-processing program in the analysis. Even with limited knowledge of word processing, you are likely to be familiar with enough commands to sort your data into the appropriate categories for your analysis.

The third option is to use a computer program that has been developed specifically to assist qualitative analysis. Programs such as *The Ethnograph* and *AskSam* are only two of the more familiar names. The software market changes so quickly that we encourage you to consult with other qualitative researchers or computer companies about what programs they recommend. While no one has yet found a way to replace the thinking that is the critical determinant of whether an analysis truly reflects the material, qualitative analysis has become simpler with the introduction of computer programs that are able to sort and organize segments of the text with relative ease. Computers can also assist in mechanical tasks, such as recording, editing, and formatting, leaving the analytical work to you.

One rationale for using computers in qualitative analysis is to free up your time so you can concentrate on interpreting the meaning of the data. It is doubtful that any computer program will ever replace your role in analysis, since you need to be intensely involved in the reading of the data in order to understand them. Please note that the analysis of qualitative data consequently draws heavily on *your own* personal skills and resources.

Most computer programs that aid in the analysis of qualitative data require you to first enter the interview data into a word processor. There are dozens of word-processing software packages available on the market. However, it is necessary to select a package that can download the text into an ASCII format, because a number of the qualitative analysis programs require that the data be in ASCII.

ASCII stands for *American Standard Code for Information Interchange*, the basic computer language for all IBM-compatible hardware. ASCII files are stripped of special formatting commands, such as tabs and special fonts. Converting a file to ASCII is quite simple.

Task 1b: Determining Who Should Transcribe the Data

The scope of a study determines the number of resources needed to complete each step and task. In smaller studies, you are likely to have the sole responsibility for all phases, steps, and tasks from beginning to end. Although Phase Three may sound like a lot of work, there is a considerable benefit to you in transcribing the interviews yourself. You will become thoroughly acquainted with the content of the interviews, a critical aspect for the process of analysis, and transcribing provides an additional opportunity to review and connect with your data.

In large studies, you may have secretarial support or a research assistant to help with transcribing your data. When you are fortunate enough to have the assistance of others, it is essential that all persons working on your project operate according to the same principles and procedures. It is up to you to provide some form of systematic training for them so that all data are treated according to the same decision-making rules. In this case, you might transcribe some of the interviews yourself at the beginning, so you can be clear with your assistants about what you want. Also, all transcribers should be informed about the importance of including nonverbal communication, such as laughs or pauses in conversation, in the data text. Despite the advantages of having additional assistance in transcribing, many qualitative researchers prefer to transcribe their own data if at all possible.

Task 1c: Considering Ethical Issues

As discussed in both Phase One and Phase Two, ethics is a critical consideration throughout the research process. In the analysis phase, confidentiality is a central ethical issue, especially when tapes and transcripts are given to research assistants or to secretaries. To safeguard the interviewee's confidentiality, no identifying information should be included on this material. Instead, you might assign a code name or number to identify the research participant at the beginning of the tape and then use only first names throughout the transcript. Do not utilize recognizable information such as birth date, social security number, or address in your code names. In addition, you must make adequate provision to protect the privacy of your research participants by ensuring that details that might identify them are concealed. For example, if you include excerpts of interviews in your final report (Phase Four), a reader could potentially identify a person on the basis of his or her professional status, the names, ages, and gender of children, and the details of the unique experience. Such recognizable information should be masked in any examples.

In our study, we had to be particularly careful to disguise identifying features because of the intensely personal nature of the situations that the women were describing. In one case, a woman's husband was being investigated as a suspect in the sexual abuse and abduction of her ten-year-old daughter. With the widespread newspaper coverage of the event, we were extremely cautious—not only did we transcribe the tape ourselves, but no details of the family's situation were typed into the transcript or the final report.

Task 1d: Transcribing Raw Data

Transcribing data from audio- or videotapes is a long and arduous process, requiring careful attention and precise transcription. In most cases, transcripts should be produced *verbatim* to allow the context of the conversation to provide as much meaning as possible. Editing and censoring during transcription can easily wipe out the context of the data and, in the process, conceal the meaning of the text.

In the example of an interview segment presented in Phase Two, you can see how the context of the conversation gives flavor and texture to the data. Most importantly, it allows you to become completely involved in the data and to view it holistically.

It is, therefore, critical for you to record nonverbal interview events such as pauses, laughs, nervous moments, and excitement. You may also choose to insert notes based on your impressions or guesses about the context of the verbal comments, such as "seems reluctant to talk about what her parents thought about her going to a shelter."

Below is part of the interview presented in Phase Two that includes the interviewer's notes about nonverbal communication in parentheses:

Interviewer: Now that we've got the ethics forms completed, I'd like to tell you how much I appreciate you taking this time to talk about your experience after leaving Transition House.

Joy: (enthusiastically) I have only good things to say about that place. It was so peaceful being there, you know, you don't have to worry, you don't have to be concerned. You know your children are safe and everything (pause) and you're safe. The counselors were really helpful, too. No, I really liked that place. That was my second time there (pause). Silly me (in an embarrassed tone, shifting in seat, sounds uncomfortable) I've got involved in the same relationship twice. (Sounding more solid) I decided to give it another chance because of the baby. Yeah, no ... I liked that place a lot, it was just excellent.

Task 1e: Formatting the Transcript for Analysis

The format of the transcripts should facilitate very easy reading and allow sufficient space for writing comments. We recommend using standard-size paper and leaving the right margin as wide as two to four inches. In this way, the transcripts are structured so that you can easily write notes, codes, and line numbering alongside the corresponding text.

Numbering each line of the transcripts helps to organize data; some word-processing or computer programs that assist qualitative data analysis, such as *The Ethnograph*, will do this for you. With such numbering you can easily identify specific sections and determine where a particular word, sentence, or paragraph begins and ends, as illustrated:

1. **Joy**: (sadly) The booze was just too much. He destroyed our house

2. and two apartments—things broken everywhere, holes in the wall,

3. doors torn off hinges, all kinds of stuff. (pause) Yeah,

4. after the last time at Transition House my initial thought

5. was to leave him and not go back, pregnant or not. And then we

6. got talking. (sighs) I didn't phone him for a long time

7. but he kept phoning me at work, trying to see me at work, you

8. know, saying, "I want to work this through." That was great,

9. I believed him, I trusted him, and then when I finally said,

10. "Okay, I'll come back," (pause) he kept to it for a little while.

11. And then he just started breaking his promises again.

12. And then he started sneaking drinks. It kept on increasing ...

13. problems, fights kept on intensifying and that was all I could take.

14. The final blow was down at the fairgrounds because he wanted a

15. gun, a little carved gun that shoots elastics ...

16.

17. **Interviewer**: You're kidding!

18.

Step 2: Establishing a Plan for Data Analysis

Having spent a great deal of time in the initial phases of your qualitative study, you may now be feeling anxious to get the data analysis out of the way quickly. Unfortunately, given the many steps and tasks and the complex thinking involved in a qualitative analysis, you can expect to expend considerably more time and patience in processing all of the data you have collected.

One advantage of a qualitative analysis is that it is not subject to the same methodological rigor as a quantitative analysis. The researcher has more freedom to consider the unique qualities of the data set, rather than being limited to how people do "on the average." This does not mean, however, that qualitative analysis is not systematic. It is essential that you document the rules and procedures used in your analysis in enough detail that the analytic procedures can be repeated and applied to each unit of data in the analysis.

While qualitative analysis is both purposeful and systematic, in the initial stages it will be guided only by *general* rules. You will develop these rules to guide you in deciding what bodies of information fit together in a meaningful way and how these should be coded, processes that we will discuss in more detail shortly. In subsequent stages of the analysis, you will clarify and refine the rules through reflection on and critical analysis of the situations in which each should be applied. By the end of the study, you must consistently apply the rules to all units of data.

Developing a preliminary plan for data analysis involves two general tasks: (1) previewing the data, and (2) planning what to record in your journal.

Task 2a: Previewing the Data

Although in some cases, you will transcribe and analyze your interviews as you collect them, in others you will start your analysis only after you have completed interviewing. Before you launch into the steps and tasks of coding and interpreting your data, it is important to become familiar with the entire data set by reading all of the available interviews. At this point, it is important not to impose a framework or categories on the data. As mentioned previously, when you first become familiar with your qualitative data, you may be tempted to begin classifying it into meaning units (or categories) from your first glance.

You might also apply theories with which you are familiar, or create hypotheses. Doing so, however, may create a funnel effect by which you screen out important information that is recorded in the latter parts of the data set. The meaning of the information in qualitative analysis should emerge from the data. Thus, if categories are prematurely imposed, the interpretation of data could be colored by preconceived notions or your own particular viewpoint.

There are several strategies that will help you to avoid becoming focused too quickly. First, if the transcripts are extensive, do not attempt to read them all at once. When your mind starts to wander or you become impatient or start feeling uninterested, it is time to pause. Remember that qualitative analysis takes time. If you want to produce a quality product, you must respect the process. To a large extent, the process cannot be forced.

Second, refrain from always reading notes and transcripts from the beginning of a document. When you begin reading, you are usually in peak form. If you always confine this energy to the first section of your data, you are more likely to exclude or overlook valuable information from later sections. Reading the last third of the interview before the first portion is one technique that may help you to shed new light on each interview.

Task 2b: Using a Journal During Data Analysis

As noted in Phase Two, we recommend that you use a journal to record the process of the research study and your reactions to the emerging issues in your analysis. Yvonna Lincoln and Egon Guba (1985) suggest that a qualitative journal should include two key components: (1) notes on the method used in your study, and (2) notes on issues of credibility and audit trail notes (to be described later). Each component should include a section on what decisions were made during the analysis and the rationale for these.

The category scheme that you will develop will be a critical segment of the methodology section of your journal. When you unitize and initially categorize (code) your data, you will come up with numerous questions and ideas about the data. Making notes in your journal about these questions or comments with respect to identifying meaning units and categories is referred to as writing "analytical memos." It is a useful strategy for organizing your thoughts. Although the format used for analytical memos tends to reflect the individual style of the researcher, Anselm Strauss and Juliet Corbin (1990) offer some hints about how to make useful analytical memos:

- Record the date of the memo.

- Include any references or important sources.

- Label memos with headings that describe the primary category or concept being earmarked.

- Identify the particular code(s) to which the theoretical note pertains.

- Use diagrams in memos to explain ideas.

- Keep multiple copies of all memos.

- Do not restrict the content of memos; allow for a flow of ideas.

- Note when you think that a category has been sufficiently defined.

- Keep analytical memos about your own thinking process to assist you in moving the analysis from description to interpretation.

In part, the process of writing analytical memos is what some authors refer to as leaving an "audit trail." An audit trail is used when an outside person is called in to review what you have done, to ensure that there were no serious flaws in the conduct of your study. This individual may retrace your steps starting from collection of the raw data, carefully examining every decision you have made in the study. Since the work you do should be open to scrutiny by others, precise journal notes about your methodology are crucial.

Your journal will also help to ensure that the rules guiding the definition of categories and the assignment of units of data to those categories become universal and are consistently applied. Keeping notes about the coding process will ensure greater consistency of coding to protect rules from any whims or impulsive decisions. You will also record the code acronym (the shortened version of the category name) that is assigned to each category, as well as the characteristics of the meaning unit that qualify it to be categorized in that particular way. Later, you may want to revise the category scheme, a point at which you again clearly record the reasons for your decision and how the characteristics of the data have changed. This process, then, will track the developmental history of your data analysis.

In Phase Two we described using a journal to record your notes about what transpired in your interviews and how you obtained your research participants. You were asked to take special note of your honest reactions to the people that you interviewed, since these comments will eventually be used to assess the credibility of the research participants in your study. If, for example, you have overrelied on one informant or developed a bias against one subset of interviewees, then your conclusions will be one-sided. Such biases will, hopefully, become more evident as you read your journal entries.

It is also essential to record other attempts at establishing the credibility of your study, such as asking others to unitize and categorize your data to provide evidence that your categorization scheme is useful and appropriate. This process, called "triangulation of analysts," will be described in more detail later. Finally, your journal should contain a section that covers your personal reactions to your study, not unlike a personal diary. Following is an example of a comment from our journal in our study. The example shows an analytical memo that speaks to issues of both credibility and reactions to the study as a whole:

May 16, 1995. I can't help but feel that the interview with Joy went extremely well. She was surprisingly open about her story and seemed very concerned that other women who might be living with men such as her ex-partner know what options they have. She is really quite remarkable to have set up a new home with two small children, and so little income. I think her narrative really adds to the interviews we've conducted so far because she is doing so well under difficult circumstances.

Step 3: First-Level Coding

Once you have transcribed your data, and reviewed it in a preliminary way, you can launch into first-level coding: a combination of identifying meaning units, fitting them into categories, and assigning codes to the categories. In this section we will describe each of these tasks individually, but, once again, in practice you may find that they overlap. For example, you may be thinking about how to categorize certain meaning units as you are identifying these units in the transcripts (and will use analytical memos to make sure that you do not forget these initial ideas).

Coding begins at the point when you first notice similarities and differences between data segments or meaning units. You may also see patterns in the data that you will mentally label. As you read new data and re-read old data, you will conceptually connect similar meaning units together as categories. You will use a procedure called the constant comparison method: meaning units of data with the same characteristics are considered as fitting within the same category and are given the same code; meaning units that are different in important ways are put into a different category and given another code.

Coding proceeds in stages, and there are several steps involved in coding at various stages of the analysis. First-level coding is predominantly concrete, and involves identifying properties of data that are clearly evident in the text. Such content is found without combing the data for underlying meaning. Second-level coding (Step 4) is more abstract and involves interpreting the meaning underlying the more obvious ideas portrayed in the data.

By the end of the analysis phase, you will have worked with both concrete and abstract content. You will start with concrete coding at the beginning of the analysis, but work toward understanding the deeper, abstract content in the final stages of analysis. Remember, qualitative research is more than description—it takes a natural interest in the meaning underlying the words.

In summary, the primary task of coding is to identify and label relevant categories of data, first concretely (in first-level coding) and then abstractly (in second-level coding). First-level coding is a lengthy and detailed process that involves five tasks: (1) identifying meaning units, (2) assigning category names to groups of similar meaning units, (3) assigning codes to categories, (4) refining and reorganizing codings, and (5) deciding when to stop. Once again, the tasks sometimes overlap one another and they should be viewed as absolutely essential in the first-level coding process.

Task 3a: Identifying Meaning Units

Once you have previewed the data they need to be organized into a manageable format. To do this, you first identify the important experiences or ideas in your data. This is the process of classifying and collapsing the data into "meaning units." You make decisions about what pieces of data fit together; ultimately, these are the segments that will be categorized, coded, sorted, and then form the patterns that will be used to summarize your interpretation of the data.

Units are the segments (or chunks) of information that are the building blocks of a classification scheme. A unit can consist of a single word, a partial or complete sentence, a paragraph, or more. It is a piece of the transcript that you consider to be meaningful by itself. At this point you are not analyzing what the data mean, you are simply identifying the important bits of what the research participants are saying.

While what constitutes a meaning unit may be clear to outside readers, this will not necessarily be the case. The developers of *The Ethnograph* computer program studied how a group of students analyzed an identical data file. While some students identified very small meaning units of 5 to 50 lines of transcript, others identified larger units, analyzing segments of between 50 and 200 lines. Further, the category labels that the students attached to the meaning units varied considerably. Some students labeled categories in a concrete and detailed manner, while others were more impressionistic and abstract. Some students identified categories similar to those of other students, but still others identified categories that were unique. This example simply illustrates the fact that different individuals will identify and label the same meaning units differently within the same data set. The lesson is that there is no inherent "right" or "wrong" way to organize qualitative data. How one chooses to reduce data into a manageable form is an individual endeavor.

In the segment of the data set previously presented from our research study, we identified the following meaning units (the first underlined, the next in italics) early in our first-level coding process:

1. **Joy**: (sadly) The booze was just too much. *He destroyed our house*

2. *and two apartments—things broken everywhere, holes in the wall,*

3. *doors torn off hinges, all kinds of stuff.* (*pause*) Yeah,

4. after the last time at Transition House my initial thought

5. was to leave him and not go back, pregnant or not. And then we

6. got talking. (sighs) I didn't phone him for a long time

7. <u>but he kept phoning me at work,</u> <u>trying to see me at work,</u> <u>you</u>

8. <u>know,</u> <u>saying</u> "<u>I want to work this through.</u>" That was great,

9. <u>I believed him,</u> <u>I trusted him,</u> <u>and then when I finally said,</u>

10. "<u>Okay,</u> <u>I'll come back,</u>" (pause) <u>he kept to it for a little while.</u>

11. *And then he just started breaking his promises again.*

12. *And then he started sneaking drinks. It kept on increasing ...*

13. *problems, fights kept on intensifying and that was all I could take.*

14. *The final blow was down at the fairgrounds because he wanted a*

15. *gun, a little carved gun that shoots elastics ...*

16.

17. **Interviewer**: You're kidding!

In our journal we recorded that the first meaning unit relates to her ex-partner's drinking (line 1), and the second is about his past destructive behavior (lines 1-3).

The third meaning unit (lines 3-10) is rather long and may need to be broken down into more than one category later on. It describes the process of reuniting with a partner after a previous shelter stay. The final meaning unit (lines 11-15) documents the experience that prompted the final shelter stay. The topics in the meaning units may become categories if the content is repeated later on in this interview or if other interviewees identify similar issues.

The first run-through to identify meaning units will always be somewhat tentative and subject to change. If you are not sure whether to break a large meaning unit into smaller ones, it may be preferable to leave it as a whole. You can always break down meaning units more finely later on in your study. This process is somewhat easier than combining units later, especially once second-level coding (Step 4) begins.

Task 3b: Identifying Categories

Once you have identified the meaning units in the transcripts, your next task is to consider which of them fit together into categories. Especially in first-level coding, the categories you identify should logically and simply relate to the data they represent. The categories may emerge from the questions you ask, or they may simply reflect the critical events that you identify in your research participants' stories. As mentioned previously, though, while the rationale behind the categories does not have to be explained at the beginning, you must clearly explain your grounds as the data analysis proceeds and becomes more complex. The categories and their respective codes must all be defined by the end of the study.

Earlier, we introduced the method of constant comparison, which is the major technique guiding the categorization process. Constant comparison begins after the complete set of data has been examined and meaning units have been identified. Each unit is classified as either similar or different from the others. If the first two meaning units possess somewhat similar qualities, they are tentatively placed in the same category and classified by the same code created for that category.

Remember to make notes about the characteristics of the meaning units that make them similar, and record these observations in your journal. If the first two meaning units are not similar in these identified qualities, a separate category and a new code are produced for the second one. Again, the information about what defines the second category should be recorded, since the process will solidify the rules governing when to include specific meaning units in that category.

You simply repeat these steps to examine the remaining meaning units. For example, the third meaning unit is examined for similarities and differences with the first and the second category. If it differs, a third category and code are created. Constant comparison continues until all meaning units are classified into either previously described or new categories.

To illustrate how to create categories from meaning units, we will use the previous excerpt from our study. The first meaning unit identified, "the booze was just too much" (line 1), fit with a number of Joy's other comments, as well as comments from other research participants relating to their ex-partner's abuse of substances. The category was hence labeled "Partner's Substance Abuse." The rule was that past and present substance abuse issues of the ex-partner would be included under this category.

However, issues related to any substance abuse by the interviewee herself were placed in a different category: "Research Participant's Substance Abuse." Thus, each meaning unit is considered in comparison to other similar meaning units, and the category is a way of identifying important similarities within and across individuals.

The number of categories will expand every time you identify meaning units that are dissimilar in important ways from those you have already categorized. However, you also need to attempt to keep the number of categories within manageable limits. At the beginning of constant comparison, new categories will be created quickly, and then more slowly after you have analyzed between four and five dozen data segments. Sometimes, meaning units cannot be clearly placed into any of the categories developed in the analysis and fall into the category of "miscellaneous." These misfits should be set aside in a separate "pile" with other units that are difficult to classify. Make special note of why they do not fit. At some point, such unclassifiable meaning units may begin to resemble one another and can be placed in a category of their own. After reviewing all the categories, inspect the miscellaneous pile to decide what units might fit together in a new category or a new set of categories.

If you find that you are throwing data into the miscellaneous pile too often, you may be fatigued. This would be a good time to pause and return to the analysis when you are refreshed. The use of a miscellaneous pile will prevent you from throwing out what seem to be irrelevant meaning units. Such tossing is a risky move, because in some situations you may decide that your categorization scheme needs massive revision and that you must start the whole process again from scratch. We recommend that miscellaneous units make up less than ten percent of the total data set. More than that suggests that you have a problem with your original categorization scheme.

Occasionally, you will need to stop and reaffirm the rules that qualify the meaning units to be placed within each category. These decisions need to be justified, a factor that will later serve as the basis for tests of whether others who utilize your rules identify similar meaning units and categories.

The categories for your study will develop and change over time. It is natural for some categories to change or to become irrelevant (decay) in the later stages of analysis. In such instances, new categories can be created and old categories can be either revised, merged with others, or eliminated completely.

The number of categories in a study depends upon the breadth and the depth you seek in your analysis of the data. Some topics require very detailed and precise analyses, with nearly every line of the transcript coded into different categories. For less detailed work, it is possible to code larger segments, for example, every 50 or even every 200 lines.

The complexity of the categorization also needs to be considered. One meaning unit may, in fact, fit into more than one category. It is also possible to code meaning units that overlap with one another. In another case called a nested code, smaller categories fit within larger, more inclusive ones. Furthermore, there can also be a complex combination of multiple, nested, and overlapping categories.

For example, in the interview with Joy, the large meaning unit talking about the couple's reconciliation (lines 3-10) could also be considered as fitting into two smaller categories, one labeled "Partner's Past Reconciliation Attempts" (lines 5-10) and another called "Reasons for Past Breakdown of Reconciliation" (lines 11-13). These may overlap with the category "Partner's Substance Abuse," (lines 1 & 12) so that substance abuse issues will sometimes be coded into the category of "Reasons for Past Breakdown of Reconciliation."

The categories must be clear enough to simplify the data and prevent the generation of unnecessary backtracking and recoding. The category labels must also reflect the substance of the meaning units. For example, in our study many women reported having low self-esteem, which they found interfered in their ability to feel successful or to live independently from their abusive partner. In the first round of categorization, meaning units reflecting the self-esteem issue were categorized as "Self-concept: Valueless." These words did not adequately reflect the meaning of the segments in the interviews, since not one interviewee reported that she was valueless, but many noted that they had low self-esteem. The relabelled category "Low Self-esteem" more accurately reflected what the data meant.

Task 3c: Assigning Codes to Categories

Codes are simply a form of the category name that becomes a short-hand method of identifying the categories. Codes typically take the form of strings of letters and/or symbols. The form of the code used in *The Ethnograph*, for example, can assume up to ten letters and can also include symbols. Codes are usually displayed in the margins (often the right margin) of the transcribed text.

As you can see from our example, we've already made some distinctions that should be included in part of the code. One obvious issue is that some comments are about the woman herself, some about her partner, and some about her children. Thus we used *W* as the first letter of the code name if related to the woman, *P* if related to her partner, and *C* if related to her children. A second important distinction was whether issues were past (*P*), current (*C*), or anticipated in the future (*F*). Finally, in a list of categories about the problems encountered, the substance abuse category was labeled *SA*. Thus, the code that we wrote in the margin next to the meaning unit "The booze was just too much" was *P-P-SA*, standing for the partner's past substance abuse. As the analysis becomes more complex, the codes become longer.

In the initial stages of second-level coding, the codes in the margins will be used to collect together all the meaning units from all of the interviews that fit within a particular category.

Task 3d: Refining and Reorganizing Coding

Before moving on from first-level coding, we suggest that you make a final sweep through the data to ensure that your analysis reflects what your research participants have said. Pause and reflect upon your analysis thus far, considering the logic of the ideas that form the basis of the rules for each category. Rather than discovering at the end of your analysis that you have made an error in judgement, now is the most appropriate time to reexamine your thinking.

You may, for example, be confused about why you created some categories, or feel uncertain about the rules of categorization for others. You may find that some categories are too complex and may be effectively split into several new categories. This is the time to clarify and confirm what qualifies each meaning unit to fit within a particular category.

You should review all the categories to see how the units "fit" with each. You can now tighten your rules to ensure that there is no vagueness about how any meaning unit is categorized. If you have conceptualized the meaning units accurately, the categories will "hang together" internally and be easily distinguished from other categories.

You might find that some categories are not completely developed or are only partially defined. Similarly, you might discover that categories that you had originally thought would emerge from the data are completely missing. You are most likely to discover missing categories while you are thinking about the underlying logic of your categorization scheme. In such a case, make a note of the missing categories, as well as of incomplete or otherwise unsatisfactory categories. You may, in fact, wish to conduct additional interviews to address any of these gaps.

This would be a good time to ask a colleague to code one or two of your interviews using the rules that you have devised. This process is a check to ensure that the categories and the rules that define them make sense. If your colleague codes meaning units in a significantly different way than yours, your categorization scheme may need to be substantially revised.

Task 3e: Deciding When to Stop

What are the indicators that signal that this may be an appropriate time to stop first-level coding? We described some of these in Step 5 of Phase Two. Several of the same signs are relevant here. The most common indicator, though, is that when you interview new research participants the meaning units fit easily into your current categorization scheme and no new categories emerge. This process is called "category saturation." In essence, the data become repetitive and further analysis only confirms the ground that you have already covered. This is a good point in time to perform one final review of all the categories to ensure the thoroughness of your analysis. We will now turn our attention away from first-level coding and address the next step in the data analysis process—second-level coding.

Step 4: Second-Level Coding

When completed thoroughly, the tasks of initial coding (Step 3) produce a solid foundation from which to further refine the data analysis process. By this point, your data have been reduced and transformed in several ways. Sections from the transcribed interviews have been selected and identified as meaning units. The units have been subsequently classified as fitting into categories, with an identifying code attached. You have read through your entire set of transcripts, coding the appropriate meaning units with the category code name. As a part of this process you have also reviewed the rules that you have developed to ensure that you can clearly explain what types of information are included in each category.

As noted earlier, second-level coding is more abstract, and involves interpreting what the first-level categories mean. Reporting on abstract content demands that you produce detailed examples of the transcript to back up each interpretation. Bruce L. Berg (1995) suggests that you need at least three independent examples to support each of these interpretations. In second-level coding, you will pull together or "retrieve" the meaning units that fit within each category, either by computer or by cutting and pasting. This process allows you to examine the units in the categories away from any association with the person who originally stated the idea. The focus of the analysis thus shifts from the context of the interviewee to the context of the categories. In so doing, the analysis has become one level more abstract, because it is one step further removed from the original interviews.

The major task in second-level coding is to identify similarities and differences between the categories in an attempt to detect relationships. In sum, the next step of coding involves two tasks: (1) retrieving meaning units into categories, and (2) comparing categories.

Task 4a: Retrieving Meaning Units into Categories

Earlier you identified distinct units of data and grouped and coded these based on similarities and differences. During second-level coding, you will retrieve the coded units of each category, either by cutting and pasting the typed manuscript or by using a computer program. Via this process all the meaning units that fit within the first category are grouped together, as are the units that fit within category two, and so on. Remember that the meaning units have been collected from a number of different interviewees. Thus, this process pulls each unit away from the context of the individual's story. A drawback of the process, then, is that you might lose or misinterpret a meaning unit once it is separated from the context of each research participant's experience. The advantage is that you can consider the information in each category in a different way, across individuals. You can thus see how important it is that your rules for placing a meaning unit into a particular category were clarified during the initial coding process (Task 4a).

Task 4b: Comparing Categories

Whereas previously you looked for similarities and differences between meaning units to separate them into distinct categories, the next step is to compare and contrast the categories themselves in order to discover the relationships between them. At this point in the analysis, your goal is to integrate the categories into themes and subthemes based on their properties. Finding themes involves locating patterns that repeatedly appear in your data set. Once a theme is identified, you will develop a code for it in the same manner as you coded categories. The themes will, in most cases, form the basis of the major conclusions emerging from your analysis.

What possible types of relationships among categories might you find?

- There might be a temporal relationship, so that one category always precedes another. In cases such as this you may be able to identify a process that has some importance to the issue at hand. For example, in our study we found that although children often initially react positively to living away from their abusive father, later they are likely to push for a reconciliation.

- There may be a causal relationship, so that one category is the cause of another. For example, we found that the women who had no further contact with their assaultive partners after leaving the shelter seemed generally able to function better. Note, though, that it is risky to assume that one category caused another when, in fact, the opposite may be true. In this example, perhaps it is the fact that the women were functioning well that led them to cease contact with their ex-partners.

- One category may be contained within another category or may be another type of the first category. In our study, we originally saw the category wherein the men beseeched and even bribed the women to return to the relationship as different from the category of threatening the women with, for example, further abuse or no support payments if they did not return. However, in this phase of analysis we shifted to seeing the "loving" pleas as related to the threats. The new theme combining these was called "Partner's Strategies to Reunite."

Obviously, you may find other types of relationships between categories, but the previous examples are commonly found. Some categories may contain enough information to be considered themes in and of themselves.

As another example of combining categories into themes, consider our study on abused women. The three categories of "Custody Issues Regarding Children," "Separation or Divorce Proceedings," and "Obtaining Restraining Orders" all involve relationships with various aspects of the legal system, including the police, lawyers, and judges. The substance of the three categories was similar in that the women were more likely than not to have had difficulty in adequately dealing with these systems. Furthermore, the experience was likely to reignite marital issues, putting the women at risk of further abuse. The theme "Difficulties with the Legal System" was, therefore, created by combining the three categories.

LOOKING FOR MEANING AND RELATIONSHIPS

In addition to organizing the data, coding also brings meaning to the information being examined. However, once you move to the "formal" step of interpreting the data, coding at both levels is considered complete. Two important steps are involved in looking for meaning and relationships in your data. First, you will have to develop an interpretation of your data. Interpretations are sometimes descriptive, but may also suggest causal explanations of important events. Second, the research process and the conclusions must be assessed for credibility and dependability.

Step 5: Interpreting Data and Theory Building

Drawing meaning from your data is perhaps the most rewarding step of qualitative data analysis. It involves two important tasks: (1) developing conceptual classifications systems, and (2) presenting themes or theory.

Task 5a: Developing Conceptual Classification Systems

The ultimate goal of qualitative research is to identify any relationships between the major themes that emerge from the data set. To do this you must develop logical interpretations of the themes that remain consistent with your earlier categorization schemes and meaning units. One idea that may help you to get a sense of the relationships between the themes and the overall nature of the data is to visually display themes and categories in a diagram. The visual representation of your themes may help you to organize the write-up of your conclusions. It may also help you to clearly identify the interconnections between themes and categories or to identify missing categories among the data set. Matthew B. Miles and Michael A. Huberman (1994) suggest several strategies for extracting meaning from a data set:

- *Draw a Cluster Diagram:* This form of diagram helps you to think about how themes and categories may or may not be related to each other. Draw and label circles for each theme and arrange them in relation to each other. Some of the circles will overlap, others will stand alone. The circles of the themes of more importance will be larger, in comparison to themes and categories that are not as relevant to your conclusions. The process of thinking about what weight to give the themes, how they interact, and how important they will be in your final scheme will be valuable in helping you to think about the meaning of your research study.

- *Make a Matrix:* Matrix displays may be helpful for noting relations between categories or themes. Designing a matrix involves writing a list of categories along the side of a piece of paper and then another list of categories or themes across the top. In each cell you will document how the two categories fit or do not fit together. For example, using our study, along the side you could write categories that reflect the theme "Partner's Strategies to Reunite." Across the top you could write categories from the theme of "Women's Beliefs about Leaving Their Abusive Partner." Where two categories intersect on the matrix you could note with a plus sign (+) beliefs that fit with the ex-partner's desire to live together once more, and mark with a minus sign (-) those at odds with each other. Such a matrix will give you a sense of the balance of the push to leave the abusive relationship and the pull to return.

- *Count the Number of Times a Meaning Unit or Category Appears:* Although numbers are typically associated with quantitative studies, it is acceptable to use numbers in qualitative ones to document how many of the participants expressed a particular theme. You might, for example, be interested in finding out how many of your interviewees experienced different problems after separating from their abusive partners. You would write the code names for the women down the left side of a piece of paper and the list of problems across the top. To fill in the chart, you would simply place a check mark beside each woman's name if she experienced that particular problem.

  Numbers will help to protect your analysis against bias that occurs when particularly poignant but rare examples of themes are presented. For example, in our study, one woman described the death of her daughter at the hands of her ex-partner, an event that immediately preceded their separation. Although an emotionally laden event, it was certainly not typical of the experience of most of the other women. A majority of the women, however, did express concerns about past abuse of their children by their ex-partners. Although we do not discount the experience of the woman whose daughter died, that event could be better discussed in the context of the range of severity of abuse of the children.

- *Create a Metaphor:* Developing metaphors that convey the essence of your findings is another mechanism for extracting meaning. For example, in her qualitative study of battered women who remain with their partners, Lenore Walker (1979) identified a cycle that commonly occurs whereby tension builds between a couple until the husband beats his wife. This abusive incident is followed by a calm, loving phase until the tension starts to build once again.

Walker's name for this process, "the cycle of violence," is an example of a metaphor that so effectively describes this pattern that the metaphor has been extensively adopted.

- *Look for Missing Links:* If two categories or themes seem to be related, but not directly so, it may be that a third variable connects the two.

- *Note Contradictory Evidence:* Remember that contradictory evidence must be accounted for. The chain of evidence must be thorough, so that any connections between categories and themes are accounted for. While we traditionally focus on looking for evidence to support our ideas, we must also identify themes and categories that raise questions about our conclusions. Such evidence can ultimately be very useful in providing exceptions to the process that you have described.

Task 5b: Presenting Themes or Theory

Although many qualitative researchers conclude their studies by presenting descriptions of the major themes that emerged from their data, others utilize the themes and their interpretations to create hypotheses or theory. In our study on abused women we simply presented the major themes that emerged from the data without any attempt to formulate these into a theory. Even so, the themes could have been reworded as questions that could then become hypotheses in future research efforts. For example, one core theme was that the ex-partner's access to children created a situation wherein women were placed at risk of continued abuse. As a hypothesis, this could be reworded as, "Women whose abusive partners visit with their children after a marital separation are more likely to experience continued abuse than women who do not see their partner under such circumstances."

In contrast, theories answer questions such as "Why does a phenomenon occur?" or "How are these two concepts related?" If theory does develop from the study, it will not be apparent at the beginning, but will grow out of the process of analysis. This is most likely to occur during the stage of classifying the categories into themes and looking for relationships between those themes.

An example of a theory that emerged from a different qualitative study of battered women is Lenore Walker's (1979) "cycle of violence," mentioned previously as an example of a metaphor. The development of theories such as Walker's involves a shift from looking at specific instances to examining general patterns. With each step of data analysis, your thinking becomes more abstract; in other words, you become further removed from the concrete examples on the original transcript. By using the constant comparison method, you arrive at an understanding of basic patterns or ideas that connect the categories and themes developed earlier.

Step 6: Assessing the Trustworthiness of Your Results

Although developing interpretations and theory can be an exciting step in qualitative analysis, throughout the research process you must act responsibly to ensure the trustworthiness of the conclusions that you finally draw. Qualitative researchers have identified a number of issues to think about to enhance the believability of your research findings. Approaches and emphases vary (as does the depth of detail in discussions of techniques that can be employed). These issues will be revisited again in Phase Four, since they are relevant to report writing. At this point, we will discuss the challenges that are important to address during the analysis. The three tasks include: (1) establishing your own credibility, (2) documenting what you have done to ensure consistency, and (3) documenting what you have done to control biases and preconception.

Task 6a: Establishing Your Own Credibility

Since a qualitative study depends so much on the human judgement and discipline of the researcher, it is necessary for you to indicate why you should be believed. This is partly a matter of indicating your relevant training and experience and partly a matter of recording, in your journal, the procedures you followed, the decisions you made (with the rationale for them), and the thought processes that led you to your conclusions. Meticulous records of this sort will do much to convince those who must assess your work that they can believe in it.

Task 6b: Document What You Have Done to Ensure Consistency

Consistency (which is sometimes called dependability) is another key to establishing the believability of your study. While qualitative work is influenced by the unique events and relationships that unfold in the course of the study, a reasonable degree of consistency is still desirable. Hopefully, you have been rigorous in your interviewing and in developing the rules for coding, and have written detailed records of your decision making. If this is the case, another researcher should be able to follow your process and arrive at similar decisions. Also, if you yourself redo parts of the analysis at a later date, the outcome should be closely similar to that produced in your original analysis. Specific issues and procedures that you may need to address to ensure consistency include:

- Specify the Context of the Interviews and How You Incorporated This in Your Analysis: Some data collection circumstances yield more credible information than others, and you may thus choose to weight your interviews accordingly. For example, some authors claim that data collected later in the study may be more relevant than those gathered in the beginning, likely because your interviewing style will be more relaxed and less intrusive. In addition, information obtained firsthand is considered stronger than that reported by a third person. Data provided voluntarily can be assumed to be more trustworthy, as are data collected when the research participant is alone with you.

- *Triangulation:* This is a common method to establish the trustworthiness of qualitative data. There are several different kinds of triangulation, but the essence of the term is that multiple perspectives are compared. This might involve having a colleague use your data collection rules to see if he or she makes the same decisions about meaning units, categories, and themes; or it may consist of collecting multiple sources of data in addition to your interviews. The hope is that the different perspectives will confirm each other, adding weight to the credibility of your analysis.

- *Member Checking:* Obtaining feedback from your research participants is an essential credibility technique that is unique to qualitative methods. While feedback from research participants should be part of the ongoing process of the qualitative research study, it is particularly useful when your analysis and interpretations have been made and conclusions drawn. In other words, you go back to your research participants asking them to confirm or refute your interpretations.

    Note that research participants may not always agree with the data, with each other, or with your interpretations. In such cases you need to decide whether to exclude the data to which the research participants object, or to record the dissenting opinion in some way and indicate your position in relation to it.

Task 6c: Document What You Have Done to Control Biases and Preconceptions

When you report your findings, it is useful to include a careful inventory of your biases and preconceptions. Cataloguing these will remind you to keep checking to ensure that your conclusions are dictated by the data rather than by your established beliefs. A list of this sort is also useful to readers, who will want to assess how successful you have been in keeping your biases under control during data collection and analysis.

Your journal recording analytical memos and a record of your decision-making process will also be valuable for this purpose. Someone who wishes to scrutinize your work especially closely will be interested in the evidence these offer regarding your attempts to be open to what your research participants had to say. Below are a few threats to the credibility of qualitative research studies, which are relevant to the question of bias, and which you may wish to think about (and address in your journal):

- Your personal bias and life view may affect your interpretation of the data. Bias is a natural human quality, and as we move from the particular to the general there is a tendency to manipulate data to fit with what we already believe.

- You may draw conclusions before the data are analyzed or before you have decided about the trustworthiness of the data collected.

- You might censor, ignore, or dismiss data as irrelevant. This may occur as a result of data overload or because the data contradict an already established mainstream way of thinking.

- You may make unwarranted or unsupported causal statements based on your impressions rather than being founded on solid analysis.

- You may be too opinionated and reduce your conclusions to a limited number of choices or alternatives.

Matthew B. Miles and Michael A. Huberman (1994) have suggested strategies to deal with the above risks:

- Member checking has already been described in the above task, but is noted again here for its utility as a way of guarding against your own biases dictating your conclusions.

- In your analysis, it is easy to unthinkingly give certain events and people more credibility than others. However, this prevents you from making accurate interpretations of your data, because the people and the events selected are not sufficiently representative. You may come to the conclusion that you relied upon information that was too easily accessible or that you weighted your results toward people you liked. To compensate for such possibilities, you can deliberately search for events and people that differ markedly from those you have already interviewed, to help balance the perspective of the data that you have collected. If you detect such a bias, you can interview more people looking especially for atypical research participants and events.

- Assess your interaction with the research participants: another source of bias is the effect that you may have upon your interviewees as well as the effect that they may have on you. Such effects are particularly powerful in qualitative methods, where data collection may involve your spending long periods of time with your interviewees. It is not uncommon for the interviewer to become personally responsive to interviewees, especially when they are revealing intimate details of their experience. While we are not suggesting that you remain aloof, if you are too responsive your interviewees may become misleading in an effort to please you.

• Looking for negative evidence resembles constant comparison, looking for outliers, and using extreme cases. Negative evidence should be actively sought at the time when preliminary conclusions are made, to see if any data contradict or are inconsistent with your conclusion. The researcher must actively hunt for contradictory data in case it counters the preliminary conclusion and what the researcher believes.

SUMMARY

This chapter presented a systematic and purposeful approach to data analysis in qualitative research studies. The predominant steps of data analysis include transcript preparation (Step 1), establishing a preliminary plan for data analysis (Step 2), first-level coding (Step 3), second-level coding (Step 4), data interpretation and theory building (Step 5), and assessing the trustworthiness of your results (Step 6). Although these steps are presented in a linear fashion, the data analysis process is not that simple. You must be flexible and move back and forth between and among the steps and tasks to produce rich and meaningful findings.

Now that you have analyzed and interpreted your data, the next phase of the qualitative research process is to write up your results so that other interested social work practitioners, policy makers, educators, and researchers have access to them. How to disseminate your findings so that they will be read is the final phase in Part One of this book.

ANNOTATED BIBLIOGRAPHY

BERG, B.L. (1989). *Qualitative research methods for the social sciences* (Chapter 5). Needham Heights, MA: Allyn & Bacon. A sophisticated, useful discussion of content analysis as a data analysis strategy in qualitative research. Readers looking for detailed examples of how to identify units and categories and how to code may find this chapter a practical addition to the information presented in our Phase Three.

LINCOLN, Y., & GUBA, E. (1985). *Naturalistic inquiry* (Chapters 11-13). Newbury Park, CA: Sage. Three chapters in this book contain information that relates to our Phase Three. As Lincoln and Guba's ideas about data analysis formed the basis of much of our thinking about this topic, Chapter 12, "Processing naturalistically obtained data," is a useful parallel to our book. Readers will find a number of examples to help clarify each step in the data analysis process, with particular attention paid to the constant comparison method.

Lincoln and Guba's discussion of issues of trustworthiness in Chapter 11, "Establishing trustworthiness," is probably the classic deliberation on ways of ensuring credibility, transferability, dependability, and confirmability. The chapter is written in detail that should provide most of what both new and experienced qualitative researchers need to know to create trust in their findings. As part of the discussion, the authors note very practical issues related to creating an "audit trail"—a record of your procedures and thinking which others can read when evaluating your research study.

Chapter 13, "Case reporting, member checking, and auditing," is discussed because of the utility of the last two topics: the importance of member checking and strategies for conducting an audit of a qualitative study. Once again, Lincoln and Guba write in a readable style, while providing both conceptual and practical information. They even provide an agenda for a meeting to member check with research participants! While the previously mentioned discussion about audit trails in Chapter 11 is primarily with respect to creating such a file, in Chapter 13 the focus is the process that an auditor might follow if he or she were to evaluate the trustworthiness of a qualitative research study. Such suggestions can also prove useful to the researcher when planning how to set up an audit trail.

MILES, M., & HUBERMAN, M. (1984). *Qualitative data analysis: A sourcebook of new methods*. Newbury Park, CA: Sage Publications. This book is rich with analytic detail. The core that describes data reduction and data display assumes that the reader knows the first stages of qualitative research. Consequently the discussion shifts rapidly into the data analysis phase.

The book is packed with detail and needs considerable time to digest. The strength of the text is its presentation of a range of options for displaying data and the suggestions are backed up with concrete examples. Nevertheless, while full of suggestions, this book is more suitable for researchers with medium to advanced knowledge of qualitative methods. The amount of detail can be confusing to novices and is not amenable to a "learn as you go" approach to data analysis.

PATTON, M.Q. (1990). *Qualitative evaluation and research methods* (Chapters 8 and 9). Newbury Park, CA: Sage. Two of the chapters in this book are relevant to our Phase Three. However, while there is much useful information in Chapter 8, titled "Qualitative analysis and interpretation," it is sometimes difficult to identify because of the complexity and the number of topics presented. For example, the author addresses not only across-case analysis, the major focus of our Phase Three, but also case-study analysis, observational methods, and the analysis of phenomenological studies to name but a few. This chapter is recommended for researchers with a good grasp of the differences between various qualitative approaches.

In contrast, Chapter 9 titled, "Enhancing the quality and credibility of qualitative analysis," is a useful and easy-to-read discussion of the techniques available to increase the credibility of a qualitative research study. This chapter builds on a similar chapter in Lincoln and Guba's book (1985 below), as well as addressing some of Miles and Huberman's (1994 below) suggestions with respect to ensuring the rigor of data collection as a safeguard to credibility.

SEIDEL, J., KJOLSETH, R., & SEYMOUR, E. (1988). *The Ethnograph (Version 3.0).* Corvallis, OR: Qualis Research Associates. This straightforward manual that accompanies *The Ethnograph* software package is designed to instruct the novice qualitative researcher on the use of *The Ethnograph* data analysis program. The book outlines each step in a clear and concise manner.

Beyond discussing the actual mechanics of this particular software program, the manual weaves its instructions together with some very useful suggestions for coding qualitative data. It also bridges the gap between some popular word-processing packages and how they may be used for qualitative data analysis. Chapter 7, "Coding Rules and Code Mapping," is particularly relevant for those new to qualitative data analysis. It presents the complexity of coding schemes (e.g., overlapping and nested segments) visually and conceptually. The manual is recommended for those who want to avoid the more philosophical debates of qualitative research. The book's major strength lies in it practical and demystified description of qualitative data analysis.

STRAUSS, A., & CORBIN, J. (1990). *Basics of qualitative research: Grounded theory, procedures and techniques.* Newbury Park, CA: Sage. This book uses a step-by-step approach to explain the procedures and techniques of a grounded theory approach to qualitative research. The purpose of this approach is to build theory by using a systematic set of procedures, similar to many of those included in our Phase Three. Each chapter thoroughly details a specific concept or skill of qualitative research. Part Two identifies various coding strategies, offers suggestions about how to avoid bias and maintain objectivity during analysis, and explains how theory is generated from data. Part Three provides the reader with various useful techniques for enhancing data collection procedures and data analysis strategies. The book is a useful resource for the beginning researcher and is helpful for all stages of a qualitative research study.

TAYLOR, S., & BOGDAN, R. (1984). *Introduction to qualitative research methods: The search for meaning* (Chapter 6). New York: Wiley & Sons. As mentioned in our Phase Three, this chapter analyzes qualitative data by first identifying the major themes, which are then broken down into sub-themes and categories, the opposite of the method outlined in our book. If you have chosen this approach, the chapter by Taylor and Bogdan provides an easily read, basic description of how to analyze data using this approach. As mentioned earlier, we recommend starting the data analysis process with the categories rather than the overall themes because, in our experience with Taylor and Bogdan's approach, a beginning researcher is likely to disregard the meaning in what the research participants say if he or she becomes preoccupied with fitting meaning units to preestablished themes.

REFERENCES AND FURTHER READINGS

Altheide, D., & Johnson, J. (1991). Criteria for assessing interpretive validity in qualitative research. In N.K. Denzin & Y. Lincoln (Eds.), *Handbook of qualitative research* (pp. 485-499). Newbury Park, CA: Sage.

Charmaz, K. (1983). The grounded theory methods: An explication and interpretation. In R. Emerson (Ed.), *Contemporary field research* (pp. 109-126). Boston: Little, Brown.

Crabtree, B., & Miller, W. (1992). A template approach to text analysis: Developing and using code books. In B. Crabtree & W. Miller (Eds.), *Doing qualitative research* (pp. 93-109). Newbury Park, CA: Sage.

Denzin, N.K. (1994). The art and politics of interpretation. In N.K. Denzin & Y. Lincoln (Eds.), *Handbook of qualitative research* (pp. 500-515). Newbury Park, CA: Sage.

Ely, M., Anzul, M., Friedman, T., Garner, D., & McCormack-Steinmetz, A. (1991). *Doing qualitative research: Circles within circles.* New York: Falmer Press.

Erlandson, D., Harris, E., Skipper, B., & Allen, S. (1993). *Doing naturalistic inquiry: A guide to methods.* Newbury Park, CA: Sage.

Fielding, N.G., & Fielding, J.L. (1986). *Linking data: Qualitative research methods series No. 4.* Newbury Park, CA: Sage.

Fielding, N.G., & Lee, R. (Eds.). (1992). *Using computers in qualitative research.* Newbury Park, CA: Sage.

Glaser, B., & Strauss, A. (1967). *The discovery of grounded theory: Strategies for qualitative research.* New York: Aldine De Gruyter.

Glesene, C., & Peshkin, A. (1992). *Becoming qualitative researchers: An introduction.* White Plains, NY: Longman.

Huberman, A.M., & Miles, M. (1994). Data management and analysis methods. In N.K. Denzin & Y. Lincoln (Eds.), *Handbook of qualitative research* (pp. 428-444). Newbury Park, CA: Sage.

Kirk, J., & Miller, M. (1986). *Reliability and validity in qualitative research.* Newbury Park, CA: Sage.

Krefting, L. (1991). Rigor in qualitative research: The assessment of trustworthiness. *The American Journal of Occupational Therapy, 45,* 214-222.

Lincoln, Y., & Guba, E. (1985). *Naturalistic inquiry.* Newbury Park, CA: Sage.

Miles, M., & Huberman, M. (1994). *Qualitative data analysis: A sourcebook of new methods* (2nd ed.). Newbury Park, CA: Sage.

Mostyn, B. (1985). The content analysis of qualitative research: A dynamic approach. In M. Brenner, J. Brown, & P. Canter (Eds.), *The research interview: Uses and approaches* (pp. 119-131). New York: Academic Press.

Patton, M.Q. (1990). *Qualitative evaluation and research methods.* Newbury Park, CA: Sage.

Pfaffenberger, B. (1988). *Microcomputer applications in qualitative research.* Newbury Park, CA: Sage.

Richards, L., & Richards, T. (1991). Computing in qualitative analysis: A healthy development? *Qualitative Health Research, 1,* 234-262.

Rubin, A., & Babbie E. (1993). *Research methods for social work* (2nd ed.) Pacific Grove, CA: Brooks/Cole Publishing Company.

Schatzman, L., & Strauss, A. (1973). *Field research: Strategies for a natural sociology.* Englewood Cliffs, NJ: Prentice-Hall.

Seidel, J., Kjolseth, R., & Seymour, E. (1988). *The Ethnograph* (Version 3.0). Corvallis, OR: Qualis Research Associates.

Seidman, I. (1991). *Interviewing as qualitative research: A guide for researchers in education and the social sciences.* New York: Teachers College Press.

Silverman, D. (1993). *Interpreting qualitative data: Methods for analyzing talk, text, and interaction.* Newbury Park, CA: Sage.

Straus, A., & Corbin, J. (1990). *Basics of qualitative research.* Newbury Park, CA: Sage.

Tesch, R. (1990). *Qualitative research: Analysis types and software tools.* New York: Falmer Press.

Walker, L. (1979). *The battered woman.* New York: Harper & Row.

Weissman, H. (1981). Teaching qualitative methods. In S. Briar, H. Weissman, & A. Rubin (Eds.), *Research utilization in social work education* (pp. 59-65). New York: Council on Social Work Education.

Wolcott, H. (1994). *Transforming qualitative data: Description, analysis, and interpretation.* Newbury Park, CA: Sage.

Robert McClelland
Carol D. Austin

Phase Four

WHAT WILL YOUR FINAL REPORT LOOK LIKE?

STEPS IN THE DISSEMINATION PROCESS

Step 1: Getting Started to Write
Step 2: Writing Your Report
Step 3: Sending Your Manuscript to a Journal

SUMMARY

REFERENCES AND FURTHER READINGS

Writing Your Report

W RITING UP AND DISSEMINATING your research findings is a critical phase of the qualitative research process. Without an adequate plan and strategy for the dissemination of your findings, they will not reach practitioners who may find them useful. As far as we are concerned, too many research reports gather dust on shelves because the researchers have overlooked the significance of disseminating their findings. A commitment to adding to our knowledge base requires a carefully conceived and implemented publishing method for informing our practice community. It is extremely important for you to know that qualitative research findings can result either in improved social scientific understanding or in meaningless gibberish, as is so aptly pointed out by Bruce L. Berg (1989):

> My children, Alex and Kate, were eating alphabet soup for lunch one Sunday
> afternoon. Kate, then about four years old, was stirring her soup with great care and

deliberation. She managed to capture several of the letters on her spoon, carefully spill off the liquid, and spell out her name.

"Look daddy, I wrote my name with my noodles!" She held her spoon up for my inspection. She had arranged the letters to spell "KATIE." Alex, seeing the attention his sister had received, pulled his dripping spoon from his soup, and spilling much of it onto the floor exclaimed, "Me too!" Unfortunately, his letters spelled out "XCYU," a unique spelling of "Alex," or simply failure to "sort the noodles from the soup" in a fashion that made his noodles mean something to others.

With the above quote in mind, it must be noted, however, that your research findings may not merit dissemination. This is true regardless of the type of research undertaken—quantitative or qualitative. All researchers must assess the utility and practical significance of their findings before they decide whether a report should be written for possible publication. Several assessment criteria can be applied to qualitative research studies:

- Do your research findings extend current theory?

- Has your research study added anything to the theoretical base of social work practice?

- How well does your research study meet the test of trustworthiness? How credible is your research study?

- To what extent could your study's findings inform day-to-day social work practice activities?

Each of the above criteria must be evaluated keeping in mind the audience you want to reach. Effective distribution requires a clear idea of who should know about your study. Such clarity will greatly assist in selecting and implementing a strategy for its dissemination. There can be little doubt that the written word has dominated publication activities over time. In addition to journals and books, improved access to the literature is now available through on-line bibliographic searches. Nevertheless, publication methods have diversified and the presentation of qualitative research findings through non-print outlets is growing. Social work practitioners who are developing agency-specific models of intervention may find the non-print approach useful as a supplement to staff training.

Video- and audiotapes are particularly effective ways to disperse information that involves practice skills. Unfortunately, most of us do not have access to the means of creating non-print media products, so these approaches may prove difficult to develop. While it is clear that non-print media are emerging as powerful dissemination outlets, they usually require collaboration between you and one of your colleagues who possesses the requisite technical skills.

WHAT WILL YOUR FINAL PRODUCT LOOK LIKE?

When your qualitative study is completed, you probably hope to discover a prescribed format for reporting your findings in the form of a report, a manuscript, or class paper. However, there are no set rules for writing them. Compared to the relatively standardized format of quantitative research reports, qualitative reports are quite varied.

The form and style of your final product will depend largely on the intended audience and the medium you selected. For example, reporting your findings to an academic audience is vastly different from reporting them through publication in a professional journal. Frequently, qualitative studies are written up as books because this format lends itself well to reporting the necessary detail. A classic book based on the qualitative research approach is Elliot Liebow's (1967) *Tally's Corner,* which reported on the day-to-day routines of African-American men who frequented the streets of a particular neighborhood. To reduce Liebow's findings to a few pages would have sacrificed the rich detail that made it a seminal piece of work.

Often the first formal effort at dissemination is through a verbal presentation to your classmates, to some faculty members, or to seminars that are held at annual program meetings such as the National Association of Social Workers and the Council on Social Work Education. Fellow students and colleagues who are familiar with the questions you are exploring can help to refine your analysis and develop its relevance to social work practice. Local audiences, agency staff, administrators, and your research participants are also frequently eager to learn about your findings, in addition to local community groups. All of these outlets are important for you because they may offer you external validation at a point when your writing task seems overwhelming.

STEPS IN THE DISSEMINATION PROCESS

Whether your goal is to begin by presenting your research findings to your classmates, research instructor, thesis or dissertation committee, or a social work audience, or by writing up a manuscript for possible publication, there are three basic steps that you need to go through. Because getting started is very difficult for most people, it is useful to develop a strategy for ensuring that progress is made.

To this end, it is helpful to make yourself accountable to others by setting a realistic deadline for presenting your initial findings to your fellow classmates and/or colleagues. Peer feedback can be a valuable measure of your readiness for further dissemination possibilities. The dissemination process includes: (1) getting started to write, (2) writing your report, and (3) sending your manuscript to a journal for possible publication.

Step 1: Getting Started to Write

Starting to write up the results of your qualitative study involves two tasks: (1) deciding when in your study to begin writing, and (2) planning and choosing a focus. Let us turn to the first task, deciding when to start writing.

Task 1a: Deciding When in Your Study to Begin Writing

The first task in starting to write your report is deciding at what point in the research process to actually begin writing. Different people have different opinions on this matter. On one hand, there is a strongly held belief that the qualitative researcher must remain open to hearing what is said. Those who view openness as a priority suggest that there is a danger of premature closure if you begin to write too early. On the other hand, some people argue that it is useful to begin organizing and writing up your study as early as possible. These people believe there is a strong likelihood that the sheer amount of information you collect during your study will immobilize you. We believe it is best for you to start writing up the results of your study as early as possible.

Writing is a learned skill, and novice writers can be big procrastinators. It is common for some writers to go through ritualized diversions to delay getting started. Cleaning the desk, sharpening pencils, giving your cats a bath, going fishing with Bob who never catches any fish to begin with, cleaning the house, and even reading research and statistics books may seem more pressing than writing up your research findings. The truth is, however, that starting to write up your research findings simply requires you to write *something*. At this stage, your goal is not to strive for perfection; your goal is to produce a "working report" that can be reviewed and revised, re-reviewed and re-revised, re-reviewed and re-re-revised...

Do not fret, some of the work in writing up your findings has already been done in Phase One. Your original research proposal should have included much of the content that is required for your final report (see Figure 1.1). Thus, writing begins with a logical, lucid, rational, and coherent research proposal as outlined at the end of Phase One. If your research proposal was faulty, then rest assured that your final research report will flounder and probably will never get written in a way that makes sense to anyone but you.

Task 1b: Planning and Choosing a Focus

It should be obvious by now that your original research proposal will provide you with useful guidance in focusing your writing. Your proposal should have identified the rationale and process for investigating your research question.

Your literature review demonstrated the significance of the research question being explored and placed your particular study within the broader context of established theory (if any such theory exists).

Your proposal should have provided an overview and rationale for the methodology you selected to gather your data. It should have described and justified how and why your research participants were to be selected. It should have specified how ethical and informed consent issues were to be resolved and included a discussion of critical concepts (e.g., life events, attitudes about specific issues, metaphors) that would guide the structure of your data-gathering method and the organization of your study's findings. These components of your proposal can now serve as a method for organizing a verbal presentation of your study or writing up your study for possible publication.

Step 2: Writing Your Report

Writing a report involves four tasks: (1) using correct terminology, (2) developing evidence of trustworthiness, (3) choosing a writing style, and (4) organizing your report.

Task 2a: Using Correct Terminology

Curiously, you may at first find yourself writing up your findings using a quantitative frame of reference. This is a big error. Qualitative research findings cannot be framed in terms that are applicable to reporting findings of a quantitative research study. If this is done, it will lead to a mismatch in terminology. If you use quantitative terminology throughout your report, you may end up being viewed by others as a "quantitative wolf dressed up in a qualitative sheep's clothing" (Miles & Huberman, 1994). As you know, the qualitative research approach is based on a different set of assumptions than the quantitative approach. Thus, methodological terminology used to report qualitative findings must be consistent with and accurately reflect a qualitative—not quantitative—research design.

Qualitative research studies use different standards than quantitative studies when it comes to demonstrating rigor. For example, in quantitative studies tests for threats to validity and reliability are familiar. In naturalistic studies, the analogous concept is trustworthiness. In reporting your qualitative findings, you need to demonstrate to the reader that you paid careful attention to meeting the standards of trustworthiness in the observations and insights you report. To achieve this, you will need to consider whether your written report provides sufficient evidence of the extent to which your trustworthiness has been established. These considerations are critical in developing the conceptual framework that guides the writing process, particularly in the discussion of your study's methodology.

Task 2b: Developing Evidence of Trustworthiness

There is a set of standards that provide evidence of trustworthiness, addressing four major concerns: credibility (truth value), transferability (applicability), dependability (consistency), and confirmability (neutrality). These are the rough equivalents of the quantitative research concepts of internal validity, external validity/generalizability, reliability, and objectivity, respectively (Guba, 1981). The demonstration of credibility is particularly important and is built on the following aspects of your study:

- Prolonged engagement with your research participant(s), persistent observation, and triangulation.

- Peer debriefing through systematic review of your study's substantive, methodological, legal, and ethical matters with your fellow students and colleagues.

- Negative case analysis, which involves revising your analysis until it accounts for all of the known cases.

- Referential adequacy, which provides you with a record of interviews and observations, such as videotapes or audiotapes, case notes, and transcriptions.

- Member checks, where you ask the research participant(s) to provide feedback on the information you collected and the conclusions drawn.

The concept of triangulation is worth examining more closely because it may take more than one form. The most common form of data triangulation is corroborating information from other sources (e.g., other research participants or agency documents). Another approach involves theoretical triangulation, which explores competing theories during the interviewing process. It is worth noting that the latter may involve a more proactive interviewing style than some qualitative researchers would feel is appropriate. Its value lies in relating your findings to a theoretical perspective.

Concerns over transferability are addressed through a rich description of your study. The reader needs sufficient information by which to judge whether your findings are based on case material that is similar to his or her own context. This requires detail in the description of the research participants and their circumstances, since there are no statistical assumptions of generalizability in a qualitative research study.

Dependability is built upon the techniques described under credibility. In particular, efforts to demonstrate triangulation of information will contribute to the assessment of dependability. A process audit conducted by your peers may provide additional evidence of an effort to maintain consistency throughout your study.

Confirmability can be demonstrated by establishing an audit trail and through triangulation. Your journal should provide ample evidence of your effort to remain critically aware of the energetic and dynamic relationship between the interviewer/researcher and the interviewee/research participant. Over time, this journal may help to integrate your observations, your self-awareness, your knowledge base, and your insight development into a coherent whole. It discloses the degree of impartiality that you bring to the entire research process. This is a valuable process guide, and it leaves a record if you want to establish an audit trail.

Evidence of attention to these criteria for assessing the trustworthiness of your study should be embedded in your final research report. This will allow the reader to judge the quality of the research process. A plan for producing evidence of trustworthiness in subsequent research findings is one of your major responsibilities during the design phase. The seeds of your ability to produce research findings that meet the standards of trustworthiness are planted long before the point where you start to write up your findings.

Task 2c: Choosing a Writing Style

John Van Maanen (1988) describes the product of a qualitative research study as reporting "tales" with varying amounts of author involvement acknowledged. Realistic tales are reported in the third person voice and may produce an academic-sounding journal article. Confessional tales are in the first person and acknowledge the author's participation in the observer role. Impressionistic tales, also in the first person, are characterized by vivid stories that frequently include the author's thoughts and opinions.

Illustrative quotes from research participants are used to help the reader better understand the topic being explored. The goal of the interviewer/author is to capture and convey important personal exchanges that provide evidence of the insights being discussed. Direct quotes from a research participant do not have to be referenced, and real names should never be used.

After you have engaged in an extensive interviewing process, your personal impressions become pertinent and relevant. Your thoughts during the interviewing process may be a significant part of your study. Therefore, you may choose to acknowledge your own feelings about a conversation you are reporting because those emotions influenced your conclusions. The suppression of this information could diminish the reader's understanding of the dynamic being described.

This is quite a different style of writing than is found in conventional research reports. It takes some practice to use the style consistently, since most educators discourage writing that is personal, metaphorical, or interpretive. Therefore, your goal is to present a credible and compelling report that will be taken seriously by the reader.

There may also be times when a more traditional reporting style is called for. Sometimes academic committees who are charged with reviewing formal theses and dissertations prefer a traditional style of writing, in which you then must use the third person when reporting observations. Likewise, some professional journals may prefer a more traditional style. Basically, you will want to modify your writing style to suit the reader as long as it does not damage the accuracy of your findings. If the particular audience is known in advance, it makes sense to select a writing style that will be acceptable to them.

Task 2d: Organizing Your Report

Attention must also be directed to the organization of your final report. Qualitative analyses and findings should be presented in an orderly, coherent, plausible, credible, and compelling format. To achieve this, there are six standardized parts to a good qualitative research report: (1) an abstract, (2) the introduction and literature review, (3) a discussion of methodology, (4) a presentation of findings and analysis, (5) a conclusion or discussion of the significance of the study's findings, and (6) a list of references. We will demonstrate how these six parts can be written by using our example of women who plan to separate from their ex-partners after they have left a women's emergency shelter. The writing style that we have used is most appropriate for a journal audience.

ABSTRACT. An abstract must be included at the beginning of your final report. It is a short statement, usually about 150 words, that indicates the purpose of your study and its conclusions. It usually starts by indicating your central thesis or research question and the theories being explored (if any). This is followed with a statement about the methodology you used to gather the data. If there is something unique about the research design or research participants, this may be delineated as well. Finally, the major findings are briefly stated and your conclusions summarized. An abstract of the example that we have been using throughout this book would go something like this:

While emergency shelters have become the primary means of providing aid to women who have been physically abused by their partners, such facilities are typically able to provide only short-term assistance. As an initial step in evaluating the efficacy of follow-up services to former shelter residents, this study identified the major needs expressed by women who have left an assaultive partner. Information was gathered in interviews with 18 women in a small city in southern Ontario, Canada. A content analysis indicated that the research participants' primary concerns involved dealing with their previous partners and with the courts, and coping with low self-esteem and with their children's reactions to the changes in their lives. The implications of the study are discussed in relation to the need for expanding services to women who wish to leave abusive partners.

INTRODUCTION. An introduction to a qualitative report examines the nature of the question or questions being explored and their significance to our profession. In order to demonstrate the significance of your research question, you need to present a conscientious review of the literature. This discussion usually consists of an historical summary of the literature as well as current theoretical or scholarly literature related to your subject. The length of the introductory literature search varies dramatically, from one page to many, but should assure the reader that you are familiar with the current research findings in your study's topic area. If the purpose of your study is to reconceptualize or add to theory, you must include enough discussion of the literature to provide a foundation for the analysis that you present later. Further discussion of the relevant literature will be presented in the analysis and discussion of findings. Continuing with our example, we produced an introduction that was broken into three overlapping parts: (1) research on women who have been abused by their partners, (2) research on women and shelters, and (3) evaluations of services to women who have been abused by their partners.

Research on Women Who Have Been Abused by Their Partners: Much of the early information collected about men who assault their partners was gathered from women who sought refuge in emergency shelters. Such women have also been the focus of considerable study, primarily in a search for variables that could explain why a women would stay with a man who was physically and emotionally abusive. The descriptions of wife assault victims in the literature have suggested some common characteristics, such as a feeling of helplessness (Hilberman & Munson, 1978; Walker, 1978), traditional sex-role orientation, social isolation (Wetzel & Ross, 1983; Pressman, 1989), and low self-esteem (Carlson, 1977; Hilberman & Munson, 1978; Hartik, 1982).

However, Hotaling and Sugarman (1990) recently concluded that "after 15 years of empirical research on wife assault, few risk markers have been found that identify women at risk to violence in close relationships ... it is evident that researchers should focus greater attention on the perpetrators, the dynamics of the relationship, and the social environment in which the relationship exists" (*p.* 12). While it is not appropriate to focus on characteristics of the victim in order to understand how women might end up in battering relationships, these traits remain of interest since they may be seen as the result of living in such a relationship (Tutty, Bidgood, & Rothery, 1993).

Low self-esteem is one of the most commonly described of these results and is thought to be caused not only by the physical violence directed toward these women, but by the emotional abuse that is normally part of an assaultive relationship (Pressman, 1989; Follingstad, Rutledge, Berg, Hause, & Polek, 1990). A pervasive feeling of helplessness is another feature of women who have been physically abused and is used to explain why many stay in abusive relationships. Feeling powerless to leave, women who have been victimized may lapse into depression, anxiety, and passivity (Hilberman & Munson, 1978; Walker, 1978).

In contrast, authors such as Bowker (1984) and Gondolf and Fisher (1988) see these women as "survivors" rather than "victims." They describe the often ingenious attempts that these women have made to alleviate violence while remaining within the relationship. In Bowker's (1983) research study, these women did not passively accept violence, but tried every strategy they could think of to stop it—hiding, threatening to leave, fighting back, and talking to friends. Nothing, however, changed a spouse's violent behavior.

Many assaulted women experience a high degree of social isolation (Wetzel & Ross, 1983; Pressman, 1989) that may, in part, be a response to embarrassment about visible injuries, coercive restraints by a jealous husband, and withdrawal by family members and friends who are frustrated by a woman's inability to leave a painful situation (Mardoyan, 1985). Follingstad et al. (1990) reported that 75% of the spouses of 234 women restricted their wives' activities by denying them access to social supports or finances.

These characteristics remain key targets for change in supportive intervention with these women (e.g., Bidgood, Tutty, & Rothery, 1991) since they will likely interfere in any transition to independence, leaving the woman vulnerable to returning to a battering relationship. The pervasiveness of such problems also suggests why emergency shelters alone cannot address all the needs of women who have been assaulted and why additional resources are necessary to facilitate a woman's move to independence. Rather than simply describing the plight of these women, the next generation of research studies must focus on their needs and what resources might assist their struggle to make a new life once they have left emergency shelters.

Research on Women and Shelters: Many women remain in assaultive relationships for years before they make the decision to leave. The question of how and when a woman makes this decision has been the focus of a number of research articles. In one study, the choice to leave for a shelter was made two weeks to several months after a critical abusive incident (Giles-Sims, 1983). This incident was not necessarily the most violent, but was characterized by three themes: (1) fear that the children would be hurt, (2) resentment at the husband for letting the children see their mother beaten, and (3) exposure of the violent pattern to people outside the family.

Moore (1979) identified the presence of a strong support group, the absence of children, and an increase in severity and frequency of the beatings as being associated with leaving sooner. Gelles (1976) found the most predictive factor to be financial independence. Interestingly, in one study of women who used a nonresidential advocacy clinic, no relationship was found between the frequency, severity, or the duration of the abuse and the decision to leave (Greaves, Heapy, & Wylie, 1988).

While shelter services and the safety they provide to assaulted women represent vital crisis intervention, entering a shelter does not necessarily mark the end of a battering relationship. Many women return directly to their spouses (55% in Snyder & Scheer, 1981; 49% in Aguirre, 1985). Of the women in one study (Giles-Sims, 1983), 58% returned to their homes at least temporarily after staying in the shelter. After six months, 33% of the women were still in the abusive relationship, 25% were separated, and 33% divorced.

Giles-Sims has suggested that, on the average, women who have been abused by their partners leave and return four to five times before a separation becomes permanent. Okun (1988) has proposed that the cycle of leaving and returning to an abusive spouse does not indicate failure of the shelter staff or inconsistency on the part of the woman, but is, in itself, a process that eventually culminates in the woman leaving for good. Wilson, Baglioni, and Downing (1989) concur with this view, stating that "women returning to a shelter should be indicative of a greater sense of control over one's physical security, and greater social involvement" (*p.* 276).

Little is known about what distinguishes women who return home directly from the shelter, those who attempt independent living, and those who successfully manage to live independently. A study by Schutte, Bouleige, and Malouf (1986) found a significant relationship between low self-esteem, a perception of self-blame for the violence, and a decision to return to the abusing partner. Cannon and Sparks (1989) reported that only 50% of the women followed through their initial plan to live independently after leaving the shelter. In a study of a second-stage shelter, McDonald, Chisholm, Peressini, and Smillie (1986) found that 78% of the residents believed that, apart from the Transition House, their only choice was to return to the battering relationship.

Ninety percent of the women who arrived at the second-stage shelter had no possessions, clothing, or money, indicating the extent of their need. After leaving the second-stage shelter, the women were found to have "more internal control and more social independence at six-month follow-up compared to what they experienced when they entered the house" (McDonald, 1989, *p.* 122). Even so, in a small study, three of nine women returned to their spouses after residing for six months in a second-stage shelter (Barnsley, Jacobson, McIntosh, & Wintemute, 1980). Similarly, in Smillie's study (1991) three women who successfully lived independently in the community for over a year after residing in a second-stage shelter ultimately returned to their husbands.

From a different perspective, a further study (Johnson, Crowley, & Sigler, 1992) found that many women return to an assaultive relationship because of fear of their partner, particularly in the face of inadequate legal restrictions (restraining order) or police enforcement. While a woman may find security in a shelter, realistic fears about her own safety and that of her children are likely to return once she must reestablish herself in the community. The first hazardous period for women after leaving extends for several months, long past the residency allowance in most emergency shelters (Ellis, 1992).

Wilson et al. (1989) studied factors related to women's readmission to a shelter after having moved home. These included lack of income and having more and younger children. The authors conclude that "an important step in preventing recurring battering is to facilitate the involvement of the battered woman in a supportive network of friends, relatives, and fellow workers. Participating in self-help groups, working away from the home, and maintaining supportive relationships outside the immediate family represent important ways that a battered woman can become embedded in social networks" (p. 282).

Interestingly, it was not the amount of earned income that determined a woman's readmission to a shelter, but whether she earned income at all, suggesting that working outside the home is an important strategy.

Those who choose not to return to their spouse must face many difficult issues, including housing, employment, child care, children's emotional reactions to the separation, a possible lack of social support, and the difficult extended tasks of a single parent. Speculation is that, after the initial crisis and separation from her spouse, a woman will need to work toward greater levels of autonomy. Follow-up support will be critical in this process, especially where second-stage shelters are not available (Scyner & McGregor, 1988).

Although it is argued that family violence occurs independently of socio-economic status or employment (Greaves et al., 1988), the women who use shelters are often disadvantaged by not being employed (60% in Wilson et al., 1989). A successful transition to independent living often entails job training or upgrading, both of which typically involve spending money, not bringing in income.

It has been noted that women leave battering relationships as much for the sake of their children as for themselves (Wilson et al., 1989). As mentioned previously, Giles-Sims (1983) found that two critical reasons prompting a woman to leave had to do with her children: (1) fear that the children might be hurt, and (2) resentment that the children were witnesses to the abuse. MacLeod's Canadian study (1987) found that abuse of children by their father or father-figure was cited as a major reason for seeking admission to an emergency shelter. A study that looked at the beliefs that serve to keep a woman from leaving a battering relationship found one central belief to be that she must stay for the sake of the children (Hilberman & Munson, 1978).

Children who have witnessed violence between their parents are at high risk for developing behavioral problems (Fantuzzo & Lindquist, 1989; Jaffe, Wolfe, & Wilson, 1990; Moore, Peplar, Mae, & Kates, 1989), especially if they have been abused themselves (Hughes, 1988). A study of an emergency shelter (Sample Survey and Data Bank Unit, 1984) found that mothers reported at least one general difficulty for approximately 63% of the children—the most common problem being that the children were withdrawn. Jaffe et al. (1990) identified two patterns in children who had witnessed parental violence, either withdrawal or aggression. In Smillie's (1991) interviews with women who returned to their husbands despite having maintained themselves independently in the community for a period of time, the women reported difficulties both with the stresses of being a single parent and with their children's behavior. Given the multiple needs of women and their children in establishing a new, autonomous life, programs that extend shelter support beyond residency appear to be critical.

Evaluations of Services to Women Who Have Been Abused by Their Partners:
Services to women who have been physically abused by their partners are seldom
evaluated. There is only beginning to be empirical evidence that shelters themselves
are helpful (McDonald, 1989), although reports from these women about the
protection they offer has made their utility abundantly clear. Many of the research
studies on women in shelters have focused on identifying common characteristics
of women who are abused, or organizational issues, and on the shelters' features.
Only one study was found that evaluated the impact of an emergency shelter upon
battered women (Cannon & Sparks, 1989).

Although only six residents responded both when they entered the shelter and
either four weeks later or immediately prior to leaving, improvements were found
in these women's acceptance of others. Interestingly, there were no increases in
acceptance of self, which was found to be markedly low for the women as they
entered the shelter. Few research studies have followed women through this
experience and identified what happens to them after they leave the shelter and what
needs to happen to facilitate their living independently.

More evaluations have been conducted on second-stage shelters. McDonald,
Chisholm, Peressini, and Smillie (1986) found that, after leaving the shelter, women
had more internal control and more social independence at six-month follow-up than
when they entered the shelter. Russell (1990) compared reports on four second-stage
shelters from a consumer's point of view. The four shelters included Monroe House
in Vancouver (Barnsley et al., 1980), Safe Choice in Vancouver (Russell, Forcier, &
Charles, 1987), Discovery House in Calgary (McDonald et al., 1986), and Women In
Second-Stage Housing (WISH) (Scyner & McGregor, 1988).

Although the results of the four diverse studies are not directly comparable, all
of the programs asked about consumer satisfaction. Individual counseling was seen
as helpful for both the women and their children. Russell (1990) concluded that
given the prevalence of psychological concerns among women in a shelter,
reluctance to provide counseling services can be viewed as counterproductive and
even dangerous.

The studies also identified several problems encountered by residents in second-
stage shelters. These included complaints in reaction to communal living, reported
by women in three of the four second-stage shelters. Conflicts also arose about
children and child care, with the exception of Safe Choice, which provided a
counseling program for children. There was variance in the extent to which women
saw a need for counseling services. Some saw short-term help as sufficient, but
others wanted longer, more extensive counseling.

Without question, research studies documenting whether the services provided
for these women and their children are adequate and appropriate are sadly lacking,
and are an essential next step in looking at how the network of services for these
women are meeting their needs.

METHODOLOGY. The discussion of your study's methodology is an opportunity
for you to address many of the issues related to trustworthiness. It includes a
rationale for using the selected approach (e.g., interviewing, participant
observation, focus groups). It also explains why and how your research
participants were selected. As you know, in qualitative research studies there is

no attempt to select a random sample. Instead, you should have identified a theoretical or purposeful sample of participants, which should consist of people who can provide data for theory development. Typically, the number of research participants is small, and is determined by the depth of interviewing.

A snowball sampling technique may be used to identify additional participants by asking for referrals from each person who is interviewed. This may be repeated until you have determined that no new information is being generated by additional referrals. The research methodology you select is dependent on the nature of your research question and your access to research participants. Anyone reading your final report will be very interested in the rationale you used to justify your particular data collection approach and the people who participated in your study.

If credibility is evaluated by evidence of prolonged engagement, persistent observation, and triangulation, then you must describe your data collection process in enough detail for the reader to judge this important aspect of trustworthiness. This is also true for the indicators used in assessing transferability, dependability, and confirmability. A chronology of your study and how it worked out is pertinent. A good description of the setting selected is also important in reporting your findings. The reader of your report will want to judge whether the influence of the research setting was appropriately acknowledged in your data analysis. Continuing with our example, we decided to break down the methodology section into two parts: (1) method, and (2) research participants.

Method: Information was gathered from 18 women who had left an assaultive relationship and who had resided in an emergency shelter in a small city in southern Ontario, Canada. The information was collected within a year of the time that they had left the shelter through both a qualitative and a quantitative component: a follow-up survey and interviews. Responses to the survey documented the concerns that each woman had encountered and the demographics of the group. Seven of the women were subsequently interviewed. The interviews lasted an average of one-and-a-half hours and provided detailed descriptions and the context of each woman's experience. The interviews were analyzed using a constant comparison method (Glaser & Strauss, 1967).

The interpretation of our results is limited by the small size of the sample of women who have responded to date. Nevertheless, given the paucity of research studies on women in such circumstances, it is argued that the exploratory nature of our study is warranted and that the results may be useful for guiding the decisions of policy-making and funding bodies.

Research Participants: Fourteen of the 18 women described in the follow-up survey were in their 20s and 30s, with two women still in their teens and two over 40. Twelve had not completed high school, with three having completed only Grade 9. Three of the women had completed Grade 12, however, and at least one had some college education. Four of the women had never married; two were divorced; 12

were separated. The length of their marital relationships varied from less than a year to 23 years. In the majority of cases, the abuse had lasted for most of the relationship. In only three of the relationships had there been no previous separations due to physical abuse. Six of the women had experienced one to two separations; another six had three to six marital separations. One women reported having been separated 15 times in reaction to her husband's abusive behavior.

All of the women had experienced emotional abuse, and all but one had been physically abused. In 12 relationships, the finances were controlled by the partner; 13 women described having had pets or property damaged. Eight women had been sexually abused by their partners. As another indicator of the serious nature of the abuse, nine women experienced abuse daily, six weekly, and two monthly. For one final participant, the frequency of the abuse was unpredictable. Objects or weapons had been used in the abuse of eight women. In eight of the families, police had been contacted to intervene, and restraining orders had been acquired in six. A partner's abuse of drugs or alcohol was implicated in the abusive behavior in 14 cases; however, only one woman reported needing support for her own alcohol- or drug-related behavior.

Of the 15 women who had children, 14 claimed that their children had also been abused by their partners. Most commonly mentioned was physical abuse, often in combination with psychological abuse. In one family, children had been both physically and sexually abused. Four mothers reported that their children were emotionally abused, in some cases because of witnessing their mother's physical abuse. Although circumstances differed widely, the nature and extent of abuse was serious and long-standing.

Of the seven women interviewed to collect more detailed information about their experiences, four had entered an emergency shelter immediately after leaving their partners. Of the other three women, two had left an abusive partner earlier and had used shelter services in other municipalities. The final participant was a young woman whose apartment and belongings had been damaged by a tenant to whom she sublet her home while she attended school in another community. She was in severe financial need, having lost most of her possessions, and had stayed at the shelter because she had no other resources.

All but the latter participant had children of varying ages: four women had preschool children living at home, two women had older children (nine to 10 years) or teenagers. In two families, there were children not living with their mothers: in one case a 15-year-old had moved back with his father, in another case one child was in foster care.

FINDINGS. The presentation of your findings and analyses uses descriptive profiles of participants and direct quotes to provide illustrations of the questions you are exploring. These quotes may conform with, contradict, or modify generally accepted theories. They should add to the reader's understanding of the specific questions being explored. The data are organized into constructs that present information systematically. As an example, you may want to compare the attitudes of your participants to a generally accepted theory of human behavior. In exploring the issue, you will need to examine the reasons why some participants fit the theory and some do not. In qualitative research studies, majority opinion is only part of your total story. A common analytic theme in qualitative studies is the search for disconfirming as well as confirming evidence. This leads to a reconceptualization of commonly held beliefs or theories. Continuing with our example:

The Critical Issues: The small body of previously reviewed research studies on what happens to women after they leave assaultive partners suggests that the key issues are housing, employment, the children's emotional reactions to the separation, the extended tasks of a single parent, and lack of social support. Many of these concerns were identified by the participants in our study as significant in maintaining a decision to remove their families and to live independently from their abusive partners.

The six issues that were most pressing to the women were, in order of concern: (1) the relationship with their ex-partners; (2) court, for those women who were pressing charges or dealing with divorce or custody issues; (3) self-esteem; (4) coping with children's responses to the separation; (5) finances and vocational training or finding a job; and (6) housing. In the following discussion of each of these areas, excerpts from the interview transcripts add a sense of the realities of these women's lives:

Relationship with Ex-partners: All 18 women expressed difficulty in dealing with their ex-partners, and this was ranked as the most serious concern, with four women rating it as their most pressing concern and another seven rating it as the second or third most important issue. This conclusion parallels the findings of another study of women who were attempting to live independently in a second-stage shelter (Russell, Forcier, & Charles, 1987). In that study, three of the top-rated concerns involved the relationship with an ex-partner: (1) dealing with fear in the aftermath of life-threatening situations, (2) dealing with the husband's behavior, and (3) making a decision about whether to return to him.

Not all of the women had remained in contact with their partners, in most cases because they had fled to another city. For those who continued to have contact with an ex-partner to allow him to visit the children, the relationship entailed continued emotional and, at times, physical abuse, or pressure to reunite the family.

Some men used threats or intimidation, many in respect to access to the children or applying for full custody, a common occurrence according to Beaudry (1985). In the current study, three of the four women who had left their partners described how they were subsequently threatened or harassed:

- Well, he leaves notes on my vehicles ... and, then when I park over here, one night he was behind a few [cars] and he was going to jump me, but the guy upstairs saw him, eh. And then he'd phone me in the middle of the night and he'd ask if the kids were in bed and ... oh, it was pretty wicked there for a while.

- No, he hasn't threatened to take [two-year-old son] since last year, so ... that's nice. *That's not a problem that he knows where you are?* No ... well in some sense there is. My sister's still really worried because she went through the same thing with her husband, so it's kind of a repeat for us girls ... I don't know what we do with men. But she's really scared too. She phoned me the other day and she said that she wished I would just leave, cause you know things could get bad. Cause we fight when we're together. Like when he comes over, we still fight a lot.

Other men entreated their ex-wives to return, and some offered bribes to them to reconcile the relationship. As is typical in most relationships in which men assault their partners, the enticements and remorse were interspersed with threats or harassment. The same two women described their experiences with such pressure:

- Exactly on the 8th of this month it'll be exactly a year I've been gone ... but he told me if I take him back he'll get me a new car. And he says, "Are you sure you want this divorce?" He still wants me. And tells me, like, he's going to forgive me, like for ... I've been in two different relationships. Definitely great! And it was just listening to that last night and "You're the best," he'd say, "I miss you in bed." ... so I don't know if he's going to change the pattern, like is he going to go back to being abusive ... like, you don't know.

- Lots of pressure to go back. Lots of "I'll change, I'll change," but in the meantime nothing was changing. The same thing was happening, but "I'll change."

Court: Issues related to dealing with the legal system are inextricably bound up with fears about the ex-partner. Although many police forces are receiving special training in how to intervene more effectively in domestic assaults (Miller, Cragg, & Rothery, 1991), skepticism about the enforceability of restraining orders and the effects on women of having the police charge their spouses continues (Fusco, 1989). Custody and access to children are clearly central issues that keep women in contact with their partners for years after dissolution of the marriage.

The initial custody battle is most likely conflictual, if only because it provides an opportunity for men to continue to attempt to control their partners. However, some couples continue to fight over custody issues long after the court case has been "settled," and several mothers reported consistently worrying about the safety of their children during their visits with their fathers. Custody and access issues are so fraught with the potential for continuing abuse that special programs to help women cope have been developed in association with shelters (e.g., the Custody and Access Support Committee of Vancouver).

In our study, four women were pressing charges against their partners for assault or were dealing with divorce or custody issues. For them, dealing with the legal system and going to court provoked anxiety. An additional four women raised potential legal issues as problematic, although it was not their most pressing concern.

- [Two shelter staff] helped me with the restraining order ... and we wrote up a statement what happened that day that I had the police come over. And other than that there were no other court ... I haven't gone for legal custody of my son yet. But I don't know ... some days I feel like I should and some days I feel like I shouldn't ... it's hard to say.

- Especially when now he [two-year-old son] asks a lot where his dad is. So that's hard too. *Does his dad get to visit him now?* His dad? Yeah ... *So it's still hard when he comes to see him?* I guess it wouldn't be so bad if we didn't have a child, but then, it's something you can't take back I guess. I mean it's something that every batterer does. You can always get children to think that it might get better, eh, and that's sad that he'd do that. *Does he still want to get back together?* Yes.

- I had to go to court for child support, sorry, custody, both, actually and I was just like a little mouse ... I didn't want to go.

Self-Esteem: Women who have been in battering relationships are commonly viewed as experiencing low self-esteem, which will interfere with their ability to make decisions and to present themselves in their best light when dealing with agency representatives or potential employers. Low self-esteem, encouraged by the often long-standing denigration of their abilities by an ex-partner, can also be a factor that leads women to marital reconciliation, despite the fact that this may not be the preferred option. Seventeen of the women talked about feelings of low self-esteem. Although it was identified as the most important concern by only two women, another 11 listed it as their second or third most pressing problem. Several of the women interviewed described their self-esteem as so low that they had contemplated suicide:

- I have a really bad thing with suicide. Sometimes everything gets overloaded and I go through a crisis with different men ... I used to be really self destructive to myself. I used to slash my knees and my wrists and suicide and usually injure myself really bad and figure that everything was my fault cause I couldn't do anything right ... I don't feel normal with all of these emotional problems that I've been having in the past, and I still have them occasionally. But I always wanted to know what normal is because when you're in a battering relationship from now, like when you look back, back then wasn't normal.

- Before I moved out here I was suicidal and since I've got out here that's just not there any more ... there's way too much to live for, there's just way too much to live for. It's the people that you meet ... people are so friendly and so willing to help. Like I said, it's just a different way of thinking I guess.

Such low self-esteem is a pervasive problem that will affect how women deal with every aspect of their lives.

Coping with Children's Reactions to the Separation: Even though women may resolve the normal emotional reaction to leaving a partner to live independently, if they have children they are likely to experience persistent problems with the continued presence of the ex-partner during visitations. In addition, the children will experience emotional reactions to their parents' separation and to any inconsistencies in their father's visitation. In Smillie's study (1991), several women who were successful in living independently in the community for over a year ultimately returned to their husbands. Two of the main reasons were to "give their children a father" and the stresses of single parenting.

Eleven of the women in our study described concerns about their children. Two indicated it was their greatest worry; five ranked it second or third in importance. Four of the women who were interviewed by the author described pressure to reconcile with their partners, either because of their children's reaction to the separation or because the partner exerted pressure through the children.

- I was tempted [to reunite] ... I really was, by him just hanging in there ... he has visitation and I have full custody of [three-year-old daughter]. *Does he come and visit?* He doesn't come in the house ... he came about a week and a half ago and took my daughter up to his place for about a week. But he hasn't really paid any child support or anything like that. But he does visit her and J's at the age where she thinks that daddy's really important, and "I love my daddy."

- Like, I could have handled him, but I couldn't handle the kids. I couldn't handle him going through the kids and the kids putting the same amount of pressure on me. I was fighting too then. And he had ... *He had visitation rights?* Yeah, I gave him just free visitation rights, I didn't stop him from at any time ... I could have, but then I would have paid for it in the end through the boys. Because "Well, mom won't let dad come see me now." That was the type of ammunition he used. And it has eased off now, he's been back working and things have been calmer.

- Does he [their dad] visit regularly? Well, it depends. Like for a while there, I had lots of dates written down saying he'd pick them up Saturday. But Friday night he'd be seen in the bar. So Saturday he's supposed to pick them up at 10 o'clock, but yet he wouldn't get ahold of our third party contact and he wouldn't show up at all to pick them up, let alone phone. But Saturday night he'd be seen in the bar again. And he would do this so finally I just started not letting him see them. And then now, he informed me after this week that he doesn't want to see them anymore.

Finances and Upgrading or Job Training: Of the seven women who disclosed their incomes, all were on social assistance with payments ranging from $400 to $1,000 per month, depending on their circumstances and the number of children. Most received $800 in assistance payments. Although 15 women identified finances as problematic, it was not the most critical issue for any. Since all of the women were already on social assistance, financial concerns may have been less pressing than some of the other issues they were facing. Rather, for several women the issue was learning how to cope on such a reduced income:

> Living on Social Services is not easy. For one thing, a lot of people they don't have phones and they don't have vehicles and once they're out there, they're out there, but they don't have the telephone or the car. So where's their communication—they can't get through.

Most of the women hoped to upgrade their schooling or to receive vocational training so that they need not remain on social assistance. As mentioned earlier, holding a job has been suggested as a key component in women being able to maintain an independent life (Wilson et al., 1989). Of the seven women interviewed, four described the need to decide about applying for vocational upgrading or training programs or for employment.

> I got a part-time job which is new, I just started ... I didn't know what a resume was ... I've been nothing but a housewife and what kind of experience have you got there?

> Well, it's not something that people would write down sometimes. I wouldn't have written it down.

Housing: Finding a place to live and settling into a new residence is obviously a first priority for women who wish to establish independent lives. Helping a woman to find accommodation is usually one of the tasks undertaken while she resides in an emergency shelter. Once accommodation is secured, many women have to begin from scratch to furnish their dwellings, as well as acquiring clothes and other basic household necessities. If a woman is unable to afford accommodation she may return to the previous relationship out of economic desperation (DeKeseredy & Hinch, 1991).

One study of homeless women (Breton & Bunston, 1992) found that one-third had previously been physically assaulted by a male partner, suggesting that women who have been physically abused by their partners are at a reasonably high risk of becoming homeless. Of the 18 women in the current study, half raised housing as a concern, although it was not the central issue for any.

CONCLUSIONS. Some people contend that the substance and conclusions of a research report belong to the author, and maintain that interpretive research must begin and end with the writer, which is you, taking responsibility for the research study. This does not preclude a final member check to review the findings with your research participants, which shows a high degree of consideration for those who made your study possible. If your participants disagree with your conclusions, this information is worth reporting and analyzing, but there is a point in the process where your study becomes more than simply reporting what was said. At this point, you, and you alone, must accept responsibility for the data analysis.

The conclusion is a discussion of the significance of your findings for your readers. Your audience wants to hear *your* opinion of the relevance of *your* findings. As an example, the readers may consist of social work practitioners dealing with related concerns. If your findings challenge existing professional wisdom and suggest a reconsideration of current practices, readers will want you to identify how these practices could be affected. As well, a discussion of the program or policy implications of your findings may be useful for an audience that includes social work administrators.

When making assertions in the conclusions section of your report, you must attempt to strike a delicate balance. Qualitative research studies are not designed to be statistically generalizable, but they should be relevant to your readers. Since your study has met rigorous qualitative standards, your conclusions should be written in a confident manner. For example, journal editors want the articles in their journals to be compelling for their readers.

Qualitative research studies often have, as one of their major objectives, the exploration of a subject that has not been well conceptualized. In the discussion section of your report, it is important to help frame new questions and to suggest new hypotheses that may be studied further. The discussion of important topics for further study is particularly valuable for others who are just beginning the inquiry process. Let us continue with our example, and how we presented our summary and conclusions:

A variety of issues were seen as critical by women making the transition to a life independent from their assaultive partners. The areas they identified are congruent with previous research findings on the experience of women after they leave abusive relationships. Interestingly, the needs of the women in our study focused less on basic needs, many of which they had previously met through the shelter, and centered more on dealing with their ex-partners, their children, and their own feelings of low self-esteem.

The concerns indicate that women trying to live independently may experience serious difficulties, especially if the previous partner is still applying pressure to reconcile or to obtain custody of the children. Issues of low self-esteem were similarly striking in the extent to which women felt incapable of success, from simple chores such as phoning an office for information to more obviously anxiety-producing situations such as going to court. For many women it was the number of new situations to which they had to react that created feelings of discomfort. Several of the women had never had to manage a household on their own before.

The serious nature of the concerns described in our study suggests that women are in need of continued support after they have left an assaultive relationship. While many women remarked that they found the counseling they received while in the emergency shelter vital to their making a decision to leave, they also commented on how difficult it was to be on their own and how strong the pull was to return to the former relationship. Continued support and information pertaining to dealing with an ex-partner, children, the legal system, and social assistance, and to making a decision about upgrading education or employment, were high priorities. Also striking was the fact that, for many of the women, the problems continued for at least a year, contrary to the expectation of shelter staff that support for three to six months would be sufficient to alleviate most distress. Considering the multiple changes involved in constructing a new household and dealing with the loss of a partner, it should not be considered unusual that these women need time to adjust to these new circumstances.

Such support can be offered through follow-up programs that are being developed as part of the continuum of services in many emergency shelters. Most follow-up programs have one or two full-time workers who are housed within the emergency shelter but visit clients in their homes. Follow-up workers must be able to respond to the diverse needs expressed by each woman, in respect to what kind of support and services she needs to help her establish herself independently and safely from her partner. The issues range from assistance with basic needs such as information about nutrition, household tasks, and budgeting, to more complex concerns such as help with the legal system or exploring possibilities for further training or employment.

A follow-up worker is, thus, expected to respond flexibly depending on the expressed concerns of the program participant. The worker may be an educator, providing information on issues from wife assault to opportunities in the community for vocational upgrading or leisure. She may act as an advocate with legal representatives, child welfare workers, or social assistance personnel. During weekly visits, the worker provides support and one-on-one counseling on issues of self-esteem, dealing with concerns about the ex-partner, or coping with the children's reactions to the separation. In many ways the worker functions as a case manager, in that he or she will, in all probability, be the only worker in the community knowledgeable about the range of services each woman receives or might benefit from in the future.

The need for such follow-up services may seem obvious to those who have talked with previous shelter residents. However, in these times of economic restraint it has been difficult to convince funders of this, despite the fact that the programs are relatively inexpensive, especially when compared to second-stage shelters. While emergency shelter services are critical, it is also time to extend adequate supports to a woman who wishes to develop an independent life after she leaves the shelter.

REFERENCES. Finally, you are expected to include a list of references that will allow the reader to locate the materials you used for documentation in the above five sections. These are an important resource for the reader, so attention needs to be paid to the accuracy of the citations. The most commonly used style manual for references, as well as overall style, is published by the American Psychological Association (1994), but some journals prefer the Chicago style (University of Chicago Press, 1982). Most journals will review a manuscript using any standard manual style and ask for revisions if the article is accepted for publication. In our study we used the APA style; the references are correctly presented as follows:

Aguirre, B. (1985). Why do they return? Abused wives in shelters. *Social Work, 30,* 350-354.

Barnsley, J., Jacobson, H., McIntosh, J., & Wintemute, M.J. (1980). *A review of Monroe House: Second stage housing for battered women.* Vancouver: Women's Research Center.

Beaudry, M. (1985). *Battered women.* Montreal: Black Rose Books.

Bidgood, B., Tutty, L., & Rothery, M. (1991). *An evaluation of the Coordinated Family Violence Treatment Program of the Waterloo Region of Ontario.* Waterloo, ON: Center for Social Welfare Studies, Wilfrid Laurier University.

Bowker, L. (1983). *Beating wife-beating.* Lexington, MA: Lexington Books.

Bowker, L. (1984). Coping with wife abuse: Personal and social networks. In A. Roberts (Ed.), *Battered women and their families: Intervention strategies and treatment programs* (pp. 56-90). New York: Springer.

Breton, M., & Bunston, T. (1992). Physical and sexual violence in the lives of homeless women. *Canadian Journal of Community Mental Health, 11,* 29-44.

Brinkerhoff, M., & Lupri, E. (1988). Interspousal violence. *Canadian Journal of Sociology, 13,* 407-434.

Cannon, J., & Sparks, J. (1989). Shelters—An alternative to violence: A psychosocial case study. *Journal of Community Psychology, 17,* 203-213.

Carlson, B. (1977). Battered women and their assailants. *Social Work, 22,* 455-460.

DeKeseredy, W., & Hinch, R. (1991). *Woman abuse: Sociological perspectives.* Toronto: Thompson.

Ellis, D. (1992). Woman abuse among separated and divorced women: The relevance of social support. In E. Viano (Ed.), *Intimate violence: Interdisciplinary perspectives* (pp. 177-189). Washington, DC: Hemisphere Publishing.

Fantuzzo, J., & Lindquist, C. (1989). The effects of observing conjugal violence on children: A review and analysis of research methodology. *Journal of Family Violence, 4,* 77-94.

Follingstad, D., Rutledge, L., Berg, B., Hause, E., & Polek, D. (1990). The role of emotional abuse in physically abusive relationships. *Journal of Family Violence, 5,* 107-120.

Fusco, L. (1989). Integrating systems: Police, courts, and assaulted women. In B. Pressman, G. Cameron, & M. Rothery (Eds.), *Intervening with assaulted women: Current research, theory, and practice* (pp. 125-135). Hillsdale, NJ: Erlbaum.

Gelles, R. (1976). Abused wives: Why do they stay? *Journal of Marriage and the Family, 27,* 659-668.

Giles-Sims, J. (1983). *Wife-battering: A systems theory approach.* New York: Guilford Press.

Gilman, S. (1988). A history of the sheltering movement for battered women in Canada. *Canadian Journal of Community Mental Health, 7,* 9-21.

Glaser, B., & Strauss, A. (1967). *The discovery of grounded theory: Strategies for qualitative research.* New York: Aldine de Gruyter.

Gondolf, E., & Fisher, E. (1988). *Battered women as survivors: An alternative to treating learned helplessness.* Lexington, MA: Lexington Books.

Greaves, L., Heapy, N., & Wylie, A. (1988). Advocacy services: Reassessing the profile and needs of battered women. *Canadian Journal of Community Mental Health, 7,* 39-51.

Hilberman, E., & Munson, K. (1978). Sixty battered women. *Victimology, 2,* 460-470.

Hotaling, G., & Sugarman, D. (1990). A risk marker analysis of assaulted wives. *Journal of Family Violence, 5,* 1-13.

Hughes, H. (1988). Psychological and behavioral correlates of family violence in child witnesses and victims. *American Journal of Orthopsychiatry, 58,* 77-90.

Jaffe, P., Wolfe, D., & Wilson, S. (1990). *Children of battered women.* Newbury Park, CA: Sage.

Johnson, I., Crowley, J., & Sigler, R. (1992). Agency response to domestic violence: Services provided to battered women. In E. Viano (Ed.), *Intimate violence: Interdisciplinary perspectives* (pp. 44-51). Washington, DC: Hemisphere Publishing.

MacLeod, L. (1987). *Battered but not beaten: Preventing wife battering in Canada.* Ottawa: Canadian Advisory Council on the Status of Women.

Mardoyan, J. (1985). *Personality characteristics of battered women: The examination of self-concept, locus of control, and irrationality.* Ann Arbor, MI: University Microfilms International.

McDonald, P.L. (1989). Transition houses and the problem of family violence. In B. Pressman, G. Cameron, & M. Rothery (Eds.), *Intervening with assaulted women: Current research, theory, and practice* (pp. 111-123). Hillsdale, NJ: Erlbaum.

McDonald, P.L., Chisholm, W., Peressini, T., & Smillie, T. (1986). *A review of a second stage shelter for battered women and their children* (Project No. 4558-32-2). Ottawa: National Welfare Grants Directorate, Health and Welfare Canada.

Miller Cragg, S., & Rothery, M. (1991). Police officers' responses to assaults against women. *Canadian Journal of Community Mental Health, 10*, 93-102.

Moore, D. (Ed.). (1979). *Battered women.* Newbury Park, CA: Sage.

Moore, T., Peplar, D., Mae, R., & Kates, M. (1989). Effects of family violence on children: New directions for research and intervention. In B. Pressman, G. Cameron, & M. Rothery (Eds.), *Intervening with assaulted women: Current research, theory, and practice* (pp. 93-110). Hillsdale, NJ: Lawrence Erlbaum.

Okun, L. (1988). Termination or resumption of cohabitation in woman-battering relationships: A statistical study. In G. Hotaling, D. Finkelhor, J. Kirkpatrick, & M. Straus (Eds.), *Coping with family violence: Research and policy perspectives* (pp. 235-243). Newbury Park, CA: Sage.

Pressman, B. (1989). Treatment of wife-abuse: The case for feminist therapy. In B. Pressman, G. Cameron, & M. Rothery (Eds.), *Intervening with assaulted women: Current theory, research, and practice* (pp. 21-45). Hillsdale, NJ: Lawrence Erlbaum.

Russell, M. (1990). Second stage shelters: A consumer's report. *Canada's Mental Health, 38*, 24-27.

Russell, M., Forcier, C., & Charles, M. (1987). *Safe Choice: Client satisfaction survey.* Vancouver: Act II.

Russell, M., Phillips, N., Lipov, E., & Sanders, C. (1989). Assaultive husbands and their wives: A Canadian-American comparison. *The Social Worker, 57*, 181-185.

Sample Survey and Data Bank Unit. (1984). *Breaking silence: Descriptive report of a follow-up study of abused women.* Regina: University of Regina.

Schutte, N., Bouleige, L., & Malouf, J. (1986). Returning to a partner after leaving a crisis shelter: A decision faced by battered women. *Journal of Social Behavior and Personality, 1*, 295-298.

Scyner, L., & McGregor, N. (1988). Women in second stage housing: What happens after the crisis. *Canadian Journal of Community Mental Health, 7*, 129-135.

Smillie, T. (1991). *Why women return to battering relationships.* Unpublished MSW project, University of Calgary, Calgary.

Smith, M. (1987). The incidence and prevalence of woman abuse in Toronto. *Violence and Victims, 1*, 173-187.

Snyder, D., & Scheer, N. (1981). Predicting disposition following brief residence at a shelter for battered women. *American Journal of Community Psychology, 9*, 559-566.

Tutty, L., Bidgood, B., & Rothery, M. (1993). An evaluation of support groups for assaulted women. *Journal of Family Violence, 8*, 325-343.

Walker, L. (1978). Battered women and learned helplessness. *Victimology, 2*, 525-534.

Wetzel, L., & Ross, M. (1983). Psychological and social ramifications of battering: Observations leading to a counseling methodology for victims of domestic violence. *Personnel and Guidance Journal, 61*, 423-428.

Wilson, M., Baglioni, A., & Downing, D. (1989). Analyzing factors influencing readmission to a battered women's shelter. *Journal of Family Violence, 4*, 275-284.

Step 3: Sending Your Manuscript to a Journal

Dissemination of your findings is usually a sequential process starting with presentations to your fellow students in classes and colleagues at professional meetings and ending with publications in journals or books. As we mentioned earlier, qualitative research studies are also uniquely suited to presentation in nonprint formats, such as videotapes, photographs, and audiotapes. These offer a powerful opportunity to capture the nuances of people's lives without having to reduce their experience to words. Nevertheless, most people who do qualitative research would like to see the results from their studies in print.

Task 3a: Choosing a Journal

You need to attend to the mechanics of publishing in addition to writing a quality report. The first task is to finalize the choice of journal. Each journal has a preference for particular kinds of reports. It makes sense to survey the field of possible journals and select one that prefers to publish findings on the subject of your research study. Journals often specialize in client focus (e.g., children) and sometimes practice method (e.g., group work). Thus, a study that focuses on children's reactions to group treatment will have a more positive response from a journal that specializes in this age group and/or this practice approach. Some journals specialize specifically in disseminating qualitative research findings.

Most journals offer a brief description of their publishing priorities at the beginning (or end) of each issue. You should make a list of potential choices and investigate the reputation of each journal. There are a number of questions to consider. What is the rejection rate? How many issues does it publish a year? Does it specialize in the topic you want to discuss? Who subscribes to the journal? How large is its readership? Is it refereed? A useful resource for gaining a comprehensive overview of many journals is *An Author's Guide to Social Work Journals* by Henry Mendelsohn (1992).

Task 3b: Preparing Your Report for Submission

As part of a final polishing process, you will want to review your final report for changes that would improve its chances of acceptance by a journal. For example, authors are expected to avoid language that may imply sexual, ethnic, or other kinds of stereotyping or bias. Gender neutrality is the norm unless a specific person (or group of people) is being discussed.

If the readership of the journal is known (e.g., social work practitioners), your narrative should acknowledge this audience. As an example, instead of discussing how your findings would be of interest to some abstract audience, it is better to discuss why social work practitioners specifically could use your findings.

Many journals have a specific format and length requirement that should be met. These are generally spelled out at the beginning (or the end) of each issue. A growing number of journals also request a copy of the manuscript on computer disk and in a popular word-processing language such as *WordPerfect* or *Word*.

Task 3c: Paying Attention to Ethical Issues

All journals assume that you have obtained prior consent to disclose the information included in your manuscript. This is particularly important in qualitative studies because rich description and direct quotes make it difficult to extend assurances of complete confidentiality and anonymity even when real names are withheld within the report. Consequently, your research participant's consent form must clearly state that you intend to publish your findings.

Qualitative research studies often produce enough information for more than one article, but identical submissions to different journals is considered unethical and may violate copyright laws. If applicable, you need to state that the manuscript you submitted for possible publication is part of a larger study that has been published elsewhere. Each new article is expected to contribute new information even if it is derived from the same initial study.

Task 3d: Taking Care of Final Details

Prior to mailing your report to a journal for possible publication, it is useful to go through a checklist of mundane concerns that include: (1) a brief cover letter to the editor, (2) a stamped, self-addressed postcard if receipt of your manuscript is to be confirmed, (3) a careful review of your manuscript to be sure it is prepared as instructed by the journal (e.g., cover page with appropriate identification, no identifiers on other pages, a running heading on each page, camera-ready charts or graphs), and (4) the correct number of copies (usually three to six) along with an original. Meeting the needs of the journal editor will facilitate the review process.

Task 3e: Submitting Your Report

The review process varies from journal to journal. One of the major distinctions is whether the journal uses a refereed-review process. This review process is characterized by peer reviewing of all manuscripts submitted for publication. Peer reviewers are selected by the editor because they are supposed to have expertise in the substantive areas covered by the journal. Usually two or three reviewers will review the submission based on criteria deemed important by the journal. Typical criteria are whether your manuscript makes a significant contribution to the social work knowledge base, whether it is methodologically correct, whether it is relevant to the readership of the journal, and whether it is well written. Each submission is evaluated by these criteria, with one of four outcomes then recommended: (1) publish without revision, (2) publish with minor revisions, (3) rewrite and resubmit, or (4) reject outright.

Task 3f: Reediting Your Report

A manuscript that is accepted for publication without revision will still need to be revised based on the recommendations of the journal's editorial staff. Their advice is most helpful, to say the least. They are, after all, quite familiar with the readers of that particular journal. On the other hand, the final product must be acceptable to you, and the journal's editor recognizes this. If acceptance of your report is contingent upon revisions, the changes you need to make are more or less specified by the reviewers. Your modifications should be made competently and quickly and the report resubmitted.

If the response from the editor is to rewrite and resubmit your manuscript, this means there is genuine interest in the report's content but major changes are needed. There will be feedback on the nature of the deficiencies, and you should take this seriously. Since interest has already been expressed in your study, you will usually want to make the modifications suggested, but sometimes the requested changes are inappropriate or may be unacceptable to you. In either case, a letter to the editor with an explanation of your concerns may produce a modified set of expectations. Otherwise, there are other journals that may be less demanding.

Task 3g: Coping with Rejection

Your manuscript may be rejected outright. In reality, this happens quite often. It does not mean that your report is unpublishable. There are many reasons why it may not have been favorably reviewed. As an example, journals frequently receive manuscripts on similar subjects. If your timing is a bit off, the journal's editor may reject your submission simply because he or she does not want to publish two articles on the same subject. More often, the reviewers who evaluated your report will have advised that your manuscript be rejected. Usually, reviewers' comments will be given to you in an effort to provide constructive feedback. Often these comments will furnish you with valuable insight into how to improve your manuscript for future submissions.

You may be inclined to take the rejection as a terminal event. This is a big mistake. You should make the changes that are relatively easy and prepare your manuscript for submission to another journal. A complete rewrite of a report is seldom necessary. Simply review the list of potential journals you previously prepared. There should be equally good prospects on the list. Since your manuscript represents a major investment in time and energy, a single rejection does not warrant abandoning it. After revising and checking to be sure your report specifically addresses the priorities of the new journal, you should resubmit your revised manuscript to this new journal.

Task 3h: Understanding Why Your Report May Get Rejected

Understanding the perspective of the reviewers can help to avoid some major pitfalls. Richard Daft (1985) offers useful insight into why manuscripts may be rejected. His comments are based on an analysis of 111 manuscript reviews for two management-oriented journals, *Administrative Science Quarterly* and *Academy of Management Journal*. These journals accept both quantitative and qualitative research findings. He identified the major problem with the manuscripts as lack of theory. Fully half of the rejected papers had little or no theory to explain the data. He goes on to note:

> The single biggest problem I found with qualitative research was lack of theory, which surprised me because the purpose of qualitative research is to build theory. The problem was that the researchers did not define concepts or create new theory ... The research goal is to end up with a well defined set of constructs and a model that can be used to guide future research.

Another common problem for qualitatively-based reports involved basic design issues. Qualitative studies are useful in exploratory, theory-building research endeavors. A design problem occurs when the wrong research approach is used to study a particular problem area. For example, when there is extensive research literature on which to formulate explicit hypotheses, a loose, open-ended qualitative approach may seem too impressionistic and vague to contribute new knowledge to a well-defined topic. Of course, if your purpose is to generate new theory, the qualitative research approach may still be applicable. The point is, you must make a case for the appropriateness of your research approach. It may not be obvious to reviewers of the manuscript.

Task 3i: Developing Important Skills Through Rewriting

You should develop three skills when doing a qualitative research study: (1) theory skills, (2) design skills, and (3) writing skills. Deficiencies in all of these areas can be overcome through the rewriting process. Most, if not all, manuscripts go through numerous revisions before they are published. You should allow enough time to set your work aside for a short period. This can often reveal major gaps in the material. Next, ask fellow students and colleagues to review your report with attention to theory, research design, and writing style. There is a point where it becomes difficult to critically review your own work. A colleague's comments can provide a fresh viewpoint at a time when your thinking has become stagnant.

SUMMARY

Getting your study published involves thinking strategically. You need to identify the correct journal and prepare a report that will be acceptable to the reviewers of that publication. This takes tenacity and patience. From first submission to seeing your work in print can take literally years. Most journals will provide reviewer feedback within two months, but some are more efficient in their reviewing and printing process than others. In fairness to the journals, you need to facilitate the process by quick responses to requests for revisions. Although the process may sometimes be tedious, seeing your work in print is very gratifying. Planning for the dissemination of your research study should not be an afterthought. Identification of target audiences, possible formats, and potential outlets are among the first considerations in designing any research study. Reporting qualitative findings requires a special set of design, analytic, and interpretive skills. You need to establish that the criteria for trustworthiness have been met.

Studies using qualitative methodology must have dissemination as a goal from the outset if your valuable insights into social work practice are to be acknowledged. By making dissemination part of your overall research plan, you will greatly increase the likelihood that your results will be positively received.

REFERENCES AND FURTHER READINGS

American Psychological Association. (1994). *Publication manual of the American Psychological Association* (4th ed.). Hyattsville, MD: Author.

Becker, H. (1986). *Writing for social scientists.* Chicago: University of Chicago Press.

Beebe, L. (Ed.). (1992). *Professional writing for the human services.* Washington, DC: NASW Press.

Berg, B.L. (1989). *Qualitative research methods for the social sciences.* Needham Heights, MA: Allyn & Bacon.

Bogdan, R.C., & Biklen, S.K. (1982). *Qualitative research for education.* Needham Heights, MA: Allyn & Bacon.

Braxton, L.A., Davis, C.A., Loomis, K.H., Pazdan, S.D. & Winchester, N.A. (1992). NASW quick guide to mechanics. In L. Beebe (Ed.). *Professional writing for the human services* (pp. 223-258). Washington, DC: NASW Press.

Cheniz, C., & Swanson, J. (1986). *From practice to grounded theory.* Menlo Park, CA: Addison-Wesley.

Campbell, D., & Stanley, J. (1963). *Experimental and quasi-experimental designs for research.* Chicago: Rand McNally.

Daft, R.L. (1985). Why I recommended that your manuscript be rejected and what you can do about it. In L.L. Cummings & P.J. Frost (Eds.), *Publishing in the organizational sciences* (pp. 35-62). Homewood, IL: Irwin.

Ely, M., Anzul, M., Friedman, T., Garner, D., & McCormack-Steinmetz, A. (1991). *Doing qualitative research: Circles within circles.* New York: Falmer Press.

Erlandson, D., Harris, E., Skipper, B., & Allen, S. (1993). *Doing naturalistic inquiry: A guide to methods.* Newbury Park, CA: Sage.

Glaser, B.G., & Strauss, A.L. (1967). *The discovery of grounded theory.* Chicago: Aldine.

Glesene, C., & Peshkin, A. (1992). *Becoming qualitative researchers: An introduction.* White Plains, NY: Longman.

Goldstein, H. (1993). The qualitative research report. In L. Beebe (Ed.), *Professional writing for the human services* (pp. 87-103). Washington, DC: NASW Press.

Guba, E.G. (1981). Criteria for assessing the trustworthiness of naturalistic inquiries. *Educational Communication and Technology Journal, 29,* 75-91.

Liebow, E. (1967). *Tally's corner.* Boston: Little, Brown and Company.

Lincoln, Y., & Guba, E.G. (1985). *Naturalist inquiry.* Newbury Park, CA: Sage.

Marshall, C., & Rossman, G. (1989). *Designing qualitative research.* Newbury Park, CA: Sage.

Mendelsohn, H.N. (1992). *An author's guide to social work journals* (3rd ed.). Washington, DC: NASW Press.

Miles, M.B., & Huberman, A.M. (1994). *Qualitative data analysis: An expanded source book* (2nd ed.). Newbury Park, CA: Sage.

Richardson, L. (1990). *Writing strategies: Reaching diverse audiences.* Newbury Park, CA: Sage.

Richardson, L. (1994). Writing: A method of inquiry. In N.K. Denzin & Y. Lincoln (Eds.), *Handbook of qualitative research* (pp. 516-529). Newbury Park, CA: Sage.

Van Maanen, J. (1988). *Tales of the field: On writing ethnography.* Chicago: University of Chicago Press.

Wolcott, H. (1990). *Writing up qualitative research.* Newbury Park, CA: Sage.

Wolcott, H. (1994). *Transforming qualitative data: Description analysis and interpretation.* Newbury Park, CA: Sage.

Part Two

Research Examples

Study A: Females Who Sexually Abuse Children   **152**
   Laurie Robinson, Nick Coady, & Leslie M. Tutty

Study B: Boards of Directors of Social Service Agencies   **174**
   David Este

Study C: A Child Welfare Tragedy   **208**
   Barbara Thomlison, Ray J. Thomlison, & Lesa Wolfe

Laurie Robinson
Nick Coady
Leslie M. Tutty

Research Study A

REVIEW OF THE LITERATURE

The Characteristics of Female Perpetrators / The Treatment of Female Perpetrators

DATA COLLECTION

Choosing the Research Participants / The Interview Format / Ethical Considerations / The Research Participants / Data Collection Recording / Method / Deciding When to Stop Data Collection

DATA ANALYSIS

Efforts to Address Credibility and Dependability

INTERPRETATION OF RESULTS

Major Theme 1: Understanding the Client / Major Theme 2: Understanding the Treatment Process / Major Theme 3: Personal/Professional Experience of Clinicians

SUMMARY AND CONCLUSIONS

Directions for Future Research / Implications for Clinical Practice

Females Who Sexually Abuse Children

<hr>

CHILD SEXUAL ABUSE is a major problem in today's society. One research study suggests that 27 percent of all women and 16 percent of all men have been victimized as children (Finkelhor, Hotaling, Lewis, & Smith, 1990). Because the majority of sexual abuse is committed by males against females, most of the research studies have focused on the male as perpetrator and the female as victim (Finkelhor et al., 1990). The extent to which children are abused by female perpetrators has received relatively little attention. Finkelhor and Russell (1984) are credited with providing the best estimate of the prevalence of the problem to date, concluding that sexual abuse perpetrated by a female occurs in about 5 percent of the abuse of girls and about 20 percent of abuse of boys.

Although the number of female sexual abusers is far less than the number of male abusers, it is clear that female perpetration is "not so rare as was once believed" (Wakefield & Underwager, 1991, p. 56). This issue has been brought to the fore by recent clinical evidence that more female clients are disclosing

EDITORS' NOTE

This study is included not only because it is a novel topic that should be of interest to social work practitioners, but also because of the careful manner in which the authors addressed methodological issues such as credibility, dependability, and ethics. In addition, the authors present a clearly articulated framework in their categorization scheme.

sexually abusive behavior (Knopp & Lakey, 1987; Lepine, 1990; Russell, 1984). In their nationwide survey of American sex-offender treatment providers, Knopp, Rosenberg, and Stevenson (1986, cited in Knopp & Lakey, 1987) were surprised to find that of 660 agencies surveyed, 392 reported they were treating some female sex offenders. In a later study, Knopp and Lakey (1987) found that 44 treatment providers reported working with a total of 476 female sexual abusers.

With the increased recognition that female perpetration of child sexual abuse is a reality, clinicians are faced with numerous questions concerning how to identify, assess, and treat these women clients. Virtually all of the current treatment approaches for sex offenders were designed for male perpetrators (Groth, 1982; Hollin & Howells, 1991), and it seems unwise to assume they will be as appropriate for female perpetrators (Grayson, 1989; Mathews, 1987).

This study's general research problem area is to develop an understanding of female perpetrators and how clinicians can most helpfully respond.

REVIEW OF THE LITERATURE

Although some qualitative research proponents argue against a preparatory review of the literature, others suggest that the benefits of conducting a review before data collection begins outweigh any possible harmful effects (Glesne & Peshkin, 1992; Patton, 1990). Agreeing with the latter, we completed an initial review of the literature on female perpetrators prior to designing and implementing the study.

First, as reported in the previous section, the literature review was used to verify that female perpetration of child sexual abuse was recognized as a legitimate problem area for social work research and that the current study had the potential to contribute to the social work profession's knowledge base on sexual abuse.

In addition, further literature research was deemed advisable to explore the characteristics of female perpetrators and possible useful treatment modalities that would be of interest to social workers.

The Characteristics of Female Perpetrators

Several authors have published casework descriptions of either the victims of female perpetrators (Goodwin & DiVasto, 1979, 1989; Krug, 1989; Margolis, 1984; Shengold, 1980; Wahl, 1960) or the female perpetrators themselves (Chasnoff et al., 1986; Lukianowicz, 1972; Wakefield, Rogers, & Underwager, 1990). The only research on the characteristics of female perpetrators was found in several small-scale descriptive projects (Faller, 1987; Finkelhor, Williams, & Burns, 1988; Mathews, Matthews, & Speltz, 1989; McCarty, 1986; O'Conner, 1987; Travin, Cullen, & Protter, 1990). A review of this literature yielded four common themes.

The first theme is that most female perpetrators were themselves sexually abused as children. This fact is not, in itself, surprising. A number of studies on male perpetrators have also identified a strong connection between victimization and perpetration (Groth, 1979). What is significant in the case of women, however, is that the severity of victimization in childhood may be a crucial factor in predisposing them to perpetrate against others (Johnson, 1989).

With reference to her sample, Johnson noted that "the sexual abuse which these children sustained was of the most serious kind, in that the frequency was high, the degree of relationship between the perpetrators was very close, [and] most of the abuse occurred over an extended period of time" (p. 581). Similarly, Mathews et al. (1989) found that one group of female perpetrators, identified as "intergenerationally predisposed," were victims of severe sexual abuse in childhood. These authors suggest that this type is the most common female perpetrator.

Second, few of the women offenders described in these studies were considered to suffer from a serious mental illness or developmental handicap. It was once thought that any women who would commit an act of paedophilia had to be crazy; however, several authors (Faller, 1987; Finkelhor & Russell, 1984) have debunked this myth.

The third major theme is that a male co-offender was present in a large number of cases of sexual abuse perpetrated by women (Faller, 1987; Finkelhor et al., 1988; Mathews et al., 1989; McCarty, 1986; O'Connor, 1987). This dynamic is rarely seen with male offenders. Faller (1987) and Mathews et al. (1989, 1990, 1991) clarified that a significant proportion of the co-offending women did not initiate the abuse but were either forced or persuaded to participate by their male partners. Consequently, Mathews et al. (1989) renamed what McCarty (1986) had previously referred to as the "co-offending" female perpetrator, to the "male-coerced" female perpetrator.

Fourth, several authors hypothesized that female perpetrators are, by means of their abusive behavior, acting out the trauma of their own severe sexual victimization (Johnson, 1989; Mathews et al., 1989; Travin et al., 1990). According to Johnson (1989), the sexual abuse perpetrated by the young girls in her study appeared to be a "compulsive reenactment of previously anxiety-producing experiences" (*p.* 582). The abuse was often interpreted as an attempt by these children to work out the distressing events of their recent past.

The Treatment of Female Perpetrators

Only a limited number of literature sources were helpful in developing a preliminary understanding of the treatment needs of the adult female perpetrator. These sources include published descriptions of clinical casework (Lepine, 1990), unpublished papers distributed by the Safer Society Program of Vermont (a clearinghouse of female child sexual abuse research), and one paper describing adolescent offenders (Scavo, 1989). While no research studies were discovered that addressed the clinical issues with this population, the review of the treatment literature yielded several major themes.

First, women who have perpetrated child sexual abuse tend to come for help in two ways. One group enters treatment as identified perpetrators, but another group discloses perpetration during treatment for their own sexual victimization.

Second, a strong, positive therapeutic relationship is considered to be crucial when working with female perpetrators (Mathews et al., 1989; Scavo, 1989). It may be a significant challenge for the clinician to move beyond an "initial repugnance for their client's behavior and to engage the shattered person" (Mathews et al., 1989, *p.* 66). However, female perpetrators are thought to feel a deep sense of shame over their own childhood victimization in addition to the sexual abuse they perpetrated (Grayson, 1989). According to Mathews et al. (1989), it is the therapeutic relationship that enables the female perpetrator to move from a position of shame to one of change and identity development.

A third issue deals with how to address disclosures of perpetration. Lepine (1990) urges clinicians to respond to the offending behavior without hesitation, and to discuss perpetration in a matter-of-fact, non-judgmental manner. This approach is thought to help the client to talk more openly about her offending behavior. According to Scavo (1989), a trusting relationship may be established by such early discussion of the perpetration.

A fourth theme raises the question of how clinicians should balance the therapeutic issues of their clients' perpetration and their victimization. Scavo (1989) argues that although female perpetrators must receive treatment for sexual victimization, the seriousness of their sexual abuse offense must not be minimized. No matter how the woman's perpetrating behavior comes to the clinician's attention, the immediate concern is to address the offending behavior and to ensure the safety of any children at risk (Carey, cited in Grayson, 1989; Lepine, 1990). Once safety issues have been addressed, the focus of treatment can shift to the process of healing (Lepine, 1990).

In contrast, Larson and Maison (cited in Grayson, 1989) argue that, since early victimization in the life of the offender is an "underlying condition which set the stage for perpetration" (*p.* 11), the victim aspect of the female offender should be the primary concern in treatment. Most authors conclude, however, that survivor issues are inextricably enmeshed with perpetrator issues (Grayson, 1989; Lepine, 1990; Mathews et al., 1989; Scavo, 1989) and that helping the female sexual abuser to take responsibility for her offending behavior is an essential component of treatment.

In summary, although a few authors have identified important themes and made some useful suggestions to guide the treatment of female perpetrators, there are several areas of disagreement, and the discussion is clearly at an exploratory level. The scant number of studies provides further support for approaching the problem as a qualitative inquiry rather than from a more traditional quantitative perspective (Rothery, 1993).

Since little is known about treating female perpetrators, this study lends itself to a method of inquiry that focuses on a process of discovery rather than one of hypothesis testing. Qualitative research methods were thus judged to be the most appropriate means of documenting the views of clinicians who have worked with a female perpetrator.

DATA COLLECTION

Choosing the Research Participants

Rather than interview female clients who had perpetrated sexual abuse, we decided to interview the clinicians who were providing counseling for these women.

The rationale for collecting data from clinicians rather than from the female perpetrator herself was threefold:

- It was anticipated that it would be difficult to persuade female perpetrators to participate in the research study.

EDITORS' NOTE

The authors provide a strong rationale for their decisions both to interview clinicians rather than female perpetrators and to use a semi-standardized interview format. The study's focus on sexual abuse also necessitated careful attention to ethical considerations.

- In order to learn about treatment issues for this population, it made sense to interview the clinicians who provide such treatment.

- Because most of the clinicians had treated a number of women perpetrators, we could learn about their experiences with a large number of clients.

The clinicians to be interviewed were chosen based on the single requirement that they had experience working with at least one female perpetrator. Initially, telephone calls to treatment agencies, follow-up letters, and announcements were used to publicize the study and to contact clinicians. Then snowball sampling, the process of getting to know some respondents and having them introduce you to others who have the desired attributes (Taylor & Bogdan, 1984), was used to connect with other appropriate clinicians. A profile of the clinicians was compiled by asking each of them to fill out a short personal information questionnaire.

The Interview Format

The preparatory literature review informed the research design, leading us to choose the semi-structured interview format as the main data-gathering tool. Semi-standardized interviews are necessarily based on prior knowledge of the issue under investigation, are formulated in words familiar to the research participants, and reflect the researcher's attempt to approach the world from the informant's perspective (Berg, 1989).

The questions that were included in the semi-structured interview were:

- How are female perpetrators coming to the attention of clinicians?

- What are the characteristics of adult female survivors of child sexual abuse who have perpetrated child sexual abuse?

- What are the differences between female survivors who perpetrate child sexual abuse and those who do not?

- What are the important treatment issues for adult female survivors who have perpetrated child sexual abuse?

- How do clinicians experience working with adult female survivors of sexual abuse who have perpetrated child sexual abuse?

The first four questions reflect the central aim of the study, which was to examine the clinician's understanding and treatment of female perpetrators. The fifth question represents the secondary focus of the study: to briefly explore the personal and professional experiences of the clinicians.

A semi-standardized format provides some initial structure to the interview, yet allows the interviewer the freedom to probe well beyond the responses to the prepared questions (Berg, 1989). Thus, although the interview guide was used as a means of exploring specific issues, a certain degree of flexibility was maintained in order to give clinicians the opportunity to "shape the direction of the content."

The use of a questionnaire does not preempt the "open-ended" nature of the qualitative interview. Within each of the questions, the opportunity for exploratory, unstructured responses remains. As is expected with this type of data collection technique, both the wording and the sequence of the questions were adapted during the actual interviews (Patton, 1990). The questions were rarely asked verbatim, but rather were paraphrased in an open-ended manner.

Using the interview guide to ensure that certain topics were consistently covered was a sound methodological strategy (Patton, 1990) and increased the likelihood that the data were comparable (Lofland & Lofland, 1984). The later analysis involved identifying elements of the experience that were common to this particular group of clinicians.

Ethical Considerations

The important ethical issues that were addressed in the current study included ensuring:

- that treatment providers were aware of their obligation to report disclosures of perpetration that they might discuss in the research interviews;

- that the clinicians understood the voluntary nature of the study and their right to discontinue involvement in it;

- that clinicians' names would not be used in the study;

- that names of perpetrator clients would not be discussed in the interviews;

- that potential identifying information related to case examples would be eliminated or disguised in the written research report;

- that audiotapes would be stored in a secure place in the researcher's home and destroyed after completion of the research study.

At the beginning of the interview, each clinician was presented with an information package that included an introductory letter explaining the study, a consent form, and the clinicians' profile questionnaire. The ethical issues that were presented in the letter and consent form were discussed, and all forms were filled out and signed before the formal interview began.

The Research Participants

Of the nine clinicians interviewed, eight were female and one was male. This male-female ratio is considered to be representative of the professional community as a whole, since few male clinicians work with female survivors. In terms of professional affiliation, six of the interviewees were social workers and three were psychologists. Five worked in private practice, two worked in public nonprofit agencies, one worked in a family service agency, and one worked in both a public nonprofit agency and private practice.

The mean age of the clinicians was 40 years, with a range of 31 to 49. The average number of years of experience in the field of counseling was 14, with a range of 2 to 27 years of experience. Of significant interest was the fact that interviewees had worked with an average of 10 female perpetrators, with a range of 2 to 25. In total, the nine clinicians reported having worked with 91 female perpetrators.

Data Collection Recording Method

All nine of the clinicians agreed to audiotaping of the interviews. Each interview was held at the clinician's place of employment. One interviewee was interviewed over three separate sittings; the remaining eight clinicians were interviewed once only.

The interviews were set up as two-hour blocks with the first half hour set aside for introductions and reviewing and signing forms. Each of the single-occasion interviews lasted approximately one and one-half hours, while the interview that spanned three separate appointments was 2½ hours long.

A second phase of the literature review occurred during the interviewing process. The literature was used to explore a variety of areas as a means of helping the interviewer to understand the various themes that were emerging during the interviews.

For example, the literature on male perpetrators of child sexual abuse was utilized in order to better understand the clinicians' experience of the contrast between work with male and with female perpetrators. It should be noted, however, that some qualitative researchers do not use the professional literature until the end of their projects.

Deciding When to Stop Data Collection

There appear to be few rules governing the number of interviews to conduct in a qualitative research project; in the current study data collection was discontinued following the ninth interview. At this point, the observations and field notes indicated that no new insights were being presented (Taylor & Bogdan, 1984). Other factors that influenced the decision to stop after nine interviews were the realities of fixed resources and time limitations (Patton, 1990).

DATA ANALYSIS

According to Taylor and Bogdan (1984), the analysis of qualitative data is directed toward developing an in-depth understanding of the phenomenon being studied, and generally entails several distinct phases. The first phase of analysis is the process of ongoing discovery that occurs throughout the time the data is being collected, and often serves to shape the content of the semi-standardized interviews through the use of unscheduled probes. The second phase occurs after the data have been collected, and involves coding and sorting categories that emerge from the researcher's in-depth review of verbatim transcripts of the interviews (Taylor & Bogdan, 1984).

The overall approach to analysis of the data was content analysis (Berg, 1989) aimed at uncovering the common themes in clinicians' interview responses. Once begun, "open coding" (Berg, 1989) took several hours of careful examination of each transcript. Open coding is described by Berg as an "unrestricted" intensive review of the document "line by line" and "word by word" (*p.* 121). Analysis began by reading the entire transcript, making tentative interpretations in the margins, and coding the central ideas found throughout the data. The themes emerged as a result of the combined process of becoming intimate with the data, making logical associations with the interview questions, and considering what was learned during the initial review of the professional literature.

As the categories, major themes, and subthemes emerged, all were specifi-

---

EDITORS' NOTE

This study is notable for the attention to Phase Three issues. The authors carefully describe the coding process and present a clear rationale for the framework that emerged from the interviews. They also systematically address issues related to credibility and dependability.

cally defined and recorded in a "code book" (Glesne & Peshkin, 1992). The code book was then consistently utilized during subsequent analysis, and new categories were added as each additional interview yielded new insights. All of the coded interviews were entered into *The Ethnograph* (1988) computer program to aid in sorting transcript segments into their respective code categories.

Every category was then systematically reviewed. According to Taylor and Bogdan (1984), this phase of the research process involves refining the analysis and enables the researcher to "understand the data in the context in which they were collected" (*p.* 134). Consistent themes were noted as well as areas for further exploration.

The fact that no new categories or themes were identified after the sixth interview indicated that "saturation" (Berg, 1989, *p.* 118) had taken place. According to Berg, saturation is often a sign that intensive coding is complete and the next phase of the analysis can begin. That saturation occurred in the sixth interview confirmed the original decision to stop collecting data after the ninth interview, as no new insights were being presented (Taylor & Bogdan, 1984). After analysis was complete, the code book consisted of three major themes, seven subthemes, and thirty-seven categories.

Efforts to Address Credibility and Dependability

Three weeks after coding of the first interview was completed the transcript was recoded, with concentration on refining the code categories and reexamining the rationale for the fit between the data and the originally assigned codes. According to Krefting (1990), this type of code-recode procedure is an excellent means of increasing dependability. Although several segments needed to be more clearly defined in terms of start and stop delineations, few changes were made to the original code categories or their assignments. Eventually, all of the interviews were coded twice.

In addition, in an effort to address issues related to credibility (Krefting, 1990; Lincoln & Guba, 1985; Patton, 1990), the strategy called "triangulating analysts" was utilized (Patton, 1990). Triangulation is described by Lincoln and Guba as the use of "multiple and different" sources to verify (or confirm) outcomes. Another professional who was familiar with qualitative research methods was engaged to partially code the first interview using the code book. This strategy was intended to test the replicability of the original assignment of code categories to segments of data (Krefting, 1990).

Overall, the results of this triangulation procedure were very positive. Comparisons of the separately coded segments showed a high degree of consistency amongst the code assignments, and even the theoretical notes referred to similar coding dilemmas. As a result of this procedure, some codes were identified as repetitive and were eventually collapsed.

The third phase of the literature review took place during, and following, the analysis of the data. Relevant literature was explored as a means of informing the results of the study and providing a rationale for future exploration.

Journal notes were used to formulate a tentative plan for presenting the written results of the research study. Before the analysis could be considered complete, however, several issues needed clarifying with the clinicians. In a process similar to "member checking" (Krefting, 1990; Lincoln & Guba, 1985), the researcher met with six of the interviewees to present the raw results of the study, clarify issues, and confirm that they agreed with the framework for the results.

The three remaining clinicians, who could not attend the information session, were sent summaries of the results and asked to contact the researcher should they identify any inconsistencies or wish to add their ideas to the analysis. The clinicians supported the tentative findings, resulting in few changes to the framework.

INTERPRETATION OF THE RESULTS

The results of this research study represent the culmination of a lengthy process of working with the data and experimenting with a variety of possibilities for displaying the outcome of the inquiry. The decision to organize the results of the study into the current form grew out of a combined process of attending to facts grounded in the details of the data, and drawing on practice experience to situate these facts within what is called a "framework" for understanding and treating female perpetrators.

The development of the framework of results involved several phases of working with the data to identify relationships between themes and test the possibilities for organizing associated concepts into unifying categories. Over time, through a process of identifying how findings overlapped and through reorganization, the number of major themes, subthemes, and categories was reduced.

The result is a framework that consists of three major themes (MT; in CAPITAL letters), seven subthemes (ST; in *italics*), and thirty-seven categories (C; in regular typeface).

The first major theme contains issues of understanding and distinguishing the female perpetrator from other clients.

The second major theme consists of treatment issues that the clinicians addressed with female perpetrators.

The third major theme describes clinicians' personal and professional reaction to their client's disclosure of perpetration. A framework of results is presented below.

MT 1: UNDERSTANDING THE CLIENT

ST 1: *Differences between Survivors and Survivor-Perpetrators*
    C 1: Dissociation
    C 2: Self-destructive tendencies
    C 3: Motivation to get help
    C 4: The severity of the victim experience

ST 2: *Signs of Perpetration*
    C 5: "Stuckness"
    C 6: Suspicious child-rearing practices

ST 3: *Characteristics of Perpetration*
    C 7: Perpetration in the past
    C 8: "Unplanned and spontaneous"
    C 9: Asexual in nature

ST 4: *Reasons/Rationale for Perpetration: Unresolved Trauma*
    C 10: Replicating childhood abuse
    C 11: Taking back power
    C 12: A cry for help/the search for meaning
    C 13: Learned behavior
    C 14: An expression of rage

ST 5: *Differences between Female and Male Perpetrators*
    C 15: "Total acceptance" of responsibility
    C 16: Self-loathing and self-incriminating
    C 17: Not paedophilia-like
    C 18: Harder to "own" perpetration

MT 2: UNDERSTANDING THE TREATMENT PROCESS

ST 6: *Working with Disclosure*
    C 19: The importance of introducing the topic
    C 20: Normalizing/educating
    C 21: The problem with early disclosures
    C 22: Self-disclosure as proof of "badness"
    C 23: Reporting
    C 24: Ensuring child safety
    C 25: Anticipating "fallout"

ST 7: *Treatment Issues and Techniques*
    C 26: The therapeutic relationship

C 27: "Stuckness" as "deserved punishment"
C 28: Address both survivor/perpetrator issues
C 29: Balance responsibility and absolution
C 30: Make amends
C 31: Adapt survivor treatment techniques

MT 3: PERSONAL/PROFESSIONAL EXPERIENCE OF CLINICIANS

C 32: Awareness is the challenge
C 33: The shock of disclosure
C 34: Reacting in a professional manner
C 35: Feelings of "compassion," not "disgust"
C 36: Taking care of yourself
C 37: Attitudes toward breaking the silence

Major Theme 1: Understanding the Client

The major theme entitled "understanding the client" contains what was identified in the analysis of the data as the clinician's attempts to understand her client. The subthemes and categories under this theme were distinguished by references to issues that affected how the client presented to the clinician. This is the largest grouping of results, consisting of five subthemes and nineteen categories.

According to the clinicians, female perpetrators are not initially identified as such; rather, they are likely to self-disclose perpetration well into treatment for their own childhood sexual victimization. Although there are similarities in the symptoms of adult female survivors of sexual abuse and survivors who also perpetrated sexual abuse, the latter are characterized by more intense symptoms, including severe dissociation and suicide attempts. Reaching an impasse in the therapeutic process and suspicious child-rearing practices are tentative signs that a female survivor may have perpetrated child sexual abuse. Nevertheless, the sexual perpetration committed by these women is typically unplanned and asexual in nature. Female survivor-perpetrators are thought to perpetrate child sexual abuse because of the unresolved trauma related to their own sexual victimization.

Further, the clinicians identified female survivors who perpetrated as different from male perpetrators in a number of ways. The foremost of these distinctions was the extent to which the women were willing to accept responsibility for the abuse and the degree of self-loathing they expressed.

Overall, the findings related to the theme of understanding the female perpetrator suggest that the majority of the clients seen by the nine clinicians closely resemble what Mathews et al. (1989) refer to as the intergenerationally predisposed female offender. This is not surprising, in that this type is considered to be the predominant type of female perpetrator (Mathews et al., 1989). In keeping with this female offender type, all of the perpetrators referred to in this study were the victims of sexual abuse in childhood and abusive relationships in adulthood. In addition, most were described as victims of sexual abuse of the severest kind. The intergenerationally predisposed offender is likely to self-report her perpetrating behavior and approach treatment with a great deal of shame, which were distinct characteristics of female perpetrators referred to by the clinicians in this study.

Although it could be argued that this finding was somewhat predictable, considering that this study specifically focused on the treatment of female sex offender clients who were also survivors of child sexual abuse, it is noteworthy that several characteristics were found to be consistent with the profile of this type of offender. It is also worth noting that none of the female survivor-perpetrators referred to by the research participants in this study were identified as being male-coerced. Although many of the women were involved in abusive relationships with males, none of the research participants mentioned male coercion. Thus, the female survivor-perpetrators referred to in this study do not fit the male-coerced type described by Mathews et al. (1989).

Major Theme 2: Understanding the Treatment Process

The theme "understanding the treatment process" includes a wide range of topics related to both the clinicians' response to disclosures of sexual abuse and the interventions that they utilized in responding to both perpetration and victimization issues.

Suggestions from clinicians about how to elicit and deal with the disclosure of perpetration included having the clinician raise the topic of female perpetration and ensuring child safety. Findings connected to both treatment issues and techniques suggest that a positive therapeutic relationship and balancing responsibility and absolution for the perpetration of sexual abuse are essential to the healing process. Many of the treatment techniques recommended for use with survivor-perpetrators are drawn from those used with female survivors.

A large proportion of the findings concerning this theme confirmed themes already identified in the literature review. Nevertheless, new ideas emerged in each of the subthemes. For example, the clinicians in this study placed considerable emphasis on the fact that the disclosures were typically unexpected and that the female clients experienced substantial shame as they reported their offenses.

A number of the clinicians indicated that their recent experiences with female survivors of sexual abuse who disclosed perpetration had prompted them to conclude that sexual offending is a critical issue that should be addressed in the treatment of most female survivors. The clinicians believe that female survivors deserve to be educated about the phenomenon of female perpetration in order to make it easier for them to disclose perpetration, if appropriate, and to heal from that experience.

Although most of the clinicians did not advocate directly asking the female survivor if she had ever perpetrated child sexual abuse, many suggested early introduction of the topic as an educational component of therapy, seeing this as the most appropriate means of communicating that sexual abuse by females is not uncommon. Most of the clinicians believed, however, that techniques should not be used to elicit confessions, because premature disclosures were seen as potentially damaging. It was suggested that the client must be "ready" to deal with all that is involved in such a revelation.

Another factor that complicates the issue of disclosure is the clinicians' belief that disclosures were often presented as further proof of the clients' "worthlessness." This issue has significant implications for balancing taking responsibility for the abuse, on the one hand, and receiving absolution for the perpetration, on the other. The clinicians noted that it is important to anticipate "fallout," such as suicide attempts, after disclosure; this is a critical consideration in the treatment of these women. The key issue is the suggestion that the treatment provider must be prepared to deal with the anticipated aftershock of disclosure.

Major Theme 3: Personal/Professional Experience of Clinicians

This theme describes those areas of their work with female perpetrators that the clinicians found personally challenging. It is clear that treating such female clients can be difficult. The personal and professional experience of the clinician has rarely been addressed in the literature on female perpetrators. The majority of the clinicians in the current study suggested that dealing with the awareness that female perpetration exists is highly challenging. Hence much of the information addressed within this theme may help other clinicians to cope better when working with this population.

The category (C 33) titled "the shock of disclosure" refers to the initial dismay three clinicians expressed after hearing their female clients disclose perpetration. All three referred to an initial hesitancy to accept their client's disclosure of sexually abusing a child, noting that they were forced to examine their own belief systems about who perpetrates child sexual abuse.

Despite the initial shock involved in hearing disclosure of female perpetration, a number of the clinicians spoke about their awareness of the need to react to that disclosure in a professional manner. Most said that what was initially experienced as amazement quickly gave way to a "heightened sense" of what was needed to be done clinically.

Rather than feel disgusted or repulsed by the behavior, clinicians reported feeling immensely compassionate toward their clients. Most focused on the client's pain rather than her behavior, and many commented on the obvious strength and courage that it took for these female clients to self-disclose perpetration. The clinicians hypothesized that their reaction was connected to the fact that female perpetrators generally take full responsibility for their behavior, and express extreme self-loathing. Such characteristics probably evoke feelings of empathy in clinicians, who have more than likely been working with their client over a long period and have developed a strong therapeutic alliance with her. This finding speaks to clinicians' allegiance to their professional role and highlights the importance of an ability to react quickly and appropriately under intensely stressful situations.

The category (C 36) "taking care of yourself" was associated with the view, held by most of the clinicians, that treating female perpetrators is emotionally demanding. Many suggested that they therefore had an obligation to take care of their own physical and emotional health. This included recognizing the "health in distraction," by occasionally getting away from the office and using breaks as an important means of rebuilding strength in order to continue such challenging and painful work.

SUMMARY AND CONCLUSIONS

This exploratory study utilized a qualitative analysis of individual interviews with nine clinicians who had worked with a total of 91 female perpetrators. The research study was designed to explore five research questions related to the characteristics and treatment needs of adult survivors of sexual abuse who have also offended. Not only has this inquiry affirmed a number of issues previously addressed in the limited literature on female perpetrators, but it also uncovered important new knowledge regarding the understanding and treatment of female survivor-perpetrators.

Two important general findings need to be acknowledged. One of the most significant findings associated with this inquiry is the surprisingly high number of female perpetrator clients that the nine clinicians reported working with. Although other quantitative research studies indicate that the prevalence of sexual abuse perpetrated by women is small, the high number of cases reported in the current study affirms the suggestion that clinicians are seeing more female clients who are disclosing sexually abusive behavior (e.g., Knopp & Lakey, 1987; Lepine, 1990; Russell, 1984). This finding alone speaks to the importance of doing research studies in the area of female perpetrators of child sexual abuse.

A second critical finding is that the vast majority of female perpetrators referred to by the clinicians in this study had come to therapy to address survivor issues, and then later freely disclosed that they had perpetrated child sexual abuse. In fact, the findings indicate that disclosure did not generally occur until "well into" the treatment process. This conclusion affirms descriptions in the limited literature on female perpetration that suggest that a number of clinicians are encountering women clients who disclose perpetration during treatment for their own victimization (Kasl, 1990; Lepine, 1990; Russell, 1984; Mathews et al., 1989; Travin et al., 1990).

Directions for Future Research

Since so few research studies have been conducted in the area of female perpetrators of child sexual abuse, we recommend continued study of the characteristics and treatment needs of adult female survivors who have perpetrated child sexual abuse. There are a number of more specific suggestions for future investigation.

First, further study is required to explore the hypothesis that clinicians are seeing more female clients who disclose perpetration during treatment for their own victimization (Kasl, 1990; Knopp & Lakey, 1987; Krug, 1989; Lepine, 1990; Russell, 1984). Except for the work of Knopp and Lakey (1987), and this qualitative inquiry, no empirical evidence exists to back up these claims. As a result, a survey of clinicians much like the Knopp and Lakey study might provide more information on the scope of the problem and areas for further study.

Second, a more in-depth exploration of the experience of the female perpetrator is critical in developing theory for the treatment of these clients. Although a number of small-scale studies have focused on the characteristics of the female sexual offender, more emphasis needs to be placed on developing a typology of female perpetrators that is based on in-depth understanding of their experiences. A qualitative inquiry into the female perpetrator's experience would be especially important for this objective.

Third, we have suggested that current research studies could be replicated by interested parties who have more access to the resources required to improve on the research methodology. Such methods as prolonged engagement (in the form of multiple interviews), further use of triangulation techniques (e.g., multiple sources, multiple researchers), use of more rigorous sampling techniques (such as interviewing research participants who had worked with a large number of female perpetrators), and use of a larger informant group are a few of the suggestions for this work.

Implications for Clinical Practice

Few research studies have been conducted on the therapeutic needs of female perpetrators. More importantly, even fewer research studies have explored the personal/professional experience of the clinician. Although the results must be viewed cautiously because of the exploratory nature of the research, some of what has been discovered represents new knowledge that has clinical implications for understanding and treatment of female perpetrators, in particular, those who are also survivors of sexual abuse.

A number of authors have commented on the various barriers to recognition of female perpetration (Allen, 1990; Groth, 1979; Kasl, 1990), suggesting that mistaken beliefs and a general lack of knowledge about the perpetration of sexual abuse by women are significant problems in society. Even professional treatment providers who work in the area of sexual abuse are thought to lack awareness of either the problem of female sex offenders or the dynamics associated with female perpetration. Thus, in a general sense, this study may serve as an educational tool to raise the awareness of social workers and all clinicians interested in the vast range of issues related to sexual abuse. This research is perhaps particularly relevant to clinicians who specialize in working with both male and female survivors of child sexual abuse.

An increased awareness of the issues related to female perpetration may allow clinicians to pass on new knowledge to clients. Educating clients about female perpetration may allow more recognition of the phenomenon from both the victim and the perpetrator. Since it is suggested that the victims of female perpetrators avoid disclosure because of the shame associated with what they consider to be a rare event (Goodwin & DiVasto, 1989; Krug, 1989), learning that others have been similarly victimized may free them to fully explore the experience during the therapeutic process. Similarly, for those female survivors who have perpetrated child sexual abuse, learning that they are not alone can be an important step toward self-disclosure and healing.

In addition, clinicians may use the research to become familiar with the special characteristics of the female perpetrator. This information should be disseminated through workshops, conference presentations, and publications in order to educate those involved in the field of sexual abuse. Clinicians, researchers, and academics have an obligation to recognize that female perpetration does exist and to be cognizant of the often serious implications of this phenomenon.

For those clinicians who have already worked with female perpetrators, the research can provide assurance that they are not alone in their struggle to provide service to this unique clientele. The research results may serve to substantiate some of their theoretical suppositions about the client group and perhaps introduce new ideas regarding treatment issues and techniques. For instance, knowing about the importance of a positive therapeutic relationship may assist clinicians in understanding the need for self-awareness and clarity about how they might respond to female perpetrators. In addition, that this type of work is likely to demand a long-term commitment by both the client and the clinician is an important factor in planning and contracting for service. Techniques such as taking a non-confrontational approach to therapy and creating safety are crucial when considering the difficulties associated with balancing responsibility and absolution. This study presents a range of issues and techniques that can serve as a valuable resource for clinicians.

On the personal/professional side, this study can serve to assure clinicians that others have experienced the shock of a disclosure by a female client, and have struggled with the fears associated with recognizing female perpetration. They can learn that despite these fears, some clinicians are recognizing that female perpetration is an important issue and that "breaking the silence" is the first step in helping clients to heal. In addition, the results can help clinicians to understand that their own emotional well-being is an important part of being an effective therapist, and that taking care of oneself means understanding that time away from the work is necessary to maintain psychological health.

REFERENCES

Allen, C. (1990). Women as perpetrators of child sexual abuse: Recognition barriers. In A. Horton, B. Johnson, L. Roundy, & D. Williams (Eds.), *The incest perpetrator: The family member no one wants to treat* (pp. 109-125). Newbury Park, CA: Sage.

Berg, B. (1989). *Qualitative research methods for the social sciences.* Needham Heights, MA: Allyn & Bacon.

Chasnoff, I., Burns, W., Schnoll, H., Burns, K., Chisum, G., & Kyle-Spore, L. (1986). Maternal-neonatal incest. *American Journal of Orthopsychiatry, 54,* 577-579.

Faller, K. (1987). Women who sexually abuse children. *Violence and Victims, 2,* 263-276.

Finkelhor, D., Hotaling, G., Lewis, I., & Smith, C. (1990). Sexual abuse in a national survey of adult men and women: Prevalence, characteristics, and risk factors. *Child Abuse and Neglect, 14,* 19-28.

Finkelhor, D., & Russell, D. (1984). Women as perpetrators. In D. Finkelhor (Ed.), *Child sexual abuse* (pp. 171-185). New York: Free Press.

Finkelhor, D., Williams, L., & Burns, N. (1988). *Nursery crimes: Sexual abuse in day care.* Newbury Park, CA: Sage.

Glesne, C., & Peshkin, A. (1992). *Becoming qualitative researchers.* White Plains, NY: Longman.

Goodwin, J., & DiVasto, P. (1979). Mother-daughter incest. *Child Abuse and Neglect, 3,* 953-957.

Goodwin, J., & DiVasto, P. (1989). Female homosexuality: A sequel to mother-daughter incest. In J. Goodwin (Ed.), *Sexual abuse incest victims and their families* (2nd ed., pp. 140-146). Chicago: Year Book Medical Publishers.

Grayson, J. (1989). Female sex offenders. *Interchange.* (Published by the C. Henry Kemp National Center for the Prevention and Treatment of Child Abuse and Neglect, Denver, CO; Newsletter of the Adolescent Perpetrator Network.)

Groth, N. (1979). Sexual trauma in the life histories of rapists and child molesters. *Victimology, 4,* 10-16.

Groth, N. (1982). The incest offender. In S. Sgroi (Ed.), *Handbook of clinical intervention in child sexual abuse* (pp. 215-239). Lexington, MA: Lexington.

Hollin, C., & Howells, K. (1991). *Clinical approaches to sex offenders and their victims.* New York: Wiley.

Johnson, T. (1989). Female child perpetrators: Children who molest other children. *Child Abuse and Neglect, 13,* 571-585.

Kasl, C. (1990). Female perpetrators of sexual abuse: A feminist view. In M. Hunter (Ed.), *The sexually abused male* (Vol. 1, pp. 259-274). Lexington, MA: Lexington.

Knopp, F., & Lakey, L. (1987). *Female sexual abusers: A summary of data from 44 treatment providers.* Orwell, VT: Safer Society Press.

Krefting, L. (1990). Rigor in qualitative research: The assessment of trustworthiness. *American Journal of Occupational Therapy, 45,* 214-222.

Krug, R. (1989). Adult male report of childhood sexual abuse by mothers: Case descriptions, motivations, and long-term consequences. *Child Abuse and Neglect, 13,* 111-119.

Lepine, D. (1990). Ending the cycle of violence; overcoming guilt in incest survivors. In T. Laidlaw, C. Malmo, & Associates (Eds.), *Healing voices* (pp. 272-287). San Francisco: Jossey-Bass.

Lincoln, Y., & Guba, E. (1985). *Naturalistic inquiry.* Newbury Park, CA: Sage.

Lofland, J., & Lofland, L. (1984). *A guide to qualitative observation and analysis.* Belmont, CA: Wadsworth.

Lukianowicz, N. (1972). Other types of incest. *British Journal of Psychiatry, 120,* 108-113.

Margolis, M. (1984). A case of mother–adolescent son incest: A follow-up study. *Psychoanalytic Quarterly, 52,* 355-385.

Mathews, R. (1987). *Genesis II female sex offender program.* Orwell, VT: Safer Society Press.

Mathews, R., Matthews, J., & Speltz, K. (1989). *Female sexual offenders: An exploratory study.* Orwell, VT: Safer Society Press

Mathews, R., Matthews, J., & Speltz, K. (1990) Female sexual offenders. In M. Hunter (Ed.), *The sexually abused male* (pp. 275-293). Lexington, MA: Lexington.

Mathews, R., Matthews, J., & Speltz, K. (1991). Female sex offenders: A typology. In M. Quinn Patton (Ed.), *Family sexual abuse: Frontline research and evaluation* (pp. 199-219). Newbury Park, CA: Sage.

McCarty, L. (1986). Mother-child incest: Characteristics of the offender. *Child Welfare, 65,* 447-459.

O'Connor, A. (1987). Female sex offenders. *British Journal of Psychiatry, 150,* 615-620.

Patton, M. (1990). *Qualitative evaluation and research methods.* Newbury Park, CA: Sage.

Robinson, L.A. (1994). *Understanding and treating female survivor perpetrators: The view of the therapist.* Unpublished masters thesis, University of Calgary, Calgary.

Rothery, M. (1993). Problems, questions, and hypotheses. In R. Grinnell (Ed.), *Social work research and evaluation* (4th ed., pp. 17-37). Itasca, IL: Peacock.

Russell, D. (1984). *Sexual exploitation.* Newbury Park, CA: Sage.

Scavo, R. (1989). Female adolescent sex offenders: A neglected treatment group. *Social Casework, 67,* 114-117.

Shengold, L. (1980). Some reflections on a case of mother/adolescent son incest. *International Journal of Psycho-Analysis, 61,* 461-476.

Stainback, S., & Stainback, W. (1988). *Understanding and conducting qualitative research.* Dubuque, IO: Kendall/Hunt.

Taylor, S., & Bogdan, R. (1984). *Introduction to qualitative research methods* (2nd ed.). New York: Wiley.

Travin, S., Cullen, K., & Protter, B. (1990). Female sex offenders: Severe victims and victimizers. *Journal of Forensic Sciences, 35,* 140-150.

Wahl, C. (1960). The psychodynamics of consummated maternal incest. *Archives of General Psychiatry, 3,* 188-193.

Wakefield, H., Rogers, M., & Underwager, R. (1990). Female sexual abusers: A theory of loss. *Issues in Child Abuse Accusations, 2,* 181-195.

Wakefield, H., & Underwager, R. (1991). Female child sexual abusers: A critical review of the literature. *American Journal of Forensic Psychology, 9,* 43-69.

David Este

Research Study B

KEY CONCEPTS

DATA COLLECTION

DATA ANALYSIS

FINDINGS

RELATIONSHIP TO THE PLANNING SYSTEM

CONCLUSIONS

REFERENCES

Boards of Directors of Social Service Agencies

C OUNTLESS SOCIAL WORK AGENCIES are governed by boards of directors, which, in theory, are critical to their effective functioning. Board members' duties are usually described in impressively worded declarations of intent suggesting they are expected to formulate the organization's mission, provide a sense of direction, and perform many other functions that will help their agencies operate effectively.

How well do idealistic ideas about what boards do conform to reality? Though much has been written about boards, the literature consists largely of statements regarding what boards *should* do; very little empirical work has been done to establish what they *do* and how well they do it. Therefore, a qualitative research study was designed to examine this problem, employing interviews with research participants (and a document review).

The reason this problem is relevant is that we can benefit from developing realistic expectations of what boards are able to do for their agencies, given the

EDITORS' NOTE

Most social workers spend their working lives in social service agencies, and many of these organizations are governed by boards of directors. These boards, together with agency managers and major funders, have considerable power to influence the policies and practices to which the social worker, as an agency employee, must adhere. This study is included as an example of a qualitative research study that focuses on what boards do and how they work—both vital organizational issues that influence the daily lives of the social worker. It is also a good example of a study that combines two data collection methods: interview data supplemented by an analysis of documents.

present context in which they must work. Understanding the relationships between the "planning system" (which is defined below) and agencies, and between the planning system, executive directors, and boards, provides insights into the way the social service system really operates, and this can suggest ways to improve board functioning.

KEY CONCEPTS

This section will discuss the planning system and the traditional expectations of boards.

The Planning System

In the past few decades, the work of social work agencies has increasingly come under the control of powerful government bureaucracies: municipalities and community organizations have become more reliant on the government for funding and policy direction.

Together with major funders such as the United Way, the government has become a high-level overseer, heavily influencing the policies and practices that were once decided more independently within the agencies themselves. This is what is meant by the planning process and system to which agency boards are accountable.

The relationship between planning systems and social service agencies has not been well researched. We do not know how well agencies can maintain a degree of autonomy, and how relationships work between agency directors, board members, and key people in the planning system to which they are accountable.

Traditional Expectations of Boards

There is a traditional view of boards of directors and the functions they perform for their organizations, which much of the literature promotes without considering whether it is true or realistic. The expectations assigned to boards in the conventional view are broad, and include governance, accountability, policy making, financial management, public relations, recruitment and supervision of the executive director, monitoring of performance, and self-maintenance.

Governance

Prescriptive writers (Duca, 1986; Houle, 1989; Wolf, 1990) have been eager to outline idealized expectations. They view boards as governing bodies that oversee all aspects of agency work, including strategic direction and external realities, policies and funding.

Accountability

Boards of governors of nonprofit organizations have inherited certain democratic expectations in that they are supposed to stay in tune with and responsible to the wishes of their communities. Therefore, the board ought to act as guardians of the public trust and upholders of community values.

A system of accountability is intended to guarantee this. A board and its agency need a mandate, the resources to fulfil it, a way of measuring progress toward it, and a system of incentives to encourage good performance. Boards are also usually accountable to government funding agencies, from which much of their operating capital is obtained. Accountability of boards is also often legally enforced, since by-laws govern many details of board operation.

Policy Making

Key among obligations prescribed for boards is policy making—broad decisions that affect overall operations. Philosophical (mission and ethics), fundamental (service and scope), and financial (resources and expenditures) policies have been posited as the primary policy types for which board members should see themselves as responsible. A focus on more pragmatic, results-oriented policy formulation, a more direct linking of means and ends, has also been suggested. Important too are policies defining the relationship between the board and its executive director. Such recommendations assume that board members are both willing and knowledgeable enough to formulate useful policies.

Financial Management

Also crucial to prescriptive expectations for boards is a commitment to (and adeptness at) financial management and fundraising. Levels of expertise and awareness of funding sources determine the board's success in this area.

Public Relations

Boards should also attend to public relations, prescriptive writers contend, in order to enhance their agency's community image. The very act of communicating effectively with the public, moreover, can help keep the agency and the board attuned to public needs.

Recruitment and Supervision of the Executive Director

The board's most important decision is seen as its selection of the executive director. The executive director is an employee of the board, but is also the chief implementor of policy, in closer touch with ongoing developments. The executive director is seen as a motivator, communicator, entrepreneur, manager, and troubleshooter, while board members are complementary leaders, communicators, negotiators, and liaison with the community.

Monitoring Performance

Performance and program evaluations are recommended as ways of keeping goals attainable and agency activities on-track. Clear expectations about criteria and timing are crucial. Despite the importance of evaluative procedures, however, they are often overlooked.

Self-Maintenance

Finally, the board needs to give continual consideration to its own composition. Who, how many, and how often are key recruiting questions, ultimately affecting the degree to which the board is effective in its work and representative of its community.

The Ideal vs. the Real

Behind popular prescriptions for board responsibilities lie crucial unasked questions regarding board functioning in the contemporary social services environment. Is it reasonable to expect voluntary boards of nonprofit organizations to be adept at all of the tasks prescribed for them? If voluntary boards cannot be expected to live up to such ideal prescriptions, what reasonable limits can be placed on expectations so that boards will be able to fulfil them?

Common descriptions of ideal board functioning are highly idealized according to some critics, who argue that:

- Nonprofit boards often seem insufficiently involved with their organizations to fulfil the tasks suggested for them.

- Boards often forgo their policy-making role as well, leaving management to fill the void as board members get bogged down in unimportant details and fail to deal with the "big picture."

- Some boards show a diminished sense of ownership in the day-to-day running of agencies.

- Recruitment of board members may emphasize attracting members of the community's elite, which can enhance the image of the board and agency without significantly augmenting board performance.

The traditional view of board responsibilities is attractive—the role it implies for these bodies expresses important democratic and social values. If the contemporary situation is such that boards are no longer able to fulfil the traditional role ascribed to them, the need for information regarding some basic questions is clear: If boards are not fulfilling the roles outlined for them, what do they do? What factors account for the activities that boards actually perform? What are boards capable of doing?

The Research Questions

A review of the literature supports the general focus of this research—there are highly relevant issues concerning the purposes and functioning of social service agency boards that require study. The literature also suggests that the ability of boards to do their work is affected by certain key people: (1) the board members themselves, (2) the planning system (in this case, government funders), and (3) agency directors. Considering the general problem in the light of the literature, the specific questions that were posed for this research were:

- What activities are being performed by the boards of directors of the participating social service agencies?

- In what ways are boards of directors accountable to their planning system, and how do they prove their accountability?

- What impact does the relationship between agencies and the planning system have on what boards do?

- What impact do relations between the planning system, executive directors, and boards of directors have on what boards do?

DATA COLLECTION

To gather the data required to answer the research questions, two primary data collection techniques were employed in the study. A variety of documents provided by the government and the participating agencies were reviewed, including (1) board meeting minutes, (2) published material describing the agency, (3) agency annual reports and service plans, and (4) government documents. Interviews with identified research participants constituted the second data collection method used.

Given the complexity of the research questions, it was necessary to speak to three types of research participants: government funders, board members, and executive directors.

Therefore, gaining entry to the service system involved several steps: soliciting support from the government; selecting appropriate agencies and obtaining agreements to participate from members of their boards and their executive directors; and identifying research participants who would be asked to agree to a series of interviews.

The Planning System

A proposal outlining the goals and plan for the research was prepared and given to individuals in the government with the authority to approve the project. Letters of introduction were sent to those who expressed interest, and meetings were arranged at their convenience.

The meetings held with government representatives were carefully planned. The proposal and letters were provided prior to the meeting, and the information about the project that they contained was reviewed verbally. Care was taken to provide considerable detail regarding the project, its rationale, and what demands it would make on participants.

Identifying Agencies

Qualitative research generally employs various nonrandom sampling methods, in which the investigator purposefully seeks "information-rich cases that will illuminate the question under study" (Lincoln & Guba, 1985; Patton, 1980).

Patton contends that purposeful sampling is used as a strategy when one wants to learn something about certain select cases without needing to generalize (*p.* 109).

The organizations asked to participate in this study all receive most of their funding from the government and maintain a close working relationship with government supervisors. Also, organizations were drawn from within a specific region.

Another factor involved in selection was the desire to have a variety of organizations included in the sample. Choosing a mixture of different organizations provides a comparative aspect to the study, and findings that are true for different organizations generate greater confidence.

Seven organizations and 25 research participants (key informants) were selected for this study. Below is a summary of the organizations selected and how many research participants were included in each organization:

- One government (program supervisors) organization with four research participants

- One children's mental health center with three research participants

- One child welfare agency with four research participants

- Two agencies providing service to people who are developmentally challenged with nine research participants

- One women's emergency shelter with three research participants

- One counseling agency with two research participants

Once the seven organizations were chosen, the process of negotiating their actual involvement began. Telephone contacts with agency executive directors were arranged, and letters describing the study were sent from the researcher to agency executive directors and board chairpersons.

Numerous meetings with the executive directors and board chairpersons were held in which full and detailed information about the research study was presented, and these resulted in the six community agencies agreeing to participate in the study.

Research Participants

The selection of research participants represented another major decision. Members of the boards of directors and executive directors were clearly important research participants, since each of these parties should be involved in budget submissions and deliberations regarding policy and service issues. They could therefore shed light on stipulated research questions: (1) What specific activities are performed by boards? and (2) What is the nature of the relationships between the planning system, boards of directors, and executive directors?

Three program supervisors from the government represented the third major grouping of research participants. These individuals are the government's front-line representatives who work with the organizations participating in the study, and it is expected that they be involved in the decision-making processes mentioned above.

Hence, the core group of informants included the executive directors and board chairpersons of the participating agencies as well as program supervisors from the government. Individuals identified by agency executive directors or board chairpersons as being active participants in the organizations also agreed to participate as research participants.

The researcher, in various contacts with the executive directors, emphasized that the study would ask research participants about their experience with two decision-making processes: (1) the development of the agency's budget submission to the government, and (2) the handling of a major policy/service issue the agency dealt with during a specified time period.

All in all, 25 research participants with broad involvement in policy issues and financial issues were recruited. They included:

- Executive directors and government supervisors

- Board chairpersons

- Executive directors

- An additional seven key organizational informants (both board and senior management personnel) identified as being involved in budget submissions and policy formulation

- Program supervisors from the government, who expressed an interest in participating in the study when the researcher's proposal was circulated in the local area office

- The budget coordinator for the government

The Research Interviews

Each of the research participants was interviewed at least twice, and most were interviewed three times. The time required for interviews ranged from 60 to 90 minutes. For the most part, the interviews were unstructured, employing open-ended questions. However, they were given a general focus designed to elicit information relevant to the research questions.

Selecting a Focus for the Interviews

The focuses for the key informant interviews were influenced by the review of the literature on board functions described earlier. During initial contacts with program supervisors and executive directors, the researcher suggested that one interview focus on the process by which the agency developed its budgetary submission to the government. In addition, each executive director was asked to provide any documentation (board minutes, finance committee minutes, descriptions of the process) that provided information on this process.

During initial contacts, the researcher asked each supervisor or director if there was a major organizational policy/service issue that might be used as a means of examining the interaction of the government, board members, and executive directors. Documentation regarding these issues (e.g., board/senior management minutes, minutes from ad hoc committees) was requested, and preparation for the interviews was enhanced by having this information in hand.

Document Review

There are several advantages to documents as data sources for qualitative research studies:

- They can be a rich source of information on the topics being investigated.

- They are a stable source of information, reflecting situations that, because they occurred in the past, can be analyzed and reanalyzed without undergoing change.

- Reviewing documents helps to ensure that the researcher stays attuned to the historical and organizational context within which findings should be understood.

- Document reviews can provide opportunities for triangulation of evidence. In this study, the information obtained from documents served to validate information obtained from interviews.

During the course of this study, the following types of documents were reviewed:

- Minutes from board meetings, board committee meetings, senior management meetings, and staff meetings

- Documents describing programs/services offered and organizational structure

- Documents describing responsibilities of the board, the executive director, and other staff

- Annual reports and service plans

- Policy and procedures manuals

- Government documents such as funding documentation

- Literature describing the government agency

The kinds of data generated by reviewing these documents were as follows:

- Descriptive background information on the agencies participating in the study

- Information on the activities performed by boards of directors, executive directors, and program supervisors

- Data on the budget submission process

- Information on decision-making processes underlying budget submissions and policy issues

Interviews with Research Participants

As discussed in Phase Two, qualitative interviewing allows individuals to share their perceptions, thoughts, beliefs, and feelings on the subject matter being investigated. One of the particular strengths of the interviewing process is that it allows the researcher to obtain full and detailed answers from research participants. In this study, two or three sets of interviews were completed with the research participants; all interviews primarily consisted of open-ended questions. The first interviews aimed to determine the specific activities performed by participants and to uncover the nature of the interactions between the major players. The second interviews were conducted to determine the role of various research participants in developing the budget submissions.

The third interviews focused on the decision-making process involving a key policy or service issue.

DATA ANALYSIS

Interviews and documents were analyzed as data collection proceeded, so that an early appreciation of potential themes could inform subsequent data collection.

All interviews were audiotaped and then transcribed (with the permission of the interviewees). All of the interviews, once transcribed, were played back and read, to fill in any gaps in the text of the transcribed interviews and to begin the process of becoming acquainted with the data. Each interview was read at least three times, initiating the process of identifying emerging patterns and making analytical notes.

Prior to and during the interviewing process, the same scrutiny was applied to documents, facilitating an early identification of common patterns and trends. A preliminary list of information categories was drawn up, with acronyms chosen for each category used in coding the data. As documents were read, typed notes were made of information pertaining to the research questions. Eventually, when information categories, or codes, were established (to be discussed below), these codes were applied to the document data. The list of codes provided a starting point for the subsequent fine-grained analysis of the data.

The researcher then utilized the software program *The Ethnograph*, with each transcribed interview being coded using that program's procedures: numbering the interviews, coding the individual transcripts, and extracting the categories. The codes that were derived during the course of the analysis are summarized below.

Codes Pertaining to Board Functions

BCACTA. Board's Actual Activities: includes information describing the actual activities that are performed by boards of directors on behalf of the organization they represent.

IDEAL. Ideal Board Activities: includes information relating to the activities that boards should be performing and/or have greater involvement in.

BDACMCSS. Board Accountability to the Government: includes information pertaining to areas for which the organizations are accountable to the planning system.

ACCOMECH. Accountability Mechanisms: includes all information relating to the ways that nonprofit social service organizations display their accountability to the planning system.

POWERPLA. Power of the Planning System: broken down into a number of subcategories, the codes for which are summarized below.

IMPACT. Impact of Power/Control of Planning System on Nonprofit Social Service Organizations: includes all information highlighting the impact of the planning system on the non-profit organization's ability to engage in meaningful planning processes.

AUTONOMY. Autonomy/Independence of Nonprofit Social Service Organizations: includes all information pertaining to the power/control of the planning system and how this affects the independence/autonomy of nonprofit social service organizations.

NONPOWER. Power of Nonprofit Organizations in Relation to Planning System: includes all information pertaining to the power/influence of nonprofit social service organizations in their relationships with the planning system.

PARTNER. Specific Reference to Partnership between Agencies and the Government: includes all information pertaining to the concept and practice of partnership between the planning system and the social service agencies.

Codes Pertaining to the Power of the Planning System

In qualitative data analysis, it is not uncommon that categories are broken down into subcategories, where a more refined analysis of a particular concept is desirable.

In this research study, the concept "the power of the planning system" (POWERPLA) was analyzed into the following five subcategories:

PFUNDER. Planning System as Primary Funder: includes manifestations of the power of the planning system resulting from its position as the primary funder to nonprofit social service organizations.

BUGETN. Budget Negotiation Process: includes information on how the planning system utilizes its power in negotiating a budget with nonprofit social service organizations.

POLSERV. Determination and Establishment of Service Priorities/ Policies: includes manifestations of the power of the planning system from its position as the dominant player in determining and establishing service priorities/policies.

LEGISLAT. Legislation/Establishment of Service Standards: includes information on how the planning system uses its power in utilizing pertinent legislation and service standards that directly affect the nonprofit social service organizations.

INFO. Control of Information as a Form of Power: includes manifestations of the power of the planning system arising from its control or awareness of information that may affect non-profit social service organizations.

FINDINGS

The findings that emerged as a result of the analysis shed considerable light on the research questions. An issue to be addressed prior to the findings themselves, however, and a special issue for qualitative research, is the credibility of those findings.

Credibility involves the confidence that the researcher, participants, and eventual readers can have in the truth of the findings. In this study, one technique for enhancing the credibility of the findings was member checking: each participant received a copy of the final findings for review and commentary.

Thus participants' perceptions were used to test the researcher's data, analytic categories, interpretations, and conclusions.

As well, the researcher used a journal containing information on his feelings, thoughts, and ideas on the logistics of the research, and comments on interviews that were reviewed shortly after they were completed. The journal also recorded feedback on the interviews received from the study's research participants.

Two common triangulation methods also served to enhance the credibility of the research. First, data were collected from interviews and from agency documentation.

Second, data collection involved three different groups of research participants and seven different organizations. Each of these factors allowed findings to be confirmed by checking for congruence across methods and across groups of research participants.

Board Functions

One of the key questions that this research addresses is, What activities are performed by the boards of directors of the agencies participating in the study?

The answers to this general question are organized as follows: (1) a general commentary on the range of activities performed by the boards, (2) a more in-depth examination of the activities performed by the boards during development of a budget submission to the planning system and during deliberations over a specific policy or service issue, and (3) a brief overview of research participants' comments about other things boards should be doing or areas where board involvement should increase.

Governance

Some research participants maintained that the primary function of a board is governance. According to one research participant:

> The board is basically responsible for everything in the organization, so they are the ultimate authority, giving direction and determining exactly what it is that the organization is going to do.

Similarly, another research participant stated that:

> This board ... takes a role largely of overseeing the operation of the agency in a general sense and approving major decisions.

This idea of governance as a board's basic *raison d'être* is echoed by an executive director:

> The board sets the direction for the agency, creating the vision as to where the agency should be going.

Policy Making

Establishment of policy was most frequently stated as the board's primary activity. As a board member stated:

> Basically the board is involved in the policy end of things as opposed to the practical end of things. A large part of our responsibilities involves preparing the service plan for the year.

Commentary provided by executive directors echoes that of board members.

One executive director remarked that "they [the board] tend to deal primarily with policy issues versus practice or implementation kinds of issues. The actual setting of policy is the responsibility of the board." In a similar vein, a senior manager stated that "the board is really the senior policy-making and decision-making body of the organization."

Strategic Planning

Both executive directors and representatives from the planning system cited the process of strategic planning as an activity of the board.

For the purpose of this discussion, strategic planning refers to the process of setting goals and determining how to achieve them. According to an executive director:

> Strategic planning or the strategic direction is [a] process we go through that involves a number of things. It involves upgrading the physical facility. It involves an upgrading of the type of service we can provide. It involves a different philosophy towards the services, [and] hiring of staff, so the board has gotten involved in some of that.

Another executive director described the agency's strategic planning process as:

> taking those strategic directions and trying to, over a five-year period, project into the future: what specific program, directions that might lead us to implement.

One board member, describing the activities associated with strategic planning, stated:

> I think about five or six years ago we developed a strategic plan, and that is reviewed annually, updated every year as to its continued value, whether circumstances have changed which may alter the direction the plan is going in.

Financial Management

In a climate of fiscal restraint, it is not surprising that financial management emerged as another major activity performed by boards of directors, one stressed by board members themselves. According to one board member:

> We [the board] are there to look at how the agency is spending the money as well as ensuring that it is spent in the best way possible.

Another remarked:

They [the board] also keep an eye on the financial situation of the agency, especially the budget, to make sure that the funding is available.

This theme also appeared in comments provided by executive directors:

The board is maintaining oversight of the [agency's] operations, making sure ... that we are using our funds in a wise and sensible fashion.

Fundraising

It appears that fundraising is an important function of some boards. As one executive director stated:

We [the agency] were quite extensively involved in fundraising in the community, and certainly the board played a primary role in that, both by members of the board participating in a fundraising committee but also by assisting in terms of making calls in the community for soliciting.

Based on the commentary provided by research participants, it appears that at least five of the boards studied are directly or indirectly involved in fundraising. The economic climate surfaced as a major reason for the attention given to this activity.

Other Activities Performed by the Boards

The research participants described a number of additional activities performed by the boards of directors, including monitoring of the programs and services provided by the agency and public relations activities designed to educate the public about the work the agency performs.

Board Activities in Selected Organizational Processes

In addition to general questions regarding the board's activities, research participants were asked about board involvement in two specific processes: budget submission and dealing with an identified policy/service issue. The findings deriving from these questions are summarized below.

Budget Submission Process

The following were identified as major activities carried out by the boards of directors in developing budgets for submission to funders (usually the government):

- *Budget preparation* — Some boards contributed to the actual preparation of the budget. Prevailing practice in most of the organizations appears to be a collaborative effort between the executive director and members of the board's finance committee.

- *Budget review* — Boards seem most active when the budget is presented to them for review and discussion. Budgetary information appears to be carefully scrutinized and discussed by the boards of directors before it is approved and eventually submitted.

- *Budget approval* — Before the budget is submitted, a final endorsement by the board is required, and this step is taken very seriously by the research participants in this study. Considerable effort goes into informing board members about the budget, and before they grant approval board members appear to be provided with regular opportunities to give input.

Service/Policy Decision-Making Processes

In order to obtain more in-depth information regarding the activities performed by the board of directors, each executive director was asked to provide a service or policy issue that the organization deliberated on during a specified period. The issues raised included: (1) downsizing programs and services, (2) determining the fate of a program after cancellation of funding by the planning system, (3) the amalgamation of three services offered by one agency, and (4) the issue of continuing to provide transportation for clients.

In decisions about service or policy issues, it appears that boards of directors are not passive bystanders. In fact, the boards spent considerable time discussing policy and service issues:

> You know we had to make some kind of decision on how to deal with that [service issue] because clearly we had to compensate for the lack of funding somehow and ... before we actually made our decision, there was a lot of discussion about the various ways to make up the funding.

> I attended the board meetings and I was there to hear the ways in which they were grappling with the issues ... It was a very clear discussion around a problem with prodding, probing, and questions.

> We formed an ad hoc committee with the board and committee [to discuss the issue].

And that became the group that really started to do some problem solving and brainstorming.

In each of the cases reviewed, the boards did not merely discuss the issues, but exercised decision-making power:

The board consulted with the staff on a number of occasions, and then the executive of the board talked to the program supervisor about the idea, all before we jumped in and made the decision and the board made the final decision.

Ideal Activities of Boards of Directors

Research participants also commented on activities they thought boards should be performing or areas where the board should have greater involvement. These included greater attention to governance functions such as providing vision, more attention to fundraising, greater involvement in strategic planning, and greater involvement in public relations activities.

RELATIONSHIP TO THE PLANNING SYSTEM

The relationship of the planning system to the agencies is an interesting balance, with the government controlling much of the funding and being responsible for broad public policy, and the agencies being the experts in delivering a service to a specific clientele in a given community. Budgeting, of course, is linked to policy making: a less-than-expected funding increase can mean a quick scramble to rethink service goals.

The aspects of this key relationship considered here are: (1) mechanisms of accountability, (2) partnership between the two parties, (3) sources of power for the planning system and how this power is manifested, (4) how the power of the planning system affects the social service agencies, (5) autonomy of the agencies in relation to the planning system, and (6) how the agencies manage or control their dependency on the planning system.

Areas of Board Accountability

With respect to accountability two key questions were addressed to participants: (1) In what areas are agency boards of directors accountable to the planning system? and (2) What mechanisms do boards of directors use to establish this accountability?

In response to the question "In what areas is the board of directors accountable to the government?" some research participants maintained that, overall, the boards are accountable for the operation of the entire organization—boards are responsible and accountable to the planning system for the governance of their agency:

> The board is responsible for the development of policies, guidelines, directives, the vision, the mission of the agency.

> We give complete responsibility for the operation of the agency to them [the board].

> I think there is just a general expectation that the board will maintain oversight over the way the staff are running the agency. They [the planning system] want to make sure that the agency is doing what they're supposed to be doing.

Financial Accountability

Research participants' comments, minutes of board meetings, and agency service plans all suggest that the major area of board accountability is financial. Research participants' comments on this issue include:

> Well, one [area of accountability] is to make sure that the funds that are provided to the agencies are utilized in a proper fashion, that they're not being wasted.

> They provide ninety or over ninety percent of our funding, so our responsibility is to make sure that we use the money in the most expeditious and proper fashion.

> For me, the bottom line is how much money you've got, don't spend more than that, and if you spend more than that, you better have a good reason.

Some research participants view boards of directors as being accountable to the public for how agency funds are used. One employee from the planning system remarked, "There's got to be public accountability because there are public funds." Another planning system representative commented that "you want to have some confidence that the dollars we are investing in the community to the agencies are being wisely spent."

This emphasis on public accountability reinforces a prevailing theme in the prescriptive literature that board members are responsible to a variety of different stakeholders, including the general public and local community, the consumers of the agency's services, and various governments and funders.

The usual means by which boards of directors demonstrate financial accountability is through financial reports:

> The board endorses the financial statements that the staff prepares ... We go over the financial statement every board meeting, which is usually every month. We do have

auditors who report to the board. The board then endorses that [statement] to the government.

They [the planning system] want a very detailed accounting system, ongoing, as to how we stand money-wise and to assure that it is under control.

What usually happens is the executive director has filled out reports for the board or specific committees of the board; the board would review those, and the board could also give direction that, yes, those reports are okay to send to us.

The board's budget submission to the government represents an important element of their financial accountability, as do periodic meetings between representatives from the planning system and the social service agencies.

Program Accountability

Boards are also accountable for programs and services. Examples of comments describing program accountability by members of the planning system include the following:

They [the boards of directors] have got to be accountable to us for the service delivery they are providing with taxpayers' dollars.

Agency accountability [is] another area [in which we] work with agencies to assist them in terms of their ... organizational effectiveness, program outcome, and quality.

Among board members, the following comment is typical: "One of the things the board must do is to make sure ... that the services that the government has contracted to be performed are in fact performed, and performed in the best possible manner."

Executive directors tended to emphasize the necessity of board adherence to program and service conditions established in legal agreements:

The second area of accountability centers on the area of practice, and that is to ensure that the services being provided are consistent with the government's expectations, and may be better than the standards in the negotiated agreement under which monies have been allocated to the organization, to ensure that services are provided at a level in a manner which is consistent with that negotiated agreement.

Another executive director pointed out the degree of specificity outlined in many program agreements, including undertakings concerning "how many you serve, who you serve, [and] what you are going to accomplish in the program." The board's challenge is to demonstrate how their agency has fulfilled that service mandate. Comments from executive directors generally suggest that agency service reports are the primary means by which agencies show their accountability to program mandates:

> In the services area, they [the government] require on a monthly basis a review of the service demand the agency's experienced, and an explanation of the numbers of clients who've been serviced in various programs and any significant trends that are emerging in terms of changes in service demands, sudden increases and decreases in different types of service usage.

One board member explained the board's own means of program accountability:

> The services committee ... reviews all of the programs within the agency. It looks at usage statistics, costs of programs, changes in programs, any difficulties any programs or services might be having, and again, that is done on a monthly basis.

However, research participants made only indirect mention of such prescriptive tools as quality assurance, evaluability assessments, and program evaluations.

In sum, annual and committee reports, as well as documents prepared by executive directors, are all additional means by which boards attempt to demonstrate their accountability to budget requirements and program and service mandates.

Adhering to Legislation

Children's aid workers responding to this study identified a final area of accountability: the expectations created by the Child Welfare Act. Existing legislation clearly outlines mandatory services, and these agencies are obligated to adhere to that legislation. According to one research participant, "with responsibility comes accountability to ensure that the legislative requirements are being met." Another stated that "very much one of the activities of the board is ensuring the legislation, through staff activities, is being followed."

The Planning System: Sources of Power

The impressive power of the planning system to influence policy and services is clear in the data gathered for this study. These data also provide useful information regarding the *sources* of that power—the variables in the current social services domain that explain why the planning system predominates to the extent it does.

Power as Primary Funder

Since each of the community agencies participating in this study receives most of its funding from the planning system, all are in a dependent relationship. The planning system, as the primary funder, has considerable power.

Senior agency managers in this study admit the government's advantageous position:

> The government, having the power of funding, ... to a large extent determines what we are able to do.

> If someone has all the money, like with my kids, I have all the money, so I give them what I think they need. I have a whole lot to say about how they spend it, and I know they know that I can withhold it if they step out of line.

Similar sentiments were expressed by a couple of board members:

> The major way that they [the government] dictate [to us, the board] is through finances. They can dictate what we can do and what we can't do because, obviously, if the budget is extremely tight or if the funds that we are given are less than what we ... need, we are restricted in our activities.

In describing the circumstances that influence an agency's decision to discontinue a program, a board member remarked, "Well, they [the planning system] forced our hand, they certainly pulled the funding, they certainly made us do that."

Boards possess very little ability to alter the dependence that results from the planning system's being the dominant funder of the agencies. The government's control of funding strongly influences programming, and may also affect agencies' structures and staffing patterns.

Policy and Service Priorities

As with funding, so with policy and service. One planning system research participant described the role of the government in the following way:

> There's a children's [policy] framework out of that corporate office. The government is saying, "This is our policy direction for children" ... So it is my job to work with this agency and say, "Look, this is the direction, how does that match with what we are doing? How can we make it match?"

Executive directors participating in this study generally concede that the planning system establishes policy directions for social service organizations.

One executive director stated that "the government is also involved in policy development within the field of social services or within the field of family violence or within the field of whatever they are funding." Another executive director commented:

> The government was taking a totally different direction, and when the government takes a different direction, without question it has an impact on how we deliver service or are going to continue.

In explaining the issue from the perspective of a board, one participant claimed:

> Every so often someone says, how can we have a board if the province is exerting this much control and in fact is setting the policy and the mission statement and therefore the service delivery system, then why don't they just take over the operation of the services?
>
> With the establishment of policy direction, the planning system in essence also determines what services should be provided in the effort to achieve the objectives of the policy initiatives:

> What we [the planning system representatives] are trying to do all the time is to continue to give the message of where the government's priorities lie. So we would continue to point out, say in the case of sheltered workshops, the expectation [that] they are to be downsized, we want to phase them out in approximately five years' time.

To ensure their continued survival, some organizations may become engaged in a process that Salamon (1987) calls "vendorism," in which the agency adheres to the policy and service agenda of the planning system. Two research participants from the executive director/senior management group alluded to this development:

> This year we talked about the new policy framework that they [the planning system] talked about.

> It is fairly clear that a priority for funding is going to be the mandatory services that need to be funded.

> This policy paper the government is coming out with seems to be oriented towards identifying up-front certain services that are mandatory and therefore will be funded to the highest priority.

With the planning system being responsible for the social service delivery system, it would appear that the ability of boards of directors to influence policy and service directions is limited. In fact, it appears that boards have three ways of responding to the planning system's leadership in the domain of policy and service:

- They may follow suit, ensuring that the programs and services offered by the agency are congruent with the direction adopted by the planning system.

- They may opt to maintain the status quo. If this clashes with the direction in which the planning system is headed, funding for the programs/-services may be jeopardized, which may in turn place the entire agency in a precarious situation.

- They may become more actively involved in raising funds to support the programs and services they provide that are not a priority of the planning system.

The Autonomy of Social Services Agencies

The degree of agency dependency evidenced in this study raises the larger issue of autonomy, which may be much diminished in light of government spending controls. The key point about agency autonomy is the degree to which board members and executive directors retain the power to enforce decisions, to choose from among different courses of action, and to carry out their wishes irrespective of others' opinions and pressures (Hatton, 1990, *p.* 128).

There is a consensus among research participants that agencies do function in an autonomous manner. In particular, participants claim that, as far as the daily operation of the agencies is concerned, the planning system allows the board of directors, and particularly the executive director, to carry out agency responsibilities as they see fit:

> One of the things that the program supervisors [representatives of the planning system] have never done is use the kind of control and power issues in the sense of telling the agency directors how they should be running the program.

This message is reinforced by a member of the planning system who states that:

> we [the planning system] are not there to manage or run the organization ... I see our position as being a liaison link, a support, a resource person, but they [the board and executive director] are responsible for running the show.

As previously stated, in an effort to ascertain what activities are performed by the boards of directors participating in the study, each executive director was asked to provide a major policy/service issue the agency dealt with during a specified time. The issues included (1) downsizing of the programs and services offered, (2) determining the fate of a program after the cancellation of funding by the planning system, (3) the amalgamation of three services offered by one agency, and (4) the issue of continuing to provide transportation for clients.

Among the agencies that provided case materials, there is a strong consensus that the agency, and in particular the boards of directors, made the final decisions regarding those particular issues. One executive director, in describing the role the planning system played in the agency's deliberations, remarked that "we felt it was our policy, not the government's." Another executive director echoed similar sentiments: "In terms of working out the various proposals [in response to the issue confronting the agency], I mean, we really did not ask them [the planning system] to play a part in that, and I am not sure they would have felt comfortable in doing so." The same research participant also commented:

> They [the planning system] did not say, hey, you guys hold on, there is no need to go do this at this point. Their view was very much that you are doing the right thing at the right time.

Representatives of the planning system acknowledged the limited role they played in the agency decisions. One said that "indirectly I did have a say in the sense that ... they were requiring information to assist them with ... budgets, concerning the direction of the government." Another planning system representative described his role as:

> providing current information but not really participating in the discussion ... I took the position that it really was a decision of the board because they have to live with that decision either way.

Board members also confirmed the planning system's limited role in internal policy decisions. As one board member said, "I don't think the government really had any contribution to make." Another board member, in recalling the degree of involvement by the planning system representative, maintained that he could "not recall the individual being involved" and could "not recall anyone saying that the individual was involved."

Both board members and executive directors valued the agencies' autonomy in dealing with internal policy and services issues. In the words of one executive director, "We will embrace a partnership, but we value our independence and our ability to speak our own mind and on the basis of our experience and knowledge to say these things work, these things do not work, or these are things that, because of the risks that we feel exist, we choose not to do."

Though the data provided by the study's research participants indicate that the boards make decisions about the operation of the agencies, it must be stressed that decisions made by the planning system can force board decisions concerning service delivery. For example, the cancellation of government funding for one service meant the board of directors had to decide about the future of that service; eventually, it voted to terminate the program. Situations of this nature illustrate the power of the planning system in establishing the context in which boards of directors function.

Managing Dependency: The Agency Perspective

Although the planning system seems to be the dominant player in the relationship, the social service agencies are not necessarily resigned to their dependent status. Research participants in this study suggested that agencies use various means to reduce their dependency on the planning system.

The most obvious strategy is to search for alternative sources of funding. As one executive director put it:

> We have been very conscious of the need to diversify our funding ... for that precise reason [to reduce the dependency on the planning system]. We did not want to be in any one particular organization's back pocket.

One agency established a separate foundation that is entrusted with the responsibility of raising funds. Members of the board of directors are involved in this endeavor. Another agency relies on an annual golf tournament to generate a substantial amount of revenue for the organization.

Another strategy employed by at least four of the agencies involves budgeting for actual amounts needed to provide and maintain services rather than likely amounts to be raised or received. In the words of one board member:

> As the board has been saying, no, we do not want to do it that way [tailoring the budget based on the amount of money coming from the planning system] because we do not want to capitulate to the belief that the money that the government is providing us is adequate to provide those services. If we continue just giving them the numbers they want, they can continue to say those are the numbers that have been asked for.

The various approaches being utilized by the agencies in an attempt to manage or decrease their apparent dependence on the planning system may indicate that the agencies disagree with the decisions made by the government. In particular, funding and service priority decisions that negatively affect the agencies may be perceived as mechanisms by which the government is exerting influence.

In an effort to increase the level of monetary support from the planning system, one agency revised its mandate—a broad mandate gives agencies greater flexibility in programming. As one executive director put it:

We can much more now do what we want as long as it is within our mandate, and we have managed to get our mandate written loosely enough.

There are other sources of power that enhance the position of the agencies. One is their role as direct service providers. Although the planning system is the dominant funder, the agency possesses the infrastructure as well as the skill and expertise required to provide services. The planning system is not equipped to take on the role of direct service provider—it needs healthy agencies able to fulfil its mandates.

With respect to managing dependency on the planning system, boards of directors are in an important position. For example, if boards become more involved in raising funds, not only will the agency potentially possess greater autonomy, but the boards may also have more latitude in determining what programs and services the agencies should and could provide.

Strategic planning as a means of lessening financial dependence on the planning system is, however, unlikely to acquire greater importance in the eyes of board members unless they have greater control over the direction of the agencies.

The current power of the planning system diminishes the perceived value of strategic planning, since boards feel they have little real ability to set goals and make plans to meet them.

Dyadic Relationships

A final set of questions that the analysis focused on dealt with the relationships between the planning system, boards, and agency executive directors. The ways in which these different players interact is a very important aspect of the decision-making process.

Planning System and Board of Directors: Distant Partners

Though boards are seen as key players in both the planning and delivery of social services, research participants to this study suggest that there is limited contact and interaction between the boards and the planning system. The following comments are indicative:

I was at one small meeting, an executive meeting with the program supervisor [the planning system representative]. The same person came to our annual meeting. That is the only time I know about.

She [the planning system representative] has come to two or three board meetings when we have invited her.

I think it was the only contact we have had with a couple of directors and myself.

A representative from the planning system remarked in response to a question about interaction with a board of directors that "I would not have any type of regular involvement with the board." Even during a process as important as the development of the agency's budget submission to the planning system, contact between the board and the planning system is limited.

The lack of contact between the two parties also leaves the board dependent on the agency director. Since the director interacts most with the planning system, the board must trust that the director will share information, especially in the areas of funding and policy/service direction.

Executive Director and Planning System: A Vital Relationship

Research participants' comments and board minutes suggest that the executive director serves as the primary contact person for the planning system:

> Most of my involvement [as a representative from the planning system] is with the executive director. When I discuss items with the executive director, it is always on the assumption, and we repeat it for clarity, that the executive director is not just speaking on behalf of himself or herself, but is speaking on behalf of the agency.

One board member also made this clear: "Most of the contact is between the executive director and the program supervisor who is a representative of the planning system."

A number of factors may contribute to the frequency and depth of the interaction between executive directors and program supervisors. As professionals, they use the same language and work the same hours, while each has the advantage of information—the executive director is in touch with the day-to-day operation of the agency (programs, waiting lists, costs), and the program supervisor is in touch with the direction of the government (budget, priorities, agendas).

Relations between executive directors and the planning system were generally characterized as positive. The following remarks are typical:

> I would say it's always been a very agreeable relationship, sometimes confrontational, but both points were well taken on both sides.

According to the research participants (especially the executive directors), the contacts and interactions with the planning system provide some concrete benefits:

> He [the government representative] has been willing to come and sit with us and

share what he can, the direction the government might be taking and whether the plans that we got have been consistent with the direction the government's going.

> It's been a very constructive relationship, and they [the planning system] have been helpful and supportive wherever they have been able to be, and I think in return they have felt they have a good handle on what is going on down here and there is a good quality of trust about it.

Also generally endorsed is the notion of open lines of communication:

> I think communicating to them [the government] regarding the agency's funding needs, both on an annual basis through the service plan and also on a regular basis throughout the year ... He [the executive director] needs to be in pretty regular communication around that.

The effectiveness of either party requires cooperation with the other. Both seem aware of the importance of working together to fulfil agency and client needs. This relationship may be one that approximates the ideal partnership model.

If information constitutes power, the planning system is most powerful, followed by the executive directors. Because boards are dependent on executive directors for information from the planning system, executive directors can influence their board's activities and levels of involvement.

Despite being in an advantageous position by virtue of their relationship with the planning system, the executive directors attempt to work with the boards in a collaborative manner. Both parties recognize the importance of working as a team in an effort to ensure the efficient and effective operation of the agency.

Executive Director and Board of Directors: The Tandem

Available job descriptions confirmed that executive directors perform three major activities. The first is keeping the board informed:

> The primary activity of the executive director is to keep the board aware of what is happening day-to-day in the organization in terms of programs, financial accountability, personnel issues that are going on in the agency, and to keep staff aware of the direction that the board is going.

Executive directors also remind board members of their responsibilities. As one executive director remarked, "My role is to help with the practical stuff: to let them know how a board works, get together an orientation package for them." Through these types of activities, executive directors take responsibility for ensuring that the board functions effectively.

The executive director also monitors the agency's environment and is—ideally—sensitive to changes. The director's contact with the planning system keeps the board in tune with government directives; board minutes suggest that meetings allow time for executive directors to bring board members up to date on government developments. As one executive director remarked, "[At board meetings] I report any dealings that I have had with the government."

Comments describing the relationship between the executive director and the boards suggest a positive working relationship:

> It is a partnership-type thing ... we do discuss concerns and problems that have arisen. It is very cooperative. It is very collegial. It is both formal and informal. I think both board members and executive director know their boundaries.

Another director said:

> The board has been very positive, very supportive, has given a great deal of direction. But when I have asked for it ... [the board] has given me a lot of autonomy.

None of the research participants noted any power differential between the two parties. One executive director pointed out that professional training and up-to-date information give him an edge in dealing with the board, but said that "we have to work very hard at counterbalancing that and sharing that power by sharing as much information with our boards as is relevant."

CONCLUSIONS

The literature describing the prescriptive model of board functioning assumes that boards operate in generic contexts, with their primary role being governance. In this "managed system" model, the board is viewed as the central entity within the organization. Theoretically, boards of directors are supposed to provide the organization with leadership—a sense of purpose and direction. Hence emerges the emphasis on boards engaging in strategic planning.

In this idealized model, it is the board that directs the executive director as its chief agent and implementor of strategy, who in turn delegates to staff. As a result, executive directors in this hierarchy are subordinates of the boards.

One of the weaknesses of this model is that it does not take into consideration that an agency's external environment (i.e., political, economic, social, cultural, technological, and environmental forces) may affect the types of activities agency players such as boards and executive directors perform or are capable of performing. The model is insular in nature, focusing on internal dynamics of the organization.

Another criticism is offered by proponents of the political conception of organizations, who maintain that organizations are arenas of competing interests. On this view, the most powerful or influential players are those individuals or organizations who control the resources (Gummer, 1990; Mintzberg, 1983; Zald, 1979). With governmental ascendancy in the funding of social services, the ideal of a government-board equal partnership is seriously flawed. Being a major funder to social service organizations, as well as the primary decision maker in determining policy and service priorities, means the planning system determines the context within which boards of directors must function. As a consequence, the agendas of boards are largely determined by decisions made by the government.

Being financially dependent on the planning system leaves boards of directors in the position of working within the parameters established by the government or exploring ways to lessen their dependency. However, it is highly unlikely that social service agencies will ever be totally independent.

Given that the activities performed by boards are increasingly contingent on decisions made by the government, boards seem to have adopted a contingency or situational model of board functioning. To ensure the ongoing operation of their organizations, boards seem to be accommodating the demands placed upon them by the planning system. This contingency approach provides boards with the opportunity to assess, first, how the decisions made by the planning system affect the organization, and second, how best to respond. The pattern of compliance or accommodation to the expectations of the government may reflect the boards' recognition of their relative powerlessness in relation to government.

With the power of the planning system, it may be very difficult for boards to perform their governance function. Not knowing what level of funding the organization is going to receive in future years, and knowing that the service priorities of the government may change, makes the task of strategic planning exceedingly difficult. In fact, the overseeing of strategic direction may no longer be the prerogative of the boards of directors.

Based on the commentary provided by community agency research participants, however, it appears that the boards of directors are not passively allowing the planning system to exert its power over the agencies. The agencies are attempting to manage or reduce their dependency, especially financial, on the planning system. And by participating in efforts to generate funds, the boards are taking greater responsibility for ensuring that their agencies possess the resources required.

REFERENCES

Duca, D. (1986). *Nonprofit boards: A practical guide to roles, responsibilities, and performance.* Phoenix, AZ: Oryx Press.

Gummer, B. (1990). *The politics of social administration: Managing organizational politics in social agencies.* Englewood Cliffs, NJ: Prentice-Hall.

Hatton, M. (1990). *Corporations and directors: Comparing the profit and not-for-profit sectors.* Toronto: Thompson.

Houle, C. (1989). *Governing boards.* San Francisco: Jossey-Bass.

Lincoln, Y., & Guba, E. (1985). *Naturalistic inquiry.* Newbury Park, CA: Sage.

Mintzberg, H. (1983). *Power in and around organizations.* Englewood Cliffs, NJ: Prentice-Hall.

Patton, M. (1980). *Qualitative evaluation methods.* Newbury Park, CA: Sage.

Salamon, L. (1987). Partners in public service: The scope and theory of government-nonprofit relations. In W. Powell (Ed.), *The nonprofit sector: A research handbook* (pp. 19-29). New Haven, CT: Yale University Press.

Wolf, T. (1990). *Managing a nonprofit organization.* Englewood Cliffs, NJ: Prentice-Hall.

Zald, M. (1979). The power and functions of boards of directors: A theoretical synthesis. In Y. Hasenfeld & R. English (Eds.), *Human service organizations* (pp. 145-157). Ann Arbor, MI: University of Michigan Press.

Barbara Thomlison
Ray J. Thomlison
Lesa Wolfe

Research Study C

PLANNING THE STUDY

    Specifying the Concepts
    Considering Methodological Issues
    Method of Data Collection
    Engaging Research Participants
    Recording Interview Data

ANALYZING THE DATA

    Ongoing Assessment of Interviews
    Data Analysis: Stage 1
    Data Analysis: Stage 2

DISSEMINATION

REFERENCE

A Child Welfare Tragedy

O N JUNE 26, 1984, 17-year-old Richard Cardinal lost what he called the biggest battle a person ever has to fight—the "battle of yourself" (Thomlison, 1984, *p.* ii). After nearly 14 years as a ward of the Crown, he killed himself; the foster parents who cared for him during the last 40 days of his life found him hanging by his neck in their backyard.

Richard was born October 7, 1966, to Metis parents, the third youngest of seven siblings. The day before his fourth birthday, Richard and his brothers and sisters were taken into the custody of the Department of Social Services and Community Health, a department of the provincial government of Alberta, Canada. This was the beginning of a life in care. At the time of his suicide, he was living in his 16th foster home placement.

Shortly after he hanged himself, Richard's last foster parents questioned the quality of care he had received from the department and requested an investigation into the matter. When their request for an inquiry was ignored, other

EDITORS' NOTE

In selecting examples of studies for this book, we wanted to expand on our basic model by indicating something of the range of methods that can be employed in conducting qualitative research and the range of purposes that its findings can serve. The Richard Cardinal study is of interest because of the seriousness of the tragedy that led to it. It is also a respectable demonstration of how different methods of data collection (interviewing and file review) can be used, and how qualitative studies can generate results that have implications for policy and organizational development as well as front-line social work practice.

concerned individuals and groups—such as members of the Legislative Assembly, the Metis Association, and the media—became involved in the cause. Realizing that no action was being taken, the foster parents wrote to the minister in July, 1994:

> Rick made himself a perfect hangman's noose, hung it from his exercise board in the yard and calmly stepped off a pail, neatly folding his legs up so he would not be standing on the ground, and did not move until he had choked himself to death. This was determination. It has been almost a month now since we came home from work to find our boy hanging in the trees. A month of reliving the whole episode from start to finish. A month of wondering what more could we have done. In that time we have not heard from anyone in Social Services.
>
> Why not? He was their child—no inquest was held. No autopsy was performed. It would appear that Richard never existed. He could no longer cause any problems. Well, maybe it's time we did. ("Tragedy of a child," 1984)

The foster parents enclosed a photograph of Richard hanging from the tree. They threatened to send the photograph to a local newspaper for publication along with a story on how the department had failed Richard. This prompted the

EDITORS' NOTE

In many respects, the focus for the Cardinal study was predetermined. Definition of the problem area was provided by the tragedy itself, as were the needs of the politicians, who required the inquiry to satisfy the demands of a concerned public. What we have described as conceptual mapping of the problem area was also relatively straightforward, since definitions of effective casework practice were already present in legislation and policy documents. Description of this and other aspects of planning the study is therefore severely abbreviated.

deputy minister to initiate a study into services that had been provided to Richard while he was a ward of the Crown.

PLANNING THE STUDY

The deputy minister who commissioned the study decided to focus it on events related to Richard's self-destructive behavior during the last months of his life, and on the efforts of the last district social services office to deal with Richard's behaviors.

The goal was to determine how well the department had carried out their case management responsibilities to Richard, and how well the child welfare practices met minimum expectations of care in his case.

Although the study was initiated by the Alberta Government, Department of Social Services and Community Health, the inquiry was an independent one in terms of the study questions that were asked. To find out if the department had carried out its responsibilities, the researcher asked the following question:

- Were responsibilities to Richard Cardinal completely and/or adequately carried out?

Two narrower questions were derived from the central question:

- What were the child welfare case management practices of the Bute Social Services District Office?

- Were the case management responsibilities vis-à-vis Richard effectively carried out?

Specifying the Concepts

The first concept for consideration in this study was case management responsibility. Case management responsibility was defined as (1) the quality of social work practice and (2) the quality of casework supervision. The definitions of these concepts were taken from legislation and policy documents that spell out what standards of service are expected of the department and its employees.

Quality of casework supervision was assessed on the basis of verbal descriptions by managers and a policy statement describing the responsibilities of clinical supervisors. These responsibilities were divided into two categories: (1) supervision responsibilities and (2) consultation responsibilities. Other relevant policy stated that minimum standards in child welfare case management included a commitment to permanency planning, among other principles.

Considering Methodological Issues

Data Sources

Interview data for this study were obtained from various sources. Organizational data came from interviews with managers and other administrative staff; information about Richard himself was obtained from foster parents and child welfare workers who had cared for him. Other sources of information included community service providers such as professional staff in group homes, physicians, psychologists, and school officials.

File data were obtained from records held in the Child Welfare Division of the department. Richard's file records for the entire time he spent as a ward of the Crown (1970 through 1984) were studied, as were the files of all six of Richard's siblings. Second, program data and organizational data were obtained from official policy and procedural documents.

Protecting the Credibility of the Study

Qualitative researchers often must take special steps to assure the credibility of their findings in the eyes of future readers, and this issue often needs to be thought about during Phase One. In this case, the contentiousness and public visibility of the study, and the potential importance of its findings to future generations of children, made protecting the credibility and integrity of this work a critical consideration. To prevent any attempts at political persuasion, the researcher established a contract in which the department agreed that there would be no effort to influence the questions asked or the content of the final report. Second, it was agreed that the final report would be made public.

The second aspect of the study context requiring careful precautions was the extensive national and international media focus on this case. Because the review was under the auspices of the department, questions were raised about the possibility that the outcome would be influenced by political opinion. In response, plans were made to state only those findings in the final report that could be fully substantiated, so that the findings could not be refuted. Second, evidence that could have been construed as inflammatory and therefore open to legal action was to be included only as part of direct quotations from the source documents. Moreover, the source documents were included in the appendix of the final report.

Third, data that could not be fully substantiated and could have been construed as inflammatory were to be omitted from the final report. Omitting this material would avoid the certain imposition of legal injunctions hampering public dissemination of the report. Thus, very high standards were set so that only the strongest evidence—evidence that could be fully substantiated and verified—was included in the final report.

Method of Data Collection

The primary method of data collection was the interview. Interviews were conducted with administrative staff. To obtain the data needed for this study, staff were asked such questions as:

- What is your job, as you understand it?

- How did you carry out the duties and responsibilities of your position?

- Describe what, if any, involvement you had with Richard.

- What would you do differently, if you had to do it again?

Interviews with the child welfare workers and foster parents asked the following questions:

- What was your relationship to Richard?

- What were your perceptions of Richard's troubles?

- What were your perceptions of Richard's strengths and weaknesses?

- Describe the events that precipitated a crisis in your relationship with Richard.

- Describe the events that led to Richard being moved to another foster home.

- What is your job, as you understand it?

- How did you receive information about what you were to do?

- Whom did you consult when you were having difficulty with Richard?

- What other information do you have about Richard?

Finally, interviews were conducted with community service providers, who were asked to describe their relationship with Richard and offer their observations of his behavior and affect. The second method of data collection was a review of records and documents within the department. This included a review of the files kept for Richard and his siblings and of the established policies and procedures that guided case management practice.

Engaging Research Participants

The researcher contracted with the research participants by (1) contacting the respondent by telephone, (2) introducing himself and the purpose of his call, (3) explaining that he was conducting a study into the death of Richard Cardinal, (4) explaining that the study was an independent inquiry although it had been initiated by the Alberta Government, Department of Social Services and Community Health, and (5) requesting an interview with the respondent. The research participant's verbal agreement to participate in an interview with the researcher was considered a formal contract.

In this way, contracts were established with more than 40 respondents. This included interviews with senior department managers. In addition, contacts for interviews were established with 9 of the 16 foster parent families who cared for Richard. Two of these interviews were conducted by telephone. Seven foster parent families could not be located. Of the 25 child welfare workers assigned to Richard during his time in care, contracts for interviews were established with four of the most recent.

As well, contacts were established with staff from three of the six group homes that cared for Richard during his lifetime, and with a number of other professionals who had been involved with him, as well as with representatives of the Metis Association, which had an obvious interest in how Richard had been so tragically failed by the child welfare system.

Recording Interview Data

While taped records of interview data are preferred, in this study hand-written notes were used. It was thought that, given the sensitive nature of the study, respondents might be unwilling to sign the written consent required for a taped interview.

Because Richard's story was so tragic and so widely publicized, considerable care had to be taken to separate facts from feelings so that the final report would accurately reflect events. The first step the researcher took to accomplish this was to obtain information from numerous sources (triangulation). The second step was to maintain an objective viewpoint as various stories about Richard were retold by the research participants; the researcher had to carefully assess respondents' emotional attachment to Richard (in degree of warmth, closeness,

EDITORS' NOTE

The analysis of data conducted in the Cardinal study required the integration of findings from a range of sources. The advantage of this is the many opportunities it yields of increasing the credibility of findings through triangulation. The actual techniques employed have already been discussed and illustrated; to avoid repetition, we will describe Phase Three of this study briefly, highlighting some of its special aspects. The findings that emerged with the analysis are presented in complete form, since they illustrate so well the breadth of information that a qualitative study can generate and its significance at the level of policy, organizational development, and front-line service delivery.

positive regard, ambivalence, and hostility) and evaluate how these feelings were influencing presentation of the facts.

ANALYZING THE DATA

Ongoing Assessment of Interviews

At the end of each stage of the data-gathering process the researcher reviewed the content of the data collected, to identify inconsistencies and gaps in the information collected up to that point. This process is necessary to allow for refocusing of a study when the data collected indicate the need. For example, the goal of the study was to determine whether responsibilities to Richard had been carried out adequately.

However, at the end of the first phase of the interviews it was evident that managers through all levels of the bureaucracy were highly confused regarding who was responsible for what—a possible consequence of a recently implemented policy of regionalization in which the goal was to decentralize authority for setting policy and delivering services. A request to the deputy minister to expand the study was granted and the initial agreement was modified to include an investigation into the impact of regionalization on child welfare practices. The analysis of the data was divided into two phases:

- The first phase consisted of an analysis tracing the chronological sequence of events in Richard's life while he was a ward of the Crown.

- The second phase consisted of an analysis of the administration and organizational functioning of the department.

Data Analysis: Stage 1

A chronology of Richard's life based on information obtained from personal interviews and file information provided a perspective on critical life events and decisions that had been made on Richard's behalf during his fourteen years as a ward. For example, during the first year that Richard was a ward, he was placed in four different foster homes. During the second year, he was moved into four more foster homes. By his sixth birthday, he had lived in a total of eight foster homes.

The chronology also highlighted important events that occurred during the time Richard was a ward. At age four, he was considered a healthy and normal child. However, by the time he was five and had been placed in his fifth foster home, he was described as aggressive and strong willed, and problems with enuresis were noted. As Richard was moved from home to home, his behavioral problems escalated and enuresis became a persistent difficulty. At age eight, when Richard was placed in his eleventh foster home, bedwetting was described as "much worse": in his thirteenth foster home at age twelve, Richard was described as being angry and irritable, sniffing glue, and engaging in inappropriate sexual behavior.

More placements followed and Richard's behavioral problems continued to escalate, eventually to include aggressiveness toward others and property offenses. More importantly, Richard began to demonstrate significant self-destructive behaviors, including several serious suicide attempts.

Findings from the investigation of direct services provided to Richard included an evaluation of case management effectiveness, the quality of the file, the quality of casework practice, the quality of casework supervision, and the extent to which the child welfare workers understood and responded appropriately to Richard's needs. The relationship between the foster parents and the department was also analyzed, as was the degree to which the department upheld its responsibility as defined in legislation, policy, and procedural documents.

Data Analysis: Stage 2

The second stage of the analysis included consideration of the administrative uncertainty that was revealed during the first phase of the study, especially the impact of regionalization.

The report concluded that the department had failed to adequately carry out its responsibilities to Richard. The findings detailing this failure were useful at the level of front-line practice as well as organizational and policy development—and they were translated into 27 recommendations. These are presented on the pages that follow:

EDITORS' NOTE

When it comes to data analysis, the seven major recommendations can be considered main themes, the 27 sub-recommendations can be considered sub-themes, and the 66 findings from the study can be considered categories.

RECOMMENDATIONS TO ENSURE
THE BEST INTERESTS OF THE CHILD

Recommendation 1: *That the department demonstrate through particular program action its declared commitment to child welfare.*

A new *Child Welfare Act* is only a foundation upon which to demonstrate this commitment. Development of supporting child welfare programs and resources will be the measure of the department's priority. It is my opinion that the department is *now* in a position to implement many of the policies, standards, and programs that are anticipated under the new *Child Welfare Act*. This should be done as soon as possible. The findings of this review indicate that:

- The Minister of the department has declared that child welfare is a top priority with this department.

- As the department began to operationalize its regionalization plan, child welfare was not a visible part of this plan.

- Some staff interviewed during this review expressed the belief that the department viewed child welfare as a low priority.

- There are virtually no appropriate treatment resources available for children of Richard's age in the Province of Alberta.

Recommendation 2: *That the department must immediately examine the care of those children who are permanent wards within both the Northwest and Edmonton Regions.* The findings of this review indicated that:

- Some people responsible for the care of these wards believe they are a second and third level priority on a caseload.

- The department's own Child Welfare Programs manual reinforces this belief by specifying casework responsibilities for the care of temporary wards (*pp.* 106–107, Child Welfare Programs) but not for permanent wards.

- In both regions the social workers significantly violated the requirements for filing the Review of Child's Progress report, leading to the speculation that the frequency of contact was also below departmental expectations.

Recommendation 3: *That the department establish a temporary and permanent ward review procedure which would insure that the care of all permanent wards is monitored and evaluated at least once per year.* The findings of this review indicate that:

- The frequency of contact between the permanent ward and the department is relatively infrequent, at least in the Northwest Region's Bute District Office.

- The quality of casework planning for the child's future was inadequate.

- Emotional and behavioral problems were repeatedly identified but no action was taken to alleviate these problems.

Recommendation 4: *That the department move immediately to establish and fund programs in the Northwest Region to assist adolescent wards in preparing for independence from the department.* The findings of this review indicate that:

- Richard Cardinal was extremely concerned about his approaching eighteenth birthday and his apparent inability to survive without the department.

- Those children in the care of the department who reach eighteen years of age, and are not in school, undergo an abrupt transition from dependence to independence.

Recommendation 5: *That the department develop a statement and a set of criteria for the recognition of a child at risk. This should be accompanied by a clear statement of procedures for helping such children.* The findings of the review indicate that:

- The series of workers involved with Richard failed to recognize the indicators that Richard was a child at risk.

- The series of workers involved with Richard did not appear to be able to identify adequate helping procedures for him.

Recommendation 6: *That the department develop a wider range of alternate care resources.* The findings of the review indicate that:

- The department has relied heavily on foster home placement as a means of caring for children. It is apparent that some children need service beyond that which can be provided in a foster home.

- There are virtually no treatment care alternatives for adolescents between sixteen and eighteen years of age.

RECOMMENDATIONS TO IMPROVE
SOCIAL WORK PRACTICE WITH THE CHILD

Recommendation 7: *That the department must identify the means by which social workers in the Northwest Region, Bute District Office can be assisted to develop a higher quality of casework planning and action.* The findings of the review indicate that:

- Few, if any, of the workers involved in Richard Cardinal's case identified a case plan for him, either as a temporary or permanent ward.

- A review of seven other files in this office indicated the absence of written case plans.

- Few workers engaged Richard in any systematic effort at change.

Recommendation 8: *That the department formulate a statement of procedures to enhance the transfer of a case from one worker to the next.* The findings of the review indicate that:

- There is a high turnover of staff in this region and casework continuity is low.

- There is a lack of consistency of service and planning from one worker to the next.

- Workers appear not to familiarize themselves with the total file at the time of transfer.

- Few, if any, workers seem to build on the work of the previous worker.

Recommendation 9: *That the department examine immediately the low staff morale and high turnover of staff in the Bute District Office.* The findings of the review indicate that:

- There is a feeling of low morale in this office and, while Richard's death is a contributing factor, it appears to be more deep rooted.

- There is a relatively high turnover of staff and a high number of unfilled positions.

Recommendation 10: *That the department re-examine its position on both academic and in-service training, with a view to: (a) reiterating its commitment to professional social work education and actively encouraging staff in the Northwest Region to pursue the Bachelor of Social Work degree, (b) mounting in-service programs on social work with Native peoples, taught by persons with knowledge and experience in working with Native peoples, (c) mounting in-*

service training programs on child abuse identification and intervention, and (d) contracting with the Suicide Prevention and Training Program to train staff in the recognition of the indicators of suicide and methods of intervention. The findings of the review indicate that:

- There are a substantial number of social workers in this region who have no professional social work education.

- The workers interviewed and the files reviewed indicated various levels of knowledge in the three areas of Native issues, child abuse, and suicide prevention.

Recommendation 11: *That the department re-evaluates its procedures for the assignment of caseloads, taking into account the variation and complexity of children's problems and the variation in level of competence and expertise of its social workers.*

Often caseload problems are viewed solely in terms of the actual number of cases for which a social worker is responsible. Greater attention should be placed on matching worker expertise and competence with the nature and complexity of the child's problems. The findings of the review indicate that:

- The quality of social work service is below that which is to be expected.

- Workers have expressed concern about the size of their caseloads, particularly where an office has unfilled social work positions.

- Caseload assignment and reassignment do not appear to be based on criteria which would take into account the varying levels of case complexity.

- Caseload size is one of a number of determinants of casework quality.

RECOMMENDATIONS TO IMPROVE SUPERVISION OF SOCIAL WORK PRACTICE

Recommendation 12: *That the department appoint an external consultant knowledgeable in the area of child welfare casework supervision to assess the supervisory needs of the Northwest Region social workers. That the department bring forward recommendations which will assist the department in elaborating and clarifying the role of the social work supervisor.*

It is my opinion that a person external to the department would be in a better position to gather an accurate perspective on the supervisory needs of the social workers. The findings of the review indicate that:

- There is no clear statement of expectations on the supervisor for social casework supervision.

- Social work supervision was qualitatively low and unsystematic.

Recommendation 13: *That the department provide educational opportunities for supervisors to improve their knowledge of contemporary social work practice in the child welfare field, as well as to improve their skills and knowledge in the methods of supervision.* The findings of the review indicate that:

- The social workers have identified a number of deficits in the knowledge and expertise of their supervisors.

- There is some question among supervisors themselves as to the priority level they should place on social work supervision.

Recommendation 14: *That the department examine the appropriateness of the social worker-supervisor relationship model known as the "social work team."* The findings of the review indicate that:

- There exists within the Northwest Region, Bute District Office frequent informal collegial collaboration.

- There is a need for collective input in casework problem-solving, due to the range of knowledge and experience within this office.

RECOMMENDATIONS TO IMPROVE
THE RELATIONSHIPS BETWEEN
FOSTER FAMILIES AND THE DEPARTMENT

Recommendation 15: *That the department strike a task force made up of members of the Foster Parents Association and departmental staff, supplemented by knowledgeable external resource people when needed, to examine the causes of foster home placement breakdown. This task force must bring forward recommendations to improve the probability of foster home placement success.* The findings of the review indicate that:

- There is a high proportion of foster home breakdown in this region, particularly with permanent wards.

- There is an indication that foster parents do not understand the depth of commitment needed in taking on this responsibility.

- Social workers have not considered the foster parents as members of the team.

- Social workers have not seen the foster family as a system through which problem-solving can be accomplished. There appears to be an attitude that problems between the child and the foster family can better be solved by moving the child.

Recommendation 16: *In addition to other suggestions for strengthening foster home placements, the task force gives consideration to a recommendation that foster parents and the department enter into a system of formalized service contracting. Such contracts would include statements of mutual responsibilities with clear statements of future planning for the child.* The findings of the review indicate that:

- Limited information is shared with the foster parents at the time of placement.

- There is limited support provided to foster parents by the department.

- Foster parents often see the social worker aligned with the child against the foster parents.

- There is a lack of replacement planning and foster family-caseworker mutual goal setting.

RECOMMENDATIONS TO IMPROVE AND STRENGTHEN RELATIONSHIPS WITH COMMUNITY RESOURCES

Recommendation 17: *That the department examine its current relationship with significant community resources with a view to recommending means by which (a) communication can be improved, (b) greater interdisciplinary collaboration can occur, and (c) greater interdisciplinary decision-making can occur.* The findings of the review indicate that:

- The department is viewed very negatively through the eyes of its community resources.

- There is little, if any, interdisciplinary team conferencing.

- There is a very low level of communication between the department and its community resources.

Recommendation 18: *That the department prepare a statement of guidelines to enhance the social workers' liaison with the school programs in which their wards are enrolled.* The findings of the review indicate that:

- School problems are recurrently identified in the Review of Child's Progress but there is little evidence of collaborative problem-solving between the worker and the school officials.

Recommendation 19: *That the department evaluate its policy and procedures governing referral to private consultants for assessment and treatment of children under its care.* The findings of the review indicate that:

- There is a strong tendency on the part of the social workers to refer to psychologists without a clear statement of the rationale and the objectives to be achieved by such referrals.

- There appears to be an unavailability and/or reluctance on the part of the psychiatric profession to assess and treat children referred by the department.

RECOMMENDATIONS TO IMPROVE RELATIONSHIPS BETWEEN MANAGEMENT AND SOCIAL WORKERS

Recommendation 20: *That the senior administration of the department clarify immediately its position on the question of regional autonomy versus central control. Specific reference must be given to such issues as budget control, policy formulation, decision making and standard setting for service delivery.* The findings of the review indicate that:

- There is currently a great deal of confusion on the degree of autonomy that exists in the regions.

- There is a range of opinion as to who is responsible for policy formulation.

- There is some degree of confusion as to the degree of autonomy a region has on budgetary matters. This, of course, affects program development and implementation.

Recommendation 21: *That the department commit itself to establishing a system of program standards and guidelines. The first system of standards and guidelines should be developed in relation to casework practice with permanent wards.* The findings of the review indicate that:

- There are no clearly identifiable statements against which to measure the quality of service delivery.

- There are few guidelines available to assist supervisors and social workers in the provision of service to children.

Recommendation 22: *That the department clarify the expectations and responsibilities on the internal monitoring of casework activity with the children in its care.* The findings of the review indicate that:

- It is unclear as to whether there is any monitoring of casework activity to ensure quality control.

- It is unclear who in the chain of authority is responsible and accountable for monitoring the quality of casework activity.

Recommendation 23: *That the department identify the reason(s) which inhibit the social workers' compliance with the required frequency of completing the "Review of Child's Progress" reports. Such a review should address procedures and technology which would assist the social workers in completing this responsibility.* The findings of the review indicate that:

- Finding a Review of Child's Progress report that was filed within the required three-month interval was more the exception than the rule.

- This appears to be a problem in other offices in other regions.

Recommendation 24: *That the department develop a case audit procedure. Such a procedure would ensure periodic external examination of the quality of service being delivered to children in the care of the department.* The findings of the review indicate that:

- There is little internal monitoring and qualitative appraisal of the services being delivered to children.

- That there are identifiable violations of departmental policy and procedures by social workers in both the Northwest Region and the Edmonton Region. It is apparent that the existing means of reviewing service is not picking up on such errors.

Recommendation 25: *That the department re-evaluate its quality review objectives and procedures. In this re-evaluation, consideration must be given to the participation of at least one member of the review committee being external (independent) from the Department of Social Services.* The findings of the review indicate that:

- There is a definite need for a periodic review of programs within the department.

- The current quality review manual, its statement of purpose, goals, and parameters needs considerable elaboration.

- Even though a quality review of the Bute District Office was done in 1980 (a review evidently initiated because of a death of a child), it appears to have had little impact on the case management and service delivery within this office.

Recommendation 26: *That the department develop a system of staff appraisal based on casework performance indicators.* The findings of the review indicate that:

- There is a wide range of performance among the social workers in relation to the quality of their casework.

RECOMMENDATION TO IMPROVE
SERVICE DELIVERY TO METIS AND INDIAN CHILDREN

Richard Cardinal was a child of Metis ancestry. Throughout his life with the department there was no evidence of the recognition of this fact. In an effort to further understand this major deficit in Richard's care, interviews were arranged with representatives from the Metis Association and the Indian Association of Alberta. Unfortunately, for unknown reasons, the meeting with the latter group did not take place as arranged. However, I had a most productive and lengthy meeting with four representatives from the Metis Association of Alberta. On the basis of their observations, concerns and frustrations with the Department of Social Services and Community Health ... I offer my final recommendation and perhaps one of the most important insofar as the case management of Richard Cardinal is concerned.

Recommendation 27: *That the department establish, as soon as possible, a task force comprised of equal representation from the Metis and Indian communities and social services personnel who have had direct work experience with the Metis and Indian communities, supplemented by knowledgeable resource people as needed, to collaborate on the exploration of Metis and Indian child welfare issues, and to recommend program alternatives for Metis and Indian children with the Northwest Region.* The findings of the review indicate that:

- A continued and more concerted effort is required to improve communication between the Metis and Indian representatives and the department on child welfare issues.

- There are successful examples of viable alternatives to child welfare service delivery to Indian children currently operating in the province of Alberta.

DISSEMINATION

Careful plans for dissemination of the document were made at the beginning of the study, for several reasons. First, the sensitive nature of the study made it necessary to think through the timing for the release of the report. Second, the potentially controversial outcome of the study made it necessary to ensure that the entire report would reach a very concerned public. Therefore, a clause outlining the process of dissemination was included in the original contract between the researcher and the department.

The agreement stated that upon completion, the report would be given to the minister in charge of the department. The minister was to examine and review

---

EDITORS' NOTE

Dissemination of the final report made it possible for many of the study's recommendations to be implemented. Many of the concerns addressed in this study have been corrected in an effort to bring about better social work services to the native children, their local communities, and the social service delivery system.

---

the report for a period of two weeks. Following this, it was agreed that the minister would provide comments and release the entire report to the public.

Despite this careful planning, certain events resulted in a change to the original dissemination plans. First, the department decided to withhold the report in spite of the original agreement. Second, parts of the document were leaked to the media, creating a dilemma for the department and the researcher and greater public interest. It was eventually decided to hold a joint news conference and release the full report to the public.

Media attention remained high throughout the period that the study was taking place, and public interest was strong at the local, national, and international levels. This ensured a thorough dissemination of the report despite the department's initial reluctance to release the report.

EDITORS' NOTE

Dissemination of the Cardinal study was unusual in that it had to be planned and negotiated at the outset. Publication of the results in some form or another was guaranteed from the beginning—the special political circumstances surrounding the study made this unusual arrangement ethically necessary.

REFERENCE

Thomlison, R.J. (1984). *Case management review: Northwest Region Department of Social Services and Community Health.* Calgary: University of Calgary, Faculty of Social Work.

Index

Abstract, in reports, 128-129
Analytical memos, 98-100
Audiotaping interviews, 67-68
Audit trail, 98-100

Biases, controlling for, 113-115

Categories
    coding, 105
    comparing, 108-109
    identifying, 102-105
    retrieving meaning units into, 107
Coding
    assigning codes to categories, 105
    first-level, 100-106

refining and reorganizing, 105-106
    second-level, 106-109
    when to stop, 106
Computer programs, in data analysis,
    92-93
Concepts, 10
Conceptual classification systems,
    109-111
Conceptual maps, 32
Confirmability, 126-127
Consent form, 64
Consistency, 112-113
Constant comparison method, 100-102
Content, complexities of, 11
Contracting, 31-32
Credibility, 112-115
Culture and research, 18-19

Data
    interpreting, 109-111
    previewing, 97-98
    transcribing, 92-96
Data analysis, 88-119
    framework for, 92-96
    purpose of, 90-92
Data collection, 50-87
Defining problem area, 26-31
Dependability, 112-115

Editing, 145-147
Engaging, 71-78
Ethical considerations, 40-43
    in data analysis, 94-95
    in submitting a report, 145-147

First-level coding, 100-106
Flexibility in research, 13-14

Gender and research, 17-18
Generalization in research, 9-10
Groundwork for research, 31-32

Interpreting data, 109-111
Interviewees, preparing, 64-67
Interviews, conducting, 71-79
    dynamics, 73-74
    reflecting about, 79-82
    terminating, 78-79
    types of questions, 74-78
Interviews, types of, 52-56
    semi-structured, 56
    structured, 53-55
    unstructured, 55-56
Interview steps, 60-82
    preparing, 60-67
Interviewer/Interviewee relationship,
    57-60
    comparison to therapeutic inter
    views, 59-60
        dealing with strong emotions, 58
    equality, 57-58

Introduction, in a report, 129-133

Journal notes
    during data analysis, 98-100
    during interview process, 67-70
Journal, professional
    sending manuscript to, 145-149

Literature review, 34-35

Meaning units
    identifying, 102-109
    retrieving into categories, 107
Member checking, 113

Negative evidence, 115
Note-taking, 68-70
Numbers, use of in research, 12-13

Objectivity, in research, 8-9

Planning your study, 23-49
Practitioners and research, 16-17
Problems, 26-31
Professional knowledge base and
    research, 15-16
Proposal writing, 43-44

Qualitative research approach, 4-5
Questions, types of, 74-78

Recording methods, 67-68
Reductionism in research, 10
Reflecting about interviews, 79-82
Report, steps in writing, 123-150
    abstract in, 128-129
    choosing a writing style, 127
    conclusions in, 140-142
    findings in, 135-140

getting started, 124-125
introduction in, 129-130
methodology in, 133-135
organization, 128-144
planning, 123-125
references, 142-144
using terminology in, 125-126
when to begin, 124
Resources, determining, 37-39
Rewriting, 147-149

Second-level coding, 106-109
comparing categories, 108-109
retrieving meaning units into
categories, 107
Sites for research, 39
Supervisors, recruiting, 35-37

Themes, 111
Theory building, 109-111
in research, 11-12
Transcripts, 92-96
choice of transcriber, 94

ethical issues in, 94-95
formatting, 95-96
raw data in, 95
Transferability, 126
Triangulation, 113
Trustworthiness, 112-115
evidence of, 126-127

Word-processing programs, 92-93
Words, use of in research, 12-13
Writing reports, 120-150
abstract in, 128-129
choosing a writing style, 127-128
conclusions in, 140-142
findings in, 135-140
getting started, 124-125
introduction in, 129-133
methodology in, 133-135
organization, 128-144
planning, 124-125
references, 142-144
using correct terminology, 125-126
when to begin, 124